DATE DUE

JUL 1 8 2001	
6-30-09	
1-1-14	
GAYLORD	PRINTED IN U.S.A.

Doing Qualitative Research

Doing Qualitative Research:
Circles within Circles

Margot Ely

with

Margaret Anzul
Teri Friedman
Diane Garner
Ann McCormack Steinmetz

 The Falmer Press

(A member of the Taylor & Francis Group)
London • New York • Philadelphia

UK   The Falmer Press, 4 John Street, London, WC1N 2ET
USA   The Falmer Press, Taylor & Francis Inc., 1900 Frost Road, Suite 101,
        Bristol, PA 19007

© M. Ely (1991)

First published 1991

British Library Cataloguing in Publication Data
Ely, Margot
    Doing qualitative research: circles within circles. —
    (Falmer Press teachers library).
    1. Social sciences. Research. Qualitative methods
    I. Title
    300.723

    ISBN 1-85000-814-0
    ISBN 1-85000-813-2 pbk

Library of Congress Cataloguing-in-Publication Data
Ely, Margot.
    Doing qualitative research: circles within circles/Margot Ely with
    Margaret Anzul ... [et al.].
        p. cm.
    Includes bibliographical references (p. 221 *ff*.) and index.
    ISBN 1-85000-813-2 (HC): ISBN 1-85000-814-0 (SC):
    1. Ethnography — Methodology. 2. Ethnography — Field
    work. 3. Participant observation. 4. Social sciences —
    Methodology.
    I. Title.
    GN345.E48 1991
    305.8′0072 — dc20

Jacket design by Caroline Archer
Set by Graphicraft Typesetters Ltd., Hong Kong.

Printed in Great Britain by Burgess Science Press, Basingstoke
on paper which has a specified pH value on final paper
manufacture of not less than 7.5 and is therefore 'acid free'.

Contents

Chapter 1

Grounding

Dear Reader,

Right at the start we planned to present you with one lucid, crystal-clear sentence to establish the character and purpose of this book. That task proved a bit like squeezing an elephant into a pint container while keeping the poor thing alive and true to form.

You will find that this book is somewhat different from most texts on qualitative research. It invites you to experience some of the struggles and questions, the insights and visions of over seventy students, their teachers, and other established researchers about learning to do naturalistic inquiry. Our book started with a collection of papers by student ethnographers to which we added accounts by more advanced doctoral and postdoctoral researchers. These sources formed a database for our studies on the process of becoming qualitative inquirers. In time we found ourselves shaping the accounts and our analyses of them into a book that might benefit future classes of student ethnographers, our professional colleagues, and other researchers.

A distinctive feature of the book is its concern with the interplay between affect and cognition — how people feel and what they learn — as they go about the very messy but exhilarating business of learning to 'do it'. Our interest in this interplay is not arbitrary. We are convinced that if practitioners of interpretive research are concerned solely with the technical aspects, they will miss the essentials of this type of research. We believe that qualitative study is forged in the transaction among what is done and learned and felt by the researcher. It is an intensely recursive, personal process, and while this may be the hallmark of all sound research, it is crucial to every aspect of the qualitative way of looking at life.

This book is predicated on the assumption that there is a need to make more public the interplay between the emotional and the intellectual in ethnographic research, since this interplay is an essential ingredient. Our perception that there is a void to be filled has been supported in our experiences as professionals and researchers and has provided us with an impetus to forge ahead. For this reason, we write directly to students of the field, whoever you are in whatever roles, beginning or seasoned.

By now you are likely to have:

1 realized that we are using different terms in a roughly synonymous way:

> naturalistic inquiry,
> ethnographic methodologies,
> qualitative research,
> interpretive research; or

2 become irked, piqued, or interested because we have used so many different terms; or

3 not noticed at all.

The first two responses have much to commend them. The field is shot through with a variety of labels and proponents of those labels. These derive from a number of theoretical models and a range of modifications and variations upon these models that guide why and how to do research (Goetz and LeCompte, 1984, p. 37; Patton, 1980, p. 203). Underlying this collection of competing labels are certain commonalities that link them together — a network of underlying principles and philosophical beliefs that constitute a paradigm or world view. We are living in an era of paradigm revolution (Kuhn, 1970). Most of us grew up in a positivist or empirical era in which the claims of empirical scientific research were held to be absolute. Particularly within the past few decades, however, this empirical world view has been challenged by an alternative paradigm, frequently referred to as naturalistic. Those who work within the naturalistic paradigm operate from a set of axioms that hold realities to be multiple and shifting, that take for granted a simultaneous mutual shaping of knower and known, and that see all inquiry, including the empirical, as being inevitably value-bound.

Lincoln and Guba (1985) and Lofland and Lofland (1984) are among many who list a variety of terms for research done within this post-positivistic, naturalistic paradigm.

> Social science is a terminological jungle where many labels compete, and no single label has been able to command the particular domain before us. Often ... researchers simply 'do it' without worrying about giving 'it' a name. (Lofland and Lofland, 1984, p. 3)

But you see, we did worry. How could we write a book about 'Unnamed Research'?

One of the more frequently used terms is 'ethnography'. There are conflicting claims, however, for what can be properly termed ethnography. There is also an interesting case made for labeling various levels of ethnography that range from the study of a complex society as a macro-ethnography to the study of a single social situation as a micro-ethnography (Spradley, 1980, p. 30). Indeed, in attempting to define the essence of ethnography, Werner and Schoepfle (1987) conclude that '. . . the ethnographic variety is almost limitless' (p. 41). It could be reasoned that the correct label for the kind of research this book is about must contain the word 'approaches', or 'methodologies', as in 'ethnographic approaches' and 'naturalistic methodologies', since such labels highlight more clearly both what researchers do in this multi-faceted research and what they cannot claim to do. For example, Harry Wolcott finds it '. . . useful to distinguish between anthropologically informed researchers who *do ethnography* and . . . researchers who frequently *draw upon ethnographic approaches* in doing descriptive studies' (1988, p. 202).

We solved our dilemma in the following ways. First, you know from the title of this book that we chose to use 'Qualitative Research' as the umbrella term. We did this because it appears to us that the term 'qualitative' has the broadest denotations. The word itself highlights the primarily qualitative-as-descriptive nature of work within this paradigm in contrast to the primarily quantitative emphasis of positivist approaches. Second, because our own research and that of our students is based on a variety of data-gathering and analysis strategies, rooted in a number of traditions, we write to researchers who work in similar ways. Third, because of this, we highlight those characteristics common to a variety of qualitative research models as we discuss the information in the chapters to come. This means that you, our reader, are asked to live with a number of research labels from now on.

And these are many! For instance, in her analysis of texts on qualitative research, Tesch (1990) compiled a list of forty-six terms that social scientists have used to name their versions of qualitative research. Even though Tesch further categorized these terms into twenty-six approaches under four basic research groups, the sheer number is mind-boggling. What is more, theorists change their labels quickly these days as their understandings of their research evolve. We were quite comfortable with Lincoln and Guba's (1985) use of the term 'paradigm of naturalistic inquiry' when they provided a rationale four years later (1989) for adopting a different label, 'paradigm of constructivism research'. We'll try to hold to a reasonable number of research labels in this book.

Now, to the definition of qualitative research, which is not as straight-forward as it seems. After serious and unsuccessful attempts to present you with a universal definition at this point, we were relieved to come across this statement by Lincoln and Guba (1985). These authors were speaking of defining naturalism, but the statement applies to defining qualitative research as well:

> ... it is precisely because the matter is so involved that it is not possible to provide a simple definition.... (p. 8)

Thus fortified, we decided that the term 'qualitative research' is perhaps better understood by the characteristics of its methods than by a definition. Several experts such as Bogdan and Biklen (1982), Lincoln and Guba (1985), and Lofland and Lofland (1984) present lists of such characteristics. We here base our description on the work of Sherman and Webb (1988) who analyzed what leading qualitative researchers had to say about their work in philosophy of education, history, biography, ethnography, life history, grounded theory, phenomenography, curriculum criticism, uses of literature in qualitative research, and critical theory (p. 2). Their analysis produced five characteristics similar to all of those species of qualitative research, and one that is characteristic of many (pp. 5–8).

1   Events can be understood adequately only if they are seen in context. Therefore, a qualitative researcher immerses her/himself in the setting.
2   The contexts of inquiry are not contrived; they are natural. Nothing is predefined or taken for granted.
3   Qualitative researchers want those who are studied to speak for themselves, to provide their perspectives in words and other actions. Therefore, qualitative research is an interactive process in which the persons studied teach the researcher about their lives.
4   Qualitative researchers attend to the experience as a whole, not as separate variables. The aim of qualitative research is to understand experience as unified.
5   Qualitative methods are appropriate to the above statements. There is no one general method.
6   For many qualitative researchers, the process entails appraisal about what was studied.

Further, from these characteristics, Sherman and Webb amalgamated the following summary:

> ... qualitative implies a direct concern with experience as it is 'lived' or 'felt' or 'undergone'.... Qualitative research, then, has the aim of under-

standing experience as nearly as possible as its participants feel it or live it. (1988, p. 7)

The essence of these characteristics weaves its way throughout this book, albeit in expanded form and different words. You may want to return to these statements by Sherman and Webb as you read, for we see this framework about qualitative research as a springboard for this entire volume.

All five of us have worked as a team on every aspect of this book. Each of us, however, served as the primary author and facilitator for one chapter, and in it inevitably touches on her own research experiences and her own perspectives on this project. Each chapter begins with an introduction to the person who shepherded that chapter to completion. Each author speaks in the first person 'I' in her chapter when she writes about her own experiences and insights, and in the first person plural 'we' when talking about the writing team. When we refer to one another, we use first names. This has not been as complicated as we first envisioned. We think you'll understand immediately as you continue.

Each chapter is composed of our text as well as that drawn from the database provided by students and other researchers. We include quotations from field logs, student articles, and excerpts from published articles and books. Our writing speaks to, with, and occasionally in opposition to what other people write as we introduce, weave strands together, pose questions, discuss, and generally say what we feel needs to be said.

Chapters 2 through 5 end with postscripts. While primary authors made the largest contributions to their specific chapters, Margot developed the postscripts so that they would provide highlighting — more discussion, new input, another point of view, challenge, or disagreement. Some consider our own affective and cognitive processes as these apply to the topic at hand.

We have provided wide margins near articles, quotations, and postscripts so that you can write your own comments and questions there, if you like to work in the 'naturalistic way'. In this book student contributors are referred to either by true name or pseudonym, according to the wishes of each. The names of people and places from researchers' logs that we have quoted have all been changed to protect their anonymity. At times the same quotation is used to support more than one section in this book. This is consonant with the way qualitative data are analyzed and presented.

We offer the following overview of the content of each chapter with the proviso that, because of the nature of this phenomenon called qualitative research, the topics are not as neatly separated and are more interwoven than is usual in many research books. Chapter 1, 'Grounding', provides an explanation about how this book is conceived, authored, and presented. Chapter 2, 'Starting', discusses those important points of beginning to learn about qualitative research and entering the field. Chapter 3, 'Doing', focuses on learning the tools that help us to see, to listen, and to interpret 'qualitatively'. Chapter 4, 'Feeling', highlights the emotional/personal aspects that are part and parcel of the research process. Chapter 5, 'Interpreting', talks of the critical tasks of final analysis and writing. Chapter 6, 'Reflecting', presents some overarching themes that resulted from a meta-analysis of the entire database on what people do, feel, and learn as qualitative researchers. The Epilogue, 'Margot's Last Word', considers social implications of the qualitative research endeavor.

And who is this 'we' so generously sprinkled throughout the foregoing pages? 'We' are the people whose voices you will hear. 'We' began with Margot, the professor who first planned and facilitated the qualitative research experiences described here. These led subsequently to the research and writing that have resulted in this book. 'We' are also a team of four who helped with every aspect of the work. Some time prior to first teaching the qualitative research course, Margot became acquainted with three graduate students who she felt might be fine members of a team to work with a class that generally has a high enrollment. Each was involved in naturalistic research. Diane was an early childhood and elementary school teacher who was completing her dissertation on children's play styles. Ann was writing a dissertation proposal while teaching at a college and negotiating an active family life. Teri was collecting data for her dissertation, a study of women police officers, and anticipating her year's clinical internship in psychology. None of these three needed any more work involvements, however fascinating they might be. They joined in right away. After the completion of the first course, we began to analyze the students' papers, and saw the value of organizing them as a support for future classes and for the profession. At this point we asked Margaret to join the team. Writing furiously at her dissertation in the nooks and crannies between being an elementary school librarian and teaching an evening course at a university, Margaret found space. It has been four years since the team first began its odyssey. This book is based on the amalgamation of our experiences and student contributions over that time. Diane, Ann, Teri, and Margaret have all earned their doctorates.

But 'we' are more than this five. 'We' include over seventy people enrolled in a doctoral level qualitative research course called 'Case Study', in three semester groups. The students were asked as part of the course requirements to write 'articles' on their most meaningful insights about learning to become qualitative researchers, and to do so in an informal manner, as if writing to other students. Into this primary database we incorporated additional personal accounts gleaned from published literature in the field so that we could amalgamate insights from experienced researchers to complement our thinking and that of our students. In the text, students and doctoral graduates are cited first by entire name and then by first name. Other authors are cited in styleguide form. The names or pseudonyms of students, as well as those of several other doctoral graduates, make up the list of colleague contributors on pages 239–40. Of no small importance in helping us integrate the work of so many people were the contributions of three colleagues and friends: Emily R. Kennedy, Belén Matías, and K. June McLeod, who provided editorial comments, moral support, and many dinners.

We wrote this book so that you might join with us in considering how affect and cognition relate to and ensue from being qualitative researchers. Throughout the book, we share some information about the course for what it can contribute to our topic. In essence, this book is the product of layers of qualitative research, and the course served as the linchpin. The course allowed us

> to establish and document the processes of helping people to learn qualitative methodologies;
>
> to think about these processes, to 'go meta';
>
> to ask students to think about their processes as they wrote the articles that are woven throughout;
>
> to study in ethnographic ways ourselves as the team as well as the class;
>
> to plan how to write this book and how to involve in it the work of other colleagues, past and present students, and authorities in the field.

The writing here comes from people who are at various stages in the ever-evolving process of qualitative research learning. As learners we range from professors and people engaged in postdoctoral research to doctoral students in the beginning stages of experiencing the methodologies. Whatever our stages, however, it seems that all of us have chosen to share a way of research life — a way of *life* — that sweeps us along in continuous circles within circles of action, reflection, feeling and meaning making.

'We' is also you. If this book is to make any difference, it will be that the collective 'we' of the qualitative research community becomes more aware and, as a result, more powerful. Thus, it is you who are also a contributor. We hope you will communicate with us about any part of this book and how the book relates to your experiences and feelings. Please write to us in care of:

Professor Margot Ely
Department of Teaching and Learning
New York University, SEHNAP
239 Greene Street
New York, NY 10003.

Chapter 2

Starting

Introducing Margot and This Chapter

I am, if nothing else, a magnificent worrier. Each time, during the months before I am slated to teach our qualitative research course, I agonize over how best to teach it. How shall I balance coverage and depth? How can I best help all the members of the class who might range from research sophisticates with tightly focused ideas to research neophytes with only the vaguest of conceptions? How will I facilitate the education of students from a variety of disciplines? For if last year were any measure, there would be people from departments of music, dance, business education, physical therapy, industrial arts, communications, English, international education, psychology, religious education, and more. How will I help people voice their objectives and fulfill them? What activities and assignments will best enable students to learn what I hope they will learn? What exactly do I hope they will learn, anyway? How can the enormous and ever-expanding fund of information in the field be considered, in at least a semi-coherent fashion, in a mere fifteen weeks, two hours and forty minutes per week? In other words, how can I do justice to the field and to my students? And why am I so prone to taking on complex projects as I have clearly done once again?

I have been a professor for many years and before that a teacher of early childhood and elementary education. My specialty is the study of human interactions and ethnographic methodologies. I have taught allied courses: The Reflective Study of Teaching, Dissertation Proposal Seminar, Theory and Research. I carry out and publish qualitative research studies, consult about this area in the wider community, and serve on the dissertation committees of scores of people who are conducting that same kind of research. Not only that, I adore teaching and have sufficient experience with it to know that things usually work well. Why worry, then? Because what is rational does not always make sense. And then, there's that edge I get from being on my toes. Perhaps that is it.

When the team was first established, we developed a framework of principles about how most productively to involve people who wish to become qualitative researchers. Over several years, we accumulated a body of experience that helped us to hone our plans and continually assess that framework, which remains our sturdy educational guide to this day. In essence, we seek to involve students in the craft of qualitative research, encourage hands-on experiences, independent learning, reflection, and create ways for people to support, network, and teach each other in small groups. We provide a variety of texts for comparison and information, and time readings to coincide with what students are doing in practice. We encourage student participation in shaping class activities and assignments. In other words, we seek to create a learning community.

The intent of this chapter is to provide information about two conjoined, inseparable 'startings': that of beginning to explore qualitative research in a university course and that of entering the field. In order to present these experiences through the eyes of beginning researchers, I have woven together stories drawn from several years.

The Beginning

Snapshot

Some students already sit in the too small room, talking, looking after-work tired, watching as the team struggles in with reams of books and handouts. We enter separately. I, hurried and hopeful as usual, sit down between two students. One of them asks me if I know the teacher. 'Yes', I say. Other people come in more slowly, having first to find the room. After a bit, the place becomes over-crowded, hot. Not an auspicious beginning. Many of the students have what I call the doctoral-student stare, the 'I challenge you' stare, or am I reading my anxiety into their faces? Some seem relaxed. One sits with eyes closed. Is she sleeping already?

At this juncture I always long for a time capsule that will bring me to the end of the first class session. I have found, then, that students show a bit more cohesion, more understanding of what we are about and of what is to come. Then some eyes meet mine with humor and recognition, even if there is also usually a bit more of selective hysteria:

'You mean I have to be in the field after only three weeks?'

'I didn't realize this course runs from 4:20 to 7 p.m.!'

'The bookstore is out of texts!'

'I'm in nursing. Is this research possible for me?'

We've made plans, revised them, and made them over again. But I am still obsessed about how to start. Last semester's first session went well, but I worry that there may be too much 'teacher talk' before we send the students out to engage in their first forty-five-minute field activity. Will they bring to bear what I know are their rich life experiences on what I say about some characteristics of qualitative research, or will my words slide over their seemingly attentive heads? And why do I, Dewey's ardent fan, begin so soon with talk? Thank heavens we involve students in a small group activity first, so that they start to get acquainted and share some of their expectations and concerns.

Somehow I forge ahead, a bit briefer on team intros and lecture, but not much. Spirited student discussion. And we were right to think that these people would have tremendously varied backgrounds and interests. But this seems an asset as we begin. Seems all right. Seems a good place to send them out for the 'coffee shop exercise'. I'll know more later when we ask people to give us feedback about tonight. (Margot, Field Log, January 1988, pp. 5–6)

Hilary Knatz's reflections on her start serve to provide a student's point of view:

'Naturalistic research is a natural!' That was my first thought after hearing the purposes and methodology described. 'I've been doing this all my life'. As someone who is no great extrovert, who has traveled widely as the child of international civil servants watching people from afar, trying to understand their feelings and behaviors, imagining and speculating about their thoughts and intentions, I felt that I had a pretty 'fine-tuned' instrument in my own observational skills. Naturalistic research attracted me immediately because it emphasizes the interactive nature of things. And as a trained counselor I am continually aware of this in my work. Naturalistic research also seemed consonant with my world view in that it endows the individual with a kind of dignity as a unique repository of important information; 'That of God in every man' as my Quaker grandmother used to say. How exhilarating, then, was the prospect of becoming a naturalistic researcher!

The Plunge

Several first-session activities relate directly to the foci of this chapter, beginning to learn about qualitative research and beginning to 'do it', and so they are described here. About halfway through the session, when the coffee-break glaze makes its debut, students are given small slips of paper. Each contains the name of a nearby eating establishment. Students are asked to take their break in one of these places and to study it by observing intensely while entering in as little as possible.

What is going on?
How is it going on?
What does the researcher feel about this observation?
No notes during these observations, please.

When students returned to class, animatedly talking together, it is usually easy for them to share their insights, experiences, feelings, and questions. The following list is drawn from what the people in one group actually said:

- I never knew I could learn so much in twenty minutes.
- It's hard not to interact — just to watch and listen.
- How can I remember everything?
- But was I being objective?
- My answers gave way to more questions in about two minutes.
- I tried to be invisible. But I think I was noticed.
- I saw old things in new ways.
- Would other people see what I saw?
- I don't think my coffee shop is representative.
- I tried not to notice, but someone from this class was in the same place. It made me nervous.
- I felt like a sneaking fool.
- I don't think I can make conclusions based on twenty minutes of observing.
- I really like this. It feels right.
- I couldn't hear them! They kept turning away!
- I liked one waitress so much more than the others.
- The sexist language! I nearly died, not speaking up.
- I need to go back to check out some things.
- My kingdom for a pencil! Why did you not allow us to write?
- I don't know if I watched the important things.

This list embraces so many important issues about qualitative research and so many topics that must be considered by qualitative researchers that its very richness provides an impetus for the semester; the teaching team is distinctly elated. No small part of this elation is the fact that the list is engendered by an activity and reflection upon it, rather than by lecture and reading. At this point, the list validates what is to come in our readings. It follows naturally that the topics engendered by this list weave their way through this book.

One student, Molly Ahye, wrote with great candor about this beginning foray into the field:

> For the first time I realized that there is an art in holding a slice of hot pizza between the fingers, that 'slice' is all you have to say on entering if you want just cheese pizza, that there are cheese calzone, meat calzone, and other such alternatives. Being in dance, I also discovered that there is a rhythm in the movement pattern of the men who work behind the counter, as each role is interplayed. Postures, stances, the attitudes in eating pizza became points of focus.
>
> In the meantime, I felt exposed like a spy behind the obvious newspaper. Twenty minutes is a long time in a pizza parlor, with a few stools and running counters which tell you to eat and go. I sat with a relaxed countenance (I thought), not gazing at anyone or any spot for too long at a time, but returning systematically to add details. I never took so long to eat a slice of pizza, but just chewing slowly helped to relax me. Yet I found myself feeling conspicuous. Why did this bother me? I have been in all kinds of situations that were comparable. I think that the fact that I was told what to do without knowing how to gauge the outcome of the instructions made me unsettled. I remember visualizing the professor's face and her elfish grin and saying to myself: 'You must be having fun'. Everyone came back to the class and with rapid fire questions she asked us to tell about our observations. We had just been in the field, and it didn't hurt a bit.

The returning students usually share Molly's enthusiasm and anxiety. Would we be sent out every time during class? several ask in wary tones. No. In fact, from then on the food break is an in-class happening as a different team of two people provide sustenance each week. This has an incredible payoff in creating seamless sessions, humor, and good fellowship, as well as in supporting small group activities.

Expectations

Toward the end of this first class, each person is asked to write a personal statement which includes reasons for taking the course, specific research interests, if any, as well as how the course might best serve him/her. You, our reader, may find yourself sharing some of their feelings and expectations as you compare your stance to theirs. The students see their statements again, read our comments, and respond to what they wrote twice more — during the second and the final course meetings.

From our analysis, the substance of their communications falls into several categories. If you suspect that we applied naturalistic methodology to establish these categories, you are correct.

1 *Some students seem refreshingly forthright about the fact that they had other reasons for taking the course than their research interests.*

I am taking this course as a research tool requirement at the suggestion of my advisor. (John Forconi)

I am interested in the content, desperately need a course to 'turn me on'. Also, it's a requirement. (Sharon Lefkofsky)

2 *Some do not describe their research interests but elaborate on their states of mind.*

I don't know yet what I want to study. I need to contend with the fact that there is no powerful man or even myself discouraging me from what I'm interested in ... I've tried so hard to bend and shape myself to play ball with the 'big boys' that I find myself a bit dumbfounded that my hopes and ideas have no need to be shoved underground for another semester. (Deborah Lamb)

Entering the course, I must admit, nothing really made sense other than the three credits I would hopefully earn (and the inch closer to the degree I would be). Fortunately for me, being somewhat ignorant was probably to my benefit. Being ignorant allowed me to be open to ethnographic research. No expectations, no biases? Of course being the only Master's student in a room full of PhD hopefuls, I must admit I was a bit biased toward the group. I automatically ass-u-me-d they knew what case study 'was all about'. (Jo Ann Saggese, Final Log Entry)

3 *Some people have research interests and seem to need to learn the tools of the trade to forge forward.*

My interest ... is either (1) adjustment to retirement; or (2) experience of depression in old age. I'd like to learn several things:
  1 how to behave — i.e., find people to interview.
  2 how to formulate questions, establish rapport, select and document responses.
  3 how to look for patterns. (Hilary Knatz)

I teach eurythmics ... I feel like bursting sometimes — I want to show others what's going on. I've been videotaping.... How do I put this material in a form which I can share? What do I distill out? How can I communicate what I see? What are the appropriate tools? And there are probably more questions I need to ask. I want to know what these questions are. (Ruth Alperson)

Issues of adult literacy and dropping out of high school interest me. I think I can find subjects for a case study within these populations. (Dorothy Deegan)

4 *Some students write about projects in ways more compatible with research paradigms other than qualitative.*

Specifically, at the moment, my dissertation problem is: Are the developmental theorists, such as Piaget and Erikson *et al.* accurate predictors of the ways in which children, adolescents, and adults understand metaphors in stories? (Steve Rosman)

I am interested in studying parents' use of denial as a defense mechanism in dealing with developmental disabilities and the effect this has on the child. If parents use denial as a defense, will the child also use denial? If parents and child deny the disability/ illness, will the child compensate in some other way? (Barbara Gagliardi)

I hope this course will help me produce a project which will be helpful to other teachers in teaching technology to Special Ed. students. (Nick Surdo)

The students' beginning statements provide us with insights about learning activities that might serve each — from the most seemingly ready for qualitative research to the least. Indeed, we see progress quickly as students start to study, discuss, and commence fieldwork. We note their increased understandings about the characteristics of qualitative research and more centered notions about choices of research paradigm for future dissertation projects. This evolution in grasp is documented in students' quotations from this point of the book forward. It is at its most vivid in their reflections at the end of their studies.

Entering the Field as an Ongoing Proposition

No doubt about it, one of the maddening though constructive truths of becoming a qualitative researcher is that one must learn by doing. Of course, reading and thinking are facets of such 'doing', but there comes a time when one must expand that repertoire. If you are fortunate, that time comes very soon, near the beginning of your foray. For the first three weeks in the course, students read about, discuss, and simulate aspects of choosing a field site. They begin their logs. They are encouraged to select a site that is of interest to them, about which they wish to know more, a site similar, perhaps, to the one they might study for their dissertation research. In Lofland and Lofland's (1984) terms, we encourage people to begin where they are — to begin not with answers but with interests, passions, and questions.

Here the issue about familiarity/unfamiliarity with what one wishes to study first comes into focus. It is important throughout the qualitative research process, and will be addressed again in this chapter and in several others. We use one of our student's stories as a device for presenting and illustrating important concepts about entering the field. Here Hilary Knatz talks about familiarity:

> Some people pick an area to study which is quite proximate to their own immediate experience. For example, a teacher studies social rules in his classroom, a daughter studies her ailing mother's hospital ward, or an individual uses his or her own work setting. This has an advantage in that there is usually little or no resistance to 'entering the field'. However, there can be research dangers in this kind of proximity to the people you wish to study. For example, I had wanted to study my great-aunt's nursing home. It became clear to me, however, that it would be difficult to establish a sufficiently detached stance or viewpoint in such a setting. In this nursing home I am known. The nursing staff has a slightly adversarial attitude towards me because I am a 'relative'. I have a slightly adversarial attitude toward the staff because I fear they neglect my aunt. And my aunt most certainly would have a negative attitude toward me if I were to arrive at her home and not devote most of my attention to her.
>
> While it is certain that almost any field setting elicits emotional responses from us as researchers because of our past experiences and associations, the setting that is too familiar can be particularly 'loaded,' and can place us in role conflicts that can be almost unbearable.

It seems particularly important that Hilary knows where her ability to be 'sufficiently detached' would be endangered. But she suggests no hard and fast rule for others. At the same time, Hilary alludes to a concept that has served many of us well; that is, being too familiar is less a function of our actual involvement in the setting than it is of the research stance we are able to adopt within it. We are too familiar when we 'know' the answers ahead of time, or when we feel too close, too distressed, too disinterested, or too biased to study the situation, or when we realize that the people in it do not accept us in our researcher roles. We are too familiar when we cannot make the familiar unfamiliar. This reasoning puts a somewhat different light on statements in the literature such as the following:

I would offer a word of caution: The more you know about a situation as an ordinary participant, the more difficult it is to study it as an ethnographer. It is no accident that ethnography was developed in the study of non-Western cultures. The *less* familiar you are with a social situation, the *more* you are able to see the tacit cultural rules at work. (Spradley, 1980, pp. 61–2)

Werner and Schoepfle (1987), however, point out that times have changed for ethnographic study:

Today we study not only people who are very different from us but also those who exhibit much smaller, more elusive cultural differences. When our consultants are almost like us, it becomes harder to see how they differ. The jarring anomaly of exotic cultures is often inescapable, precisely because it is so shocking. Today we must have methods that let us see even the most subtle departures from our expectations. (p. 61)

Moreover,

modern ethnographic work has taught us that human beings know little about cultures right around them, and that at least in substantive cultural knowledge ... great discrepancies may exist between next-door neighbors. (p. 68)

It seems that it is increasingly important to study the familiar, but without the blinders that familiarity often attaches to us.

Students are asked to choose a field site by the fourth week. Some do. They, along with those who have not yet succeeded in gaining entrée, provide tremendously valuable insight into this important, often complex and complexing step. In the following excerpt, Hilary shares her feelings at this juncture:

But wait a minute! FIRST YOU HAVE TO GET INTO THE FIELD. A cold shudder hit. It seemed to me that the selfsame shyness which helped make me an attentive observer from afar could sabotage me in my efforts to place myself in the kind of setting I wanted to explore. To be sure, a naturalistic researcher can establish him or herself as an anonymous person in a more-or-less public setting in a coffee shop, in a train station waiting room or public square, but if you want, as I did, to explore a particular and private self-contained setting, one for which you need to be granted permission and given access, you've got some work to do. Your tasks are both psychological and tangible.

What is this terror of 'entering the field' all about? Perhaps it's not a terror for everyone. Perhaps for some it's a momentary hesitance, confusion, a mild discomfort. From what I observed, however, among my fellow classmates, the sense of *angst* and inertia about entering the field is all too common. Fundamentally, I think, this feeling comes from human self-doubts and a fear of rejection. Some people, and I am among them, find it very difficult to ask for things, fearing, I think, that they will be refused. The rational counter to this kind of thinking is to say 'So? So you could be refused! So what's so devastating about that?' The trouble is that this rational line doesn't really reach what these fears may be all about. The reluctance and inertia which are promoted by self-doubts are best addressed, I think, by acknowledging the doubts and working around them.

Even before the students enter the field, they discover the value of the field log in facing and working through one's feelings. Now these logs, which are started by the second week, come alive. Some students even acknowledge that they can see why we assign, insist, and cajole them to this early start. Hilary writes:

> The first and most important thing to do, I found, was to confront my feelings directly from the start via the log, where naturalistic researchers record what they plan and feel about their experiences on any particular project. Here is a 'safe-place', a haven where feelings, fears, doubts, suspicions, intuitions all have an honored place. To sit at a desk and put these things to paper, or word processor, gets them 'up front', and gives them a reality and a sense that they are perfectly legitimate and human. This helped me feel less judgmental and self-critical. Also, I could see more clearly what I needed to do next, even before I found a place for my fieldwork. And so, the study of my log served to enable me to take further actions, both with myself and with others.

In her final sentence, Hilary makes first mention of the cycle of ongoing data collection and analysis — that continual conjoined activity that characterizes and powers qualitative fieldwork. We have found that many students are distinctly surprised to discover that they can collect and analyze data long before they are in the field. We provide more detailed information about logs in Chapter 3 (pp. 69–82).

During these early activities of entering the field, the readings we assign begin to make heightened sense to students. Now words of the authorities, words we had read about finding a gatekeeper, seeking permission, choosing a site with which one is or feels sufficiently unfamiliar, and allowing the questions to emerge become clothed with an entirely different level of awareness.

> Why was it, I wonder, such a joy to me that the questions for my possible gatekeeper came right from studying today's log? After all, I had read all about it. Now, though, I was doing it. I could 'see'.
> (Belén Matías)

While not yet in the field, Hilary suggests a variety of procedures, in addition to those related in the field log, that helped her, and others, to 'get on with it'. One of these is the dress rehearsal:

> I found it helpful to have a kind of dress rehearsal by exposing myself to an analogous but not identical setting. I paid a visit to my aunt in her nursing home. At the time I did this, I had a sneaking suspicion that it was really an exercise in procrastination — a putting off of the inevitable moment when I would have to get off my seat and go out and ask permission to enter the 'real field'. In retrospect, however, I think it was enormously valuable. For one thing, it did get me up off my seat. It made me do something, enter a setting. And the act of doing it, instead of thinking about it, was already energizing. I tried to look at my dress rehearsal site as though it were going to be my real site. I began, if only in fantasy, the process of being an observer, and this gave me a sense of excitement and impetus to go ahead with it — to get on with it.

Hilary emphasizes that throughout the pre-field activities it is helpful to ask oneself the reasons for one's choice of a particular area of inquiry:

> This can help you clarify whether you are, in fact, interested and whether or not you are likely to have a degree of comfort in the setting you have chosen. It also, fortuitously, helps you rehearse your 'sales pitch' when it comes to the crucial moment of seeking entry.

Hilary uses the metaphor of job hunting in working out her strategies for selecting a field site. In that light, she asks herself the following questions:

> Is this a place where I can learn to fit in comfortably?
>
> Is this place reasonably convenient to home, work, or school, since this is where I will spend the bulk of my time?

and very important,

> Do I know anyone with connections to this place?

As it happened, Hilary did find what she thought would be an appropriate site. To her dismay, however, her activities unearthed not a single personal contact who might make the introductions. She went ahead anyway:

> I walked into the nursing home 'cold' and asked the front desk receptionist for the names of the social service director and the

volunteer coordinator. He complied and I walked out, heart thumping wildly, to go home to prepare myself to make my 'sales pitch'. 'I'm a PhD student with an interest in aging and I'd like to talk to you about the possibility of doing a brief "observational project" in your nursing home'.

Hilary was on her way to finding a 'gatekeeper', that essential person who could provide the permission for her to study in a particular setting:

> This is the person you need to persuade: (1) that you are sympathetic to and understanding of the goals of the setting; (2) that you provide some safeguards for the setting and people in it; (3) that you won't disrupt the basic routine of the setting; and/or (4) that you can give useful feedback on the workings of the setting after your study is complete.

Sometimes gatekeepers are not easy to determine. Some students find that they interview a person they believe to be the gatekeeper only to discover that they need to start much higher on the organizational ladder. Others find, after gaining initial entrée, that they need the cooperation and permission of people lower down the hierarchy. Often, qualitative researchers determine their appropriate gatekeepers only after they understand more about the situation that they are studying. But a start must be made. In Hilary's case, she learned that she needed the cooperation from the director of social work, the activities director, and the ceramics teachers in her nursing home. While she was quite nervous about starting the process, Hilary found it was not what she expected:

> Often you are in for some surprises when you first speak with the gatekeeper, especially if you have been feeling a good deal of apprehension about it. We've discussed this in our support groups. Many a naturalistic researcher, expecting resistance and having a well-rehearsed story at his or her disposal, has found a gatekeeper quite pleased and flattered by the idea of being 'researched'. Sometimes gatekeepers hope to be able to learn about their subordinates from a third party. That's a danger to be avoided. Sometimes the research is welcomed as a public service or a way of passing on what occurs in the setting. In my case, as soon as I told her of my interest, the director of social work said, 'Fine, let's see where you can observe'.
>
> I had hardly been able to launch into my introduction, and felt a little stunned and perhaps even cheated of the chance to air it. She said, 'You look surprised. Being near a university, we often have students doing research here'.

Many students did not find gaining entrée so easy. Some of them said that they presented themselves in apologetic, self-denigrating ways, and this made their gatekeepers hesitate. Some found it necessary to change their topic altogether. Leslie Rice provides an example: she had planned to study nurses in hospitals, but found that the permission process was too long for her preliminary study:

> The emotions I had experienced had been the initial joy of choosing a topic, the rapture of feeling it was something that could be accomplished. Then the unanticipated problems started to arise and I felt frustration, anger, and panic. What was I ever going to do? The answer became clear to me. I was going to give up my idea, and try to find something else to do. This was difficult. Once an idea was in my head, I just could not move away from it. I could not think of anything else, because I was so narrowly focused. It was difficult for me to force myself to look elsewhere.
>
> I grieved for the loss of the original idea. Once I finally admitted that I had to give it up, and that there were other ideas, it became easier. Finally a new idea came to my mind. I now wished to study the experience of people who were recovering alcoholics and the whole process started over again. Instead of having a lot of frustration and anger, I was rewarded with joy when entry into the field was finally achieved.

Some students found that they took too much for granted and were too abrupt. As a case in point, Molly Ahye recounts a situation that had occurred before she studied qualitative research methods:

> As a dance choreographer and educator interested in 'dance in culture' and coming from a small nation in the West Indies, I felt I needed to study other peoples' rituals and festivals. For some years before, I had been travelling around, observing, learning, and disseminating. Now I decided to observe a very rare ceremony on another island. This was to be a six-day event for which I arrived the day before. Without wasting any time, I went to the site (the field), to the compound, to speak with the spiritual head of that religious group.
>
> This leader was a grand matriarch, tall, strong, and of African descent. She had command of her domain and had around her an aura of mystery and power. All this did not intimidate me. It fascinated me even more. I was well prepared with tape recorder, note paper, camera and the works. All I had to do was to tell her what I was there for and the rest should be easy. Well! What a shock. I thought that I was circumspect, pleasant, straightforward, and honest. But Mother Catherine saw something else which

threatened her. Could be that I was overzealous. Enough to make her balk, and she bluntly refused to talk with me.

Of course this threw me back to base, feeling angry, frustrated, and confused. Not to mention the sense of discomfort, wondering if I were still welcome there. She said it was alright for me to observe, to tape the music, to take photos of background or open activities. However, I was not permitted to attend any of the sacred rituals. I pulled back in my shell, nursed my wounds, and waited. I had risked too much to just give up and go home. Each time I went there, I tried to guard my non-verbal reactions with my life. I kept thinking that maybe I might give away something that would heighten her suspicions about me and my motives.

I realized that I had *crashed into the field*, and that my parachute was of no use to me. I was among strangers, just me and me.

Molly did receive Mother Catherine's permission to study the sacred rituals, but only after she pulled back a bit, took more time, shared more information, and showed her real respect for the people of that religious group in as many ways as she could. Not everyone in analogous situations has such victories. Some people decide to try elsewhere. We have found, however, that with a great deal of common sense and sensitivity, many researchers can and do turn around rather sticky situations and enter successfully, if more discreetly.

Some students find that the adversarial relationships internal to a situation seem to make the gatekeepers suspicious or feel too vulnerable to the presence of an 'outside' qualitative researcher. Some report that their introduction stories were contrived and unconvincing, and so they had to start again. Hilary concluded:

> ... it is particularly important that you stay with the truth, albeit generally at times, to keep yourself out of trouble. On the other hand, if you are too specific about your background or are presenting yourself in somewhat imposing terms, you may find that you have jeopardized the anonymity which can be so important to open communication on the part of those being observed.
>
> I made the mistake of presenting a résumé which described my work history as a research associate for a center on aging. This, at first, got me more attention from the nursing home staff than I really wanted. There was a good deal of effort to acquaint me with the institutional structure of the nursing home, which was not, at the time, my primary interest.

This excerpt is a good example of the fact that ethical considerations play a role in every step of qualitative research. It is essential to be honest. How that plays itself out, that is, just how much detail is needed, is specific to each research project. This decision can be made by carefully weighing the possible consequences of sharing particular information. However, while we can anticipate consequences, reality is often a different matter. The best that qualitative researchers can do is to attempt to minimize problems by being increasingly aware and reflective. At the time of writing this book, Hilary is about to begin her doctoral research — yes, in a nursing home — and she reports that this time she presented an edited résumé.

The title of this section, 'Entering the Field as an Ongoing Proposition', is Hilary's creation and we believe it carries a message that is rarely discussed in the methodological literature. Hilary proposes that entering the field is a longer, more active process than many of us envision, one that often produces surprising snags:

> I have learned that it is curious but true that the process of 'entering the field' never quite ends when you do naturalistic research. You must not only get the support of your original gatekeeper, as I have mentioned, you must get the aid of others who are more closely connected to the field that you want to observe. Often you will get the overt cooperation of such individuals because they are given no choice, but if they resent your presence or feel threatened by it some way, they can find ways of sabotaging your opportunities for observing.

An example of this is Marsha Diamond's story of her experiences as a novice researcher of classroom communication. While observing a teacher who said she welcomed the research, Marsha found that the teacher consistently spoke so softly and moved her body in such ways that Marsha could neither hear nor observe her. Hilary experienced a different kind of challenge:

> In my case, the ceramics instructor who was in charge of the class of elderly residents I had elected to observe, decided she didn't like my sitting there taking it all in but wanted me busy doing pottery like everyone else. I learned, therefore, how to pretend to be doing pottery while actually observing and storing information in my head.
>
> It is important to try to work out a relationship with the 'sub-gatekeepers' to lessen their anxiety about you. A good way, I found, was to find ways of being helpful, of showing interest and giving honest, positive feedback not related to my study, and of trying to avoid creating situations that are counter to their work style or that threaten their power.

Sometimes becoming more engaged in the context of the setting works, as it did in Hilary's example. Sometimes it does not work. Qualitative researchers depend on observing and listening. When they are so busy contributing that they miss the very information they need, and they miss it consistently over time, then they have a problem. Most people learn to walk the fine line between 'contributing' and 'researching' that serves both the research process and the social unit being studied. We will consider degrees of participation further in Chapter 3.

Even when one has found a way to participate in and to study a situation, continuous sensitivity is needed. Hilary found that:

> ... you need to monitor your degree of participation with the people you are observing so as not to upstage the person in charge, particularly if you are observing a structured setting such as a classroom. In one instance, I remember that the nursing home resident in the class whom I had interviewed brought me some pamphlets and photographs to examine. This had the effect of turning the class' and other staff members' attention toward our activity, to the apparent chagrin of the teacher of the class. It was difficult for me to regain her trust.

Often qualitative researchers in similar situations fear that all is lost. Almost always, however, they have built such previous goodwill and trust that there is sufficient 'money in the bank' to see them through with the people in their research site.

Hilary proposes that, to a degree, the final stage of entry is with the individuals one wishes to study, both as a group and as individuals. The task in group entrée is to get a degree of acceptance from people without their being overly self-conscious. Often this comes with time.

> Over a period of time you cease to be a novelty and become more of a fixture, someone they expect to see each time they are in that setting. To lessen the likelihood of their being self-conscious, it is, I think, advantageous if your power position relative to them be neutral; that you do not have a dual function. For this reason there is merit to the idea of not observing settings with which you are too closely associated already. While this is so, many researchers have successfully observed their own class or even their own staff. If you are viewed as helpful and trustworthy, you can get the cooperation, but usually this is not easy!

The challenge of earning acceptance arises again with one-on-one entry. Hilary found that the fears and doubts she had been struggling with from the start intensified again to make this level of entry every bit as anxiety provoking:

> Each individual is a field of their own and must be treated accordingly. This was certainly true in my effort to learn about how nursing home residents experienced their life in the home and how

they had experienced their life before entering the home. Certain people find it painful to share and thus avoid this kind of contact. This became frustratingly apparent to me as I sought to engage one very passive and, I thought, victimized resident whose background intrigued me. She chose simply not to be accessible to me, and I finally had to accept that fact and redefine my focus a little.

This last sentence provides an example of the shaping of qualitative research design in its very process. We'll talk of this again in following chapters.

Sometimes one-on-one entrée depends on how a qualitative researcher presents her/himself. Here is Hilary's experience of this:

> If you seem to be fulfilling a role which is aversive to them, friendship and cooperation can evaporate in a flash. I encountered this temporarily when a venerable and very articulate 94-year-old man whom I wanted to interview discovered I had training as a psychologist. He said, 'Well, you'll no doubt need to speak to someone else. I'm not a patient'. I had to make it clear that I hoped to speak to him as an equal, to be enlightened by his perspective, and not as a psychologist interviewing a patient.

Sharing vignettes such as the latter that contain the words and actions of the people we study makes qualitative research reports come alive. There is more about writing reports in Chapter 5.

As Hilary sees it, and we concur, gaining access is an ongoing process. It never ends. The trust and cooperation one establishes at one point need to be maintained. Each time a qualitative researcher defines and redefines the study, that researcher needs to speak with and/or observe different people or the same people in different and perhaps deeper ways. For this, entrée is needed. The process is worth it.

> I have learned that one shouldn't be so hard on oneself. One of the delightful things about naturalistic research is that one learns to accept that the observer is an imperfect (or should I say unique) instrument and since this is so, each study will be the outgrowth of that particular instrument, and unlike any other. Naturalistic research, fortunately, is a process which is self-generating, and the excitement of watching the unfolding and shaping of a body of work will often create the impetus to enter the field fearlessly (relatively) again and again. (Hilary Knatz)

Too Close to Home

Entering the field has its traumatic moments for most people. It also has its triumphs. The remainder of this chapter includes, among other things, some accounts by individual students that highlight what they learned and how they felt in making a start to their work.

Allie Parrish presents a particularly vibrant, if not altogether happy, account that serves to flesh out its mention in Hilary's previous contribution. This article is presented in a different way from the narrative quoted thus far, but with reason. Each of Allie's lines is numbered the same way as are the lines in our field logs (Chapter 3). In the discussion that follows her article, you'll see how I make use of line and page information. You might like to write some comments in the margin about your ideas, insights, questions, and feelings as you read Allie's lines so that you can compare your comments to mine at the end. Being too close to what you want to study is enticing to many beginning researchers, but cautioned against as well. Allie learned all about that:

Allie's Start

1 Administrator? Researcher? Student? Friend? What am I to-
2 day? Will a college administrator be accepted as a qualitative
3 researcher just because she says, 'I'm not a dean today?' Let me
4 share some of my experiences when conducting research to
5 fulfill requirements of a case study research course.
6
7   As a dean for several years at a community college, my
8 interrelationships with most faculty and students have centered
9 around my primary role as a student affairs dean. Like most
10 people, I know some of my colleagues well while I maintain a
11 formal working relationship with others.
12
13   As a doctoral student in higher education administration at
14 a large, metropolitan university, I enrolled in a course that
15 prepares students to practice qualitative research methods.
16 With the focus of the course being participant-observer metho-
17 dology, I sought out an ongoing community group that I could
18 join as an observer. When a few obstacles prevented my
19 observing this group, I felt desperate as the urgency of begin-
20 ning some kind of study met with the time pressures that I
21 would be facing. The ol' light bulb clicked on in my head and I
22 thought that observing an 'interesting' class at the college
23 would be convenient, accessible, and I could use my profes-
24 sional influence to gain entry to the field.
25
26   The social science courses had personal appeal so I set out
27 to find the 'right one'. Then, I saw it; calling out to me was a
28 seminar addressing issues concerning life and living. The course
29 was taught by a senior faculty member with whom I've had a
30 friendly though not a close friendship.

1   Approaching the professor for permission to join her class
2 as a researcher, I explained that I was taking a course and
3 needed to gain some practical experience in conducting research
4 through direct observation methods. I told her I'd like to sit in
5 on one of her social science classes for several weeks and that
6 I'd certainly try to be unobtrusive. She quickly agreed to the
7 arrangement cautioning that it was okay if I could put up with
8 her. I was all set to start attending the class at its next meeting
9 time.
10
11   On the morning of what was to be my first observation I
12 found that Professor Bartlett was ill and would not be meeting
13 her classes that day. After five days, she had not returned to
14 campus and my feelings of desperation returned. I called
15 another social science professor who teaches introductory
16 sociology and asked if I might sit in on his class. He had had
17 several run-ins with the administration as a result of complaints
18 from students. I assured him that I was asking permission to
19 join the class in my role as graduate student and not as an
20 administrator. He flatly refused me in strong terms stating that
21 the administration had given him nothing but trouble and that
22 he viewed me as part of that group. Although I assured this
23 tenured, full professor that I did not intend to use any part of
24 my study for any purposes related to our college, he would not
25 budge.
26
27   Finally, what seemed to be a very long week passed and
28 Professor Bartlett returned to the campus. On that day I began
29 my observations. I arrived at the classroom a few minutes
30 early; the professor was there and told me to take a seat in the
31 rear of the room. Since I'd previously said that my presence
32 would need to be explained, I thought she'd ask me to do that
33 when the class was ready to start. Several students recognized
34 me and looked a little puzzled. I concluded that they probably
35 thought I was there to observe the faculty member. The class
36 was held, and I sat taking pages of notes and no reference was
37 made to my being there. At the next class meeting, I stopped
38 by the professor's desk and said that the students needed to
39 know why I was there. She said, 'Why say anything? Nobody
40 has asked'. I didn't push the issue since it seemed that perhaps
41 she didn't want me to talk to her class for some reason. So, I
42 went through another class feeling a little unsettled and know-
43 ing that I might be violating research ethics by conducting
44 covert research, in effect. At the third class meeting I told
45 Professor Bartlett that it was necessary for me to say something
46 to her class to explain why I was there. I told her that the
47 professor of my university class said I must do it. After relating
48 my introduction to the class I felt that my new role had been
49 established with everybody — well, almost.

1   No sooner had I sat down from giving my account to the
2   class, Professor Bartlett added, 'It's a good idea for the dean to
3   sit in on the class because administrators are out of touch with
4   what goes on in the classroom'. Damn it! I was not there as an
5   administrator, I thought — especially not one who is out of
6   touch. On other occasions when discussing general topics like
7   preregistration procedures or obtaining information from the
8   computer center, the professor directly addressed questions to
9   me as an administrator. There seemed to be no way to avoid
10 my primary role at the college.
11
12   My role problems persisted as students directed comments
13 or questions to me as the dean — not the graduate student
14 visiting their class. One student even referred to me as 'the big
15 boss'. At least twice I found it necessary to miss a class or leave
16 early because an administrative matter took precedence. Ex-
17 plaining her absence from one of the classes, the professor told
18 the students that she missed class to attend a funeral with me
19 and referred to me by title. It was as if my being a part of her
20 reason for absence somehow lent it validity.
21
22   Occasionally, other colleagues took me out of the research
23 role by asking for my critical observations of how the class was
24 taught. Of course, I avoided direct responses to these queries.
25 Finally, I sometimes found it difficult to maintain the role of
26 researcher in my work setting. For instance, when I recognized
27 that an inaccurate statement unrelated to course content may
28 have been made to a student, or if I perceived something said as
29 inappropriate, I felt the urge to interrupt — though I didn't.
30
31   One other area of concern surfaced as I carried out my
32 research activities. In talking with students in the class, without
33 my asking, they inevitably told me what a great teacher Profes-
34 sor Bartlett was. Could some of this have been a reaction to the
35 fact that I was an administrator? Were students seeing me as an
36 evaluator? Did the professor assume that posture at times? As I
37 recall she seemed to seek my approval before cancelling the
38 class to attend the funeral that was mentioned earlier.
39
40   Reflecting on some of my experiences in trying to sand-
41 wich in a research experience in an already crowded work day,
42 I would not do it this way again. The convenience of a research
43 site might not be enough to overcome the other pitfalls one
44 might face such as the need to relinquish the researcher role
45 when you least want to, or trying to assume a role different
46 from that most people know you to have. This learning experi-
47 ence has left me with hindsight that will help in the future.
48 Perhaps the other professor's refusal to let an 'administrator' in
49 his classroom should have been taken as fair warning of possi-

1   ble problems. At any rate, I think that qualitative research,
2   accomplished through participant-observation methods at one's
3   work place, may just be too close to home.

Several thoughts about Allie's piece seem in order here. Even though her project was a course-related fieldwork trial and not her dissertation research, Allie's support group, group facilitator, professor, and class members attempted to dissuade her from her plans. She decided to go ahead. Allie shares openly the pressures of being both a professional and a student and how these pressures led her to her choice of study (see p. 26, lines 7–24). Solving the dilemma in this way is not an unusual condition for doctoral students. Many are part-time students, and, at times, they must find compromises. Given this situation, however, I am convinced that it is both important and possible to locate a social situation for study that holds more ingredients for success than did Allie's.

As I studied Allie's account, the following facts sent me some very clear danger signals: she did not describe how she provided the professor and students with a guarantee of anonymity and with detailed descriptions of her research roles as distinct from her administrative ones (p. 27:1–6; p. 27:47–49); she took copious notes (p. 27:36) in a situation where she was perceived by professor and students to be administrator rather than researcher (p. 28:2–4; 12–14; p. 28:16–20); and other professors also saw her as an administrator in this situation (p. 28:22–24).

I feel it was an excellent and honest strategy for Allie to say that her college instructor insisted she finally introduce her purpose and roles to the class, although it seemed too late (p. 27:44–47), and to be aware and concerned about the ethics that helped her to take such action (p. 27:37–44).

How did your comments compare to the intent of these? All in all, psychologically as well as experientially, Allie was too familiar, too close to home.

What Was That Question Again?

During the process of gaining entrée, the researcher continues to work conceptually on her/his project. One of the first tasks is to develop initial questions after the general area for study has been chosen. In one sense, however, selecting an area or topic for study is already an answer to one essential question: 'What topic interests or excites me as being worthy of study?' or 'What do I want to contribute to others?' or 'What do I feel I'd like to give myself to in the next year(s) of research work?' (The selection of topic is first mentioned on pp. 16–17).

Even before selecting their topic, then, qualitative researchers ask meaningful questions that arise from their life experiences. As Hilary noted (pp. 16–20), often those life experience questions draw us to study particular topics at particular sites. Emily Kennedy, for example, had been engaged for a good part of her life with issues of how people can be helped to develop personal power. She chose to study how authoritarianism-democracy and teacher expectancy played themselves out in four kindergarten classrooms. Matt Foley had dedicated his life as a priest to working with people in poverty so that they might secure decent housing, benefit from sound education, receive needed social services, find meaning in religion, and develop increased pride and dignity in these endeavors. For his doctorate, Matt documented the coping strategies of children on slum streets and produced materials for teachers based on what he found. Emily and Matt provide examples that are cases in point. In my experience, the great majority of topics for study and research questions do not arise out of a vacuum or specious choice but, instead, mesh intimately with researchers' deepest professional and social commitments. I have found this to hold for beginning qualitative researchers as well as for those engaged in dissertation and post-dissertation research. We'll be speaking more about the social implications of qualitative research in the 'Epilogue' of this book.

A key characteristic of naturalistic research is that questions for study evolve as one is studying. In fact, researchers rarely end up pursuing their original questions. This is not to say that one is a blank slate at the onset of study or changes topics at will. I believe that what is needed at the outset is at least threefold:

1 an adequate self-awareness about how the field of study relates to one's own life;
2 a sound grasp of the research method one has chosen. This assumes a sound grasp of its literature, as well as research experiences and reflections thereon.
3 a broad grasp of the literature and practices in one's field of concern and the theories and assumptions associated with these. This is tricky because such a grasp must not act as a blindfold, once the study has begun, to shut out particular leads, alternative explanations, and differing conceptual structures. In the qualitative research course, I urge people to depend first on their present tacit and overt knowledge and to go to the literature once their questions are more specific. In dissertation supervision, on the other hand, I attempt to breach the distance between qualitative research requirements and the conventional research thinking that says proposals 'must have a review of literature' by suggesting the broadest, most varied review at the start.

As questions change and become more focused, the review of literature follows their lead, is reworked, and thus becomes more pertinent
and useful. Even so, the consistent efforts of qualitative researchers, at
any point, to remain open to what they study and to examine their
assumptions as they do so seems the best defense against allowing
literature and experience to impose blindfolds. We provide examples
of students at work on this throughout.

No naturalistic researcher begins without questions, but these can and
should be as broad as 'What is going on here?' For most of us, the questions
shift, specify, and change from the very beginning in a cyclical process as the
field logs grow, are thought about, analyzed, and provide further direction
for the study. This is certainly different from positivistic research in which
questions are posed at the start and do not change, and, in this difference, it is
often discomfiting. It takes a certain emotional sturdiness for any qualitative
researcher, but particularly a beginning one, not to reach too quickly and too
firmly for 'the' question. It takes conviction and confidence to collect and
examine one's data with the view that the questions can and should change,
and to love that possibility.

Accepting the mutability of questions is one bane and joy of qualitative
research. We urge our students to consider the course project as a field trial
for their area or topic of inquiry. This does not lessen their very real, often
poignant experience of the 'changing question'. Francia de Beer provides a
time line of her adventure to determine beginning focus questions. While
what she writes is specific to her case, the phenomenon is experienced by
many others.

> I was interested in 'What are the professional perceptions of leaders
> in occupational therapy and what are the implications of these for
> present and future trends in the profession?' I thought that this
> question was clear and well focused, so I pursued it wholeheartedly.
> Little did I know that it would go through a metamorphosis.
>
> In examining how I was going to seek out people to study, I
> shared this question with several people. Their responses helped me
> to realize that what I thought was very focused initially was in
> reality still amorphous. So I changed my focus to 'What are the
> experiences of female leaders?' I went from seeking out national
> female leaders in my profession to looking for them at the local
> level. When I realized that there were very few such leaders in the
> area, I changed my focus to a study of male leaders; when I realized
> that extensive travel throughout the region would be required to
> find male leaders, I decided to change not only the population but
> also to modify the question. Instead of studying the experience of
> male leaders in a female-dominated profession, and the influence

they perceived their maleness had on their professional experiences, I was now going to study 'What are the perceptions of male students entering a female-dominated profession?' In addition, I wanted to collect data before they graduated to get their ideas about how their gender would affect their position in the field.

For me this was a radical change from the initial conceptualization of what I was going to examine. However, in analyzing the development of the question, all the stages of its metamorphosis remained within my domain of interest. In Lofland and Lofland's (1984) terminology, I still started out from where I was.

Francia's questions at this point are still more general, more topic oriented, than they will be once she collects and analyzes data. The section in Chapter 3 labeled 'What Was That Question Again? Again' considers how questions change after the beginning research phase.

Letting Go: Trusting the Process

Learning to trust the process of qualitative research is difficult for many students of the field, particularly at the beginning. It is of course essential if one wishes to be a qualitative researcher. In my experience, this learning is highlighted as students work in two arenas: learning to trust the research paradigm itself, to accept that it is worthy and respectable, and learning to trust oneself as a flexible instrument. In this section I will address both as they apply to 'starting'. Because it is an ongoing issue, the topic is also integrated into the presentations of the chapters to come.

It is certainly hard to trust a process that is so different from what most of us have come to know and respect as research:

> The first change we had to face in the course was the change in our belief system. During all our professional academic education we were brainwashed into believing that quantitative research was the only respected research in which one should be engaged. Not only were we focused toward this direction, but also to the ideal that research was done by being objective and detached rather than by being subjective and involved. (Francia de Beer and Dalia Sachs)

While the idea of qualitative research is a breath of fresh air to many, those very same people have, after all, been socialized into a particular research vision. It may well be that leading researchers are beginning to agree that various research paradigms are valuable (Sherman and Webb, 1988; Werner and Schoepfle, 1987). But this stance is not unanimous in higher education. Here, frequently, students are told verbally or non-verbally which research is 'best', which research is 'acceptable', and which research is to be believed, even before they have studied a variety of research paradigms and often before they have decided upon a topic for their work. For many novices who are drawn to qualitative research, this specter must be examined and overcome one way or the other, as an ongoing pre-and postdoctorate process (see Chapter 6). Toward this, we as teachers have found that a variety of instructional activities is useful at the beginning of a qualitative research course. One is to engage students in studying the writings of leading theorists and practitioners so that they can interact with their reasoning. A second is to find out if students have developed, in their previous studies, a solid grounding in the assumptions of a variety of research paradigms and an understanding of the kinds of questions that are congruent to each. While much has been made of the fact that some neophyte researchers fall in love with a particular research paradigm, decide that it alone will do, and only then run about looking for a question, I do not find that all too amazing. Instead, I see it as a reflection of inadequacies in how students have been taught about research. A third strategy is to organize small and large group discussions based on students' agendas that help them to share their insights and to support their emergent research understandings. Fourth, and possibly most important, students must feel that their concerns and research dispositions are respected and that they are not being manipulated to practice within only one research paradigm after the semester ends. Last, it has been immensely helpful to invite former students who have 'made it' into or past their doctoral research to testify to their process and talk to the concerns of students who are just beginning.

When the fieldwork goes into full swing, support group interactions take on heightened importance. Students explore with each other their insights and feelings as they progress in their understandings about qualitative research. Many have come to trust the paradigm and turn their concerns to other matters. For me, it is compliment enough at the end of the semester to read, as I have done, 'Well, I'm going to do survey research for my dissertation. But I surely understand more about qualitative research now and respect it immensely'.

Learning to trust oneself as a flexible instrument goes side by side with learning to trust the paradigm if there are opportunities to be that instrument. Sharon Lefkofsky tells her story of how the emergent nature of qualitative research depended in part on her.

> I knew where I should go and what I would do. First, as a coordinator for a graduate work study program, *I needed* to be in the field developing new work placements for students. Second, I wanted to conduct my observations and interviews for the designated number

of weeks at a previously chosen field site. I was using my skills in time effectiveness. *I knew* I was prepared to meet the challenge of Professor Ely's demanding class by studying the interactions of nurses and patients in one of my hospital settings.

The initial session was on how to enter the field and to plan one's introduction story. Ha! I didn't need to work much on that. I had a straightforward opening: all preplanned, all scheduled, ready to implement. So, I sat back and waited for the class to catch up with me. I turned off my listening and waited until the next problem arose. I certainly didn't have one at that moment.

When the lecture ended and our peer group organized, we met with our facilitator, Diane. Our group discussed the problems of being too close to one's setting. No problem for me, I said to myself. I've been observing professionally for thirty years. In that time I had learned how to maintain a healthy separation between myself and the group I'm observing. I knew that many of the issues presented were issues I had previously resolved before coming to class.

I should have had a clue that something was wrong with my plan when my group facilitator turned me over to the professor. T.O. is an expression used in stores when a customer isn't buying and is sent to see the manager. I had thought that all that remained for me to do was discuss with Professor Ely which one of the centers I had chosen would best fit my needs in this class. When she heard the list of things I wanted to study and the places I had chosen, she smiled, and said, 'Sharon, the topics are too narrow'. She reminded me to think about the funnel she drew on the board, a visual representation of the observation process. 'To think broader, first, and then get narrower. Choose the neonatal nursery', she suggested. 'Study life there', she said.

Think broader? Something is wrong. Even though I am in a profession that treats the patient holistically, we are trained to focus on and identify specific problems. Although puzzled and confused, I was still somewhat secure that my plan would work.

One aspect of the observations I hadn't resolved was how to set the limits for the different roles I was to manage: occupational therapist and researcher/student. I couldn't go to either of two possible centers without someone expecting something from me. That is, in my role of graduate program coordinator, my presence at these centers would put me in touch with management, therapists, teachers, nurses, and direct care workers and would have me attend meetings, discuss issues, and deal with programming problems. After much agonizing, in fact two weeks of agonizing, I realized that I couldn't enter these fields (I hope the reader notices that I was already using the jargon of this paradigm). I couldn't deal with the dual role honestly.

I felt like Tevye in *Fiddler on the Roof* dealing with major philosophical issues. He raises his hands to the sky and talks to himself, . . . And as Tevye did, I said to myself (and anyone who would listen), 'On one hand I feel relief, I feel free and honest. I don't have to misrepresent myself. But, on the other hand, I am resentful because I need to reschedule my life to fit in yet another activity'.

As it turned out, 'letting go' was not a problem for me only at the beginning of the class. I realize now, as I am writing this essay at the end of the semester, there was a pattern. There were many instances of not letting go that prevented me from moving on. When I hit this kind of block I reminded myself to trust the process. Initially that meant trusting my group and my instructor to see some of what I wasn't seeing. Later, trusting the process meant listening to my peer support group, listening carefully to what they were saying. Often it was difficult to hear, because they weren't saying what I wanted them to say. Still later, it meant that because I had trusted the process I learned to function in it.

Trusting the process allowed me to fall back on previous successes. I learn well, even when I resist. So, I knew I could learn this process. For example, I had to refocus my way of observing and interviewing to begin to formulate a broader focus before I could narrow it down, Initially I resisted letting go. When I allowed the process to flow, I was able slowly to shift my style to meet the needs of the research methodology and, so, in interviews, I began to enjoy the success of asking the lead-in question that allowed the interview to blossom.

Sharon says it so well that there is little need for more than a few brief thoughts. First, letting go, in the best sense, means that a qualitative researcher is more able intensely to 'be with' what is happening and to respond to that instead of worrying about what should or could be happening. This means that the person who is the research instrument is more in line with the needs of the study and can reflect more realistically upon possible next steps. Second, to let go in the ways that have been described indicates increased trust that, should one stumble and make mistakes, these are not the end of the world but can be used as building blocks to redo and to continue. Most of all, researchers who trust themselves as flexible instruments soon understand that they are responsible. This stance helps their participants also to trust in the qualitatitive research process and in the instrument.

The Support Group: The Tie That Binds

From the second week on, the class is subdivided, quite casually by counting off, into smaller groups of about six people each who are to meet for at least one hour as part of every ensuing class session. One member of the teaching team relates to a particular group all through the semester as a group facilitator. Serendipity! If any strategy has worked far better than originally envisioned, it has been creating and facilitating these support groups. They will be discussed throughout chapters to come. Here are some quotations that pertain particularly to this chapter's topic of getting started:

> I wrote in detail in my log exactly what I planned to do and expected to execute the same. This whole thing blew up in my face. Thank goodness for my support group.
>
> Even before I met the people in the field, the whole planned timetable became a fairy tale. A few days before the beginning of the project, the director of the clinic in charge of the designated site started to question some aspects of the project, especially the release time for employees to be interviewed. When these questions arose, it became clear that my gatekeeper had never informed the director about the project. I knew that actions had to be taken by both the gatekeeper and by me in order to smooth things over. Already, at this point, my level of anxiety was rising. After a two-week delay, the three interviews and the timetable were reestablished. At the new start, the first interviewee was ill; the second one was on jury duty for a whole week; and the third one was in a conference out of town. Now, my level of anxiety was beyond measurement.
>
> The change and adaptation that were needed in order to deal with this situation were facilitated by my support group in the research class. They offered emotional support and helped me to remember that there are things that one can change and others that are outside of one's control. (Dalia Sachs)

> So there I was, three strikes and out! Three unsuccessful attempts to gain entrée! My time was rapidly running out and I felt like the tortoise at the end of the line, doggedly plodding along. Can you imagine the frustration and the dejection, rejection, I was feeling at this point?
>
> At the very next session of our support group in class I poured out my 'expressions of woe' both in writing and in speech. You see, we had been meeting weekly since the beginning of the term in groups of five or six people, for the purpose of sharing our progress and problems and creating coping strategies for those problems.
>
> As a result of that session, I began looking, not for another class in school, but for someone in my community to study instead. This time I succeeded in finding someone who readily agreed to become 'my case study'. (Akiko Okada)

> Our peer group was a strong element in the entire course and the strength and direction of their comments began the first week. It was clear that group members wouldn't pacify each other. From them came direct head-on comments, away from familiar settings. My group members and I discussed several alternative placements

for me. Why were they seeing solutions for me so clearly? My initial plan was carefully thought out; I really didn't want to abandon it. I didn't want to 'let go'. My support group persisted until I was redirected in a more positive direction.

Phyllis Hamilton, another student, told me, 'We don't so much let go as we open our minds to another area we hadn't thought about but which becomes apparent to us. This willingness to be open to other ideas helps, but it is a long struggle'. (Sharon Lefkofsky)

Postscript

It seems clear to me upon studying this chapter and upon reflecting on the teaching team's work, that our emotions — our hopes, fears, and passions — had at least as heavy a role to play as did our cognitive grasp of the field in how we came to, planned for, and carried out our work. Our educational philosophy — that amalgam of how we believe people learn best — was shot through inseparably with both feelings and information. In hindsight, we were fortunate to bring compatible philosophies to this endeavor even if we came with differing histories and points of view about how to actualize those philosophies. While we were at different places than our students, we were quite like them in our processes because, for each of us, continuing to learn about qualitative research began again as we started to think, make decisions, and face our feelings about the endeavor.

The students show us in a variety of ways that their emotions and knowledge are of great importance to them. For some, enrolling in the course is cause for celebration, For others, it is cause for discomfort. Perhaps there are a few neutrals sprinkled through, but not many; with the exception of one they have been doctoral students. For all, it is serious business. The students bring a wide variety of personal and academic aims to the course. These goals range from general to specific, from consonant with qualitative research to consonant with other paradigms. If we do not see that students are different, I would conclude that we are not looking thoroughly enough. Qualitative researchers start at various points, unfinished and raw. This we have in common. For most of us, that rawness continues as we become more adept. Only its content changes.

At the start of each course, it is not my vision that every student will or should continue to practice as a qualitative researcher. For one thing, I feel that certain personal characteristics facilitate learning the process, although they certainly don't make it easy. Learning to become a qualitative researcher is never easy. These characteristics have to do with a person's flexible stance, trust that process leads to product, sense of human dignity, humor, and very important, an ability to create structure in progress. We provide more detail about these characteristics in Chapter 4. Since these attributes come in a myriad of garbs, it is impossible as well as patronizing for teachers to decide, first thing, that some students are meant for qualitative research while some are not. I shall admit frankly, however, that sometimes my warning bells ring very quickly. As life has played itself out, I find that I have been more right than wrong. But some of my first impressions were mightily without basis.

Would that students were better and sooner helped to develop the tools by which to match the substance and demands of each research paradigm with their own personal characteristics, professional philosophy, and contextual support system. Certainly some of this must occur prior to a course on specific methodology. For a number of our students, however, it did not, and from my experience this situation is more the rule than the exception in institutions of higher learning.

The statements students provide about their aims for the class highlight my concern about the limits of what words can do and the care that must be taken to get past the words to people's meanings. How do the students come to what they write? How do they feel about sharing their thoughts with virtual strangers? How do their past experiences with teachers, doctoral programs, courses, and writing relate to what they communicate? What of their personal lives? For example, Phyllis Hamilton traveled round trip from Baltimore to New York each week. How did this circumstance impact on her writing? What of our classroom context — that crowded, oddly shaped, drafty, poorly lit, and poorly equipped room? Of course, the students do have an opportunity to see their statements again and respond to them. But the caution about words and meaning holds, as it does throughout the qualitative research endeavor.

I am having a terrible time writing the words 'students' and 'teachers'. The artificial separation such words imply is antithetical to what I know to be true. For me, the distinction between student and teacher blurs in the doing. For example, the teaching team reflected on its work, the students reflected on theirs and ours, and we continued to do so in order to write this book. In this, all of us learned and all of us taught, often simultaneously. What is more, we learned and we taught in any manner of grouping, from whole class to an individual alone. It is probably sufficient to voice my distaste one time and to go on using such terms as students and teachers since we need to be clear about our references and I cannot find a better solution.

While I'm at it, let me add some thoughts about creating that introduction offered by a naturalistic researcher to various people in the field in order to receive permission to do the study there. This is nervous-making for many students. Some feel they must recount every detail, while some feel they must divulge none. For most, the question is 'just how much?' Certainly an introduction need not be the recounting of a myriad of details. It can, and most often should, be a broad overview. The person seeking entrée need not feel she or he is being sly or dishonest by making that introduction as general as serves its aims. Some of its purposes are to communicate about the study, the roles of the researcher that are in line with that, the ways participants will be involved and their rights, and the support that is needed, while not providing information that would impinge on the very phenomenon to be studied. This aim is not dishonest *per se*. But it does need thinking about. Members of support groups do a wonderful job of helping each other to decide on the substance of each introduction. Concerns about the ethics of doing a particular piece of research must come long before this introduction. Indeed, such concern is vital right from the inception. When the research plan has been weighed and found ethical, the introduction should present no conflict of ethics.

Chapter 3

Doing

Introducing Ann and This Chapter

I found my way into qualitative research, as I hope you will, through the research questions I raised. When I first brought my twenty questions to Margot, she looked at me and said, 'Are you sure you want to do this research?' This was not an auspicious beginning. Margot went on to explain that the questions were sound and reasonable, but much too specific, too 'set'. At that time she had no idea how flexible I could be. Her point about the nature of the questions I asked, however, was to become one of the most important lessons I learned about data gathering. I will discuss these matters in this chapter.

In addition to the nature of the research questions, a range of experiences and personality characteristics also brought me to qualitative research. I have been a college English and speech teacher for about twenty years. My professional life consists of responding to written and oral communications. I have been trained to engage the other person's point of view, to understand, and to analyze. Your profession may have trained you in a similar way. Ethnographic research requires attentive observation, empathetic listening, and courageous analysis. Ethnographers must be good at seeing 'what's there', which sounds simple, but is not.

Another personality characteristic deserves mention. I love to work with people. This is no methodology for someone who prefers the peace and solitude of the library over the rough and tumble of individual and group processes. Being 'in the field' means that you will be spending vast amounts of time observing and interacting with a wide variety of personalities — perhaps not all of whom you will like. You do not have to like all the people you study, but you must enjoy being with people.

Qualitative research isn't for everyone. For growing numbers of us, however, entering a context with questions makes more sense than going in with answers. This chapter focuses specifically on the tasks and strategies of 'doing'. The emphasis here is on the techniques involved in being in the field: choosing an observer's role, becoming an observer, conducting interviews, generating a log, beginning data analysis, striving for trustworthiness, and establishing a support group.

Participant Observation

The most essential means of gathering ethnographic data are looking and listening. Since all of us have been doing this all our lives, some of us may feel we're home free. Consider this statement overheard on the third night of the case study class: 'Well, thank heavens! I've finally come to an easy part in all this. Participant observation is a snap'. Well, it isn't. What the beginning researcher is about to learn is that an attitude of curiosity and a heightened attention are required in order to attend to those very details that most of us filter out automatically in day-to-day life.

For some of us, as we have seen in the accounts of previous chapters, gaining entrée has been a difficult, complex, and time-consuming process. By the time we are ready to begin data collection, we've made very important decisions about the research topic and site. It is understandable, then, that many people come with some sense of relief.

The stance of participant observer is basic to carrying out naturalistic research. Thus, 'participant observation', referred to by ethnographers as ongoing and intensive observing, listening, and speaking needs some explaining. At the outset it may be helpful to know that 'participant observation' is used by some researchers as an umbrella term for all qualitative data-gathering techniques. It is often used, however, to designate only one of the techniques. In this sense, participant observation joins interviewing, filming, and the analysis of written records as well as the study of other artifacts (Wolcott, 1988, p. 192). We use the term in the latter way and will discuss the various tasks and strategies of participant observation as systematically as possible.

Participant observation covers a broad continuum of kinds and degrees of participating. We will look at that continuum more closely at the beginning of the next section. Here, however, I would like to emphasize the point Lofland and Lofland (1984) make regarding 'the mutuality of participant observation and intensive interviewing':

> Classic participant observation ... always involves the interweaving of looking and listening ... of watching and asking — and some of that listening and asking may approach or be identical to intensive interviewing. Conversely, intensive interview studies may involve repeated and prolonged

contact between researchers and informants, sometimes extending over a period of years, with considerable mutual involvement in personal lives — a characteristic often considered a hallmark of participant observation. (p. 13)

It seems that at least one student in each of our qualitative research semesters walks in 'knowing' that the intensive interview is her or his method of choice. Usually it is a surprise for this student, and sometimes it is an annoyance, that we hold firm to our view that interviewing cannot be divorced from looking, interacting, and attending to more than the actual interview words and that, because of this, all aspects of both techniques must be learned.

Steve Spitz provides a case in point. His was an ethnographic interview study of men who were the major caregivers of their children. Here he describes how observation served his interviews and so, his study:

> Observing Barry's children's drawings on his apartment walls, having Mark proudly point to a plaque that his wife received for community service, feeling Bob's warm glow as his son sidled up next to me during our first interview were an indispensable part of the research and again confirmed my feelings about the value of the naturalistic mode of inquiry. Bob's son sitting next to me precipitated a discussion about his thoughts about his influence on his son. These experiences were an integral part of the study and provided some of the triangulating data. A different research method may well have missed these invaluable pieces of data.

We have, in a certain sense, all been doing participant observation to various extents all our lives. Remember Hilary Knatz's feeling when first becoming acquainted with the characteristics of qualitative research? 'I've been doing this all my life.... I had a pretty fine tuned instrument in my own observational skills'. Spradley (1980) likens participant observation to what we do when we encounter the unfamiliar social situation. He gives this example from his own life:

> I recall the day I was inducted into the United States Army. I reported to the induction center feeling like a stranger among all the other draftees and military personnel. As I took the oath of allegiance, underwent a physical exam, listened to orientation lectures, and left for Fort Ord, California, I frequently felt at a loss as to how to conduct myself. Because I could not participate with the ease of someone who had done prior service, I adapted by watching carefully what other people said and did. During the early weeks of basic training I continued to act much like a participant observer, trying to learn how to behave as a private in the Army. When walking about Fort Ord, I would watch other people to see if they saluted

> passing cars or people who looked like officers. Taking my cue from
> them, I would imitate their actions. Slowly I learned the culture of
> Army life, felt less like a stranger, and became an ordinary partici-
> pant who gave little thought to the social situations I encountered.
> (p. 53)

Perhaps the essence of the difference between being a participant-
observer in ordinary life and being one as a qualitative researcher is found in
Spradley's final phrase: '. . . and became an ordinary participant who gave
little thought to the social situations I encountered'. Wolcott (1988) says:

> We are ethnographic observers when we are attending to the cultural con-
> text of the behavior we are engaging in or observing, and when we are
> looking for those mutually understood sets of expectations and explanations
> that enable us to interpret what is occurring and what meanings are prob-
> ably being attributed by others present. (p. 193)

The distinguishing characteristic, then, of being a participant observer is
that it demands a shift of attention. This shift shows itself in a variety of
ways:

> The role of participant observer will vary from one social situation to
> another, and each investigator has to allow the way he or she works to
> evolve. But as your role develops, you will have to maintain a *dual purpose*:
> You will want to seek to participate and to watch yourself and others at the
> same time. Make yourself *explicitly aware* of things that others take for
> granted. It will be important to take mental pictures with a *wide-angle lens*,
> looking beyond your immediate focus of activity. You will experience the
> feeling of being both an *insider* and *outsider* simultaneously. As you partici-
> pate in routine activities, you will need to engage in *introspection* to more
> fully understand your experiences. And finally, you will need to *keep a
> record* of what you see and experience. These six features of the participant-
> observer role distinguish it from what you already know as an ordinary
> participant. (Spradley, 1980, p. 58)

It seems safe to say that even though these features sound evident, their
skillful application and orchestration remain the ongoing challenge of each
participant observer. For us, the hard-won bonus is to see far more than we
ever expected.

Choosing a Participant Observer Role

Perhaps one of the first questions the researcher raises is what kind of
observer role would be appropriate to the field and both physically as well as

emotionally possible. While they provide different labels for the continuum, experts (Bogdan and Biklen, 1982; Patton, 1980; Spradley, 1980; Wolcott, 1988; and Yin, 1984) agree that the meaning of participant-observer ranges from full participant, that is, actually living and working in the field as a member of the group over an extended period of time, to mute observer, who attempts to replicate the fly on the wall. Researchers generally find a level somewhere between these two extremes.

Wolcott (1988) distinguishes three different participant-observer styles: the active participant, the privileged observer, and the limited observer. The active participant has a job to do in the setting in addition to the research; the privileged observer is someone who is known and trusted and given easy access to information about the context; and the limited observer, the role most of us play, observes, asks questions, and builds trust over time, but doesn't have a public role other than researcher. Taking on any one of these styles depends on the opportunities the setting provides as well as the re-searcher's abilities and desire to do so (p. 194).

> Even if we could assume that every ethnographer was equally capable of getting as involved as he or she wanted, and of always having an exquisite sense of just how involved that should be, there are other constraints on the extent to which one can engage in or observe human behavior. (Wolcott, p. 193)

Wolcott here alludes to institutional constraints, such as those imposed parti-cularly by the strict rules of schools. It follows that each researcher has the job of defining what the term 'participant-observer' means within the particu-lar circumstances of a specific study, and to make that public:

> I think it is fair to ask anyone who claims title as a participant-observer to provide a fuller description about how each facet — participant, observer, and the precarious nexus between them — is to be played out in an actual research setting. (Wolcott, p. 193)

Even when the participant-observer role has been carefully planned, there are often unexpected snags. Laura Berns, for example, planned to be a privileged observer with access to files and personnel. She had been a teacher in a computer lab similar to the one she wished to observe and had experience interacting with students there. She was known and trusted by the people who were in charge of the computer lab. They welcomed her and told her that she had unlimited access to the lab, students, teachers, and files. Her start, however, was more like that of a limited observer.

> I have always hated knocking on doors and asking strangers to buy Girl Scout cookies. And then yesterday afternoon, starting my first

observation in the computer lab, I felt an intruder really. This is not what I had planned or expected. I had entered a tiny room so cluttered with college students busily typing papers that not a single seat was vacant. So I dragged in a folding chair and sat awkwardly for the first half hour in the center of the room, gripping my spiral notebook and trying to look inconspicuous, as students detoured around me on their way to and from the printer.

Matt Cariello planned to be an active participant. He intended to study himself as a poet in the schools in interaction with groups of children. Matt learned a painful lesson:

I couldn't seem to establish rapport with one class. Ms X seemed to be skeptical about my teaching methods. She would ask me in the middle of a poetry lesson '*What* do you want them to do?' in a loud voice that made every child sit up and wonder. She would question my use of certain poems. But worst of all were the faces she made while listening to me and the class — screwed up expressions of who knows what — and head shaking and sighing. The class seemed confused most of the time, as if they never quite knew what was happening. Soon after, the other teacher, with whom I had had excellent rapport, became critical of what I did in her class.

I was being treated as an outsider, and a dangerous one at that. Any trust I thought I had developed was apparently an illusion.

Matt left this site to find another more amenable to his study. That decision was not made lightly:

Naturalistic research lets you explore those things that arise naturally in social situations, but you have to remember that 'arise naturally' means 'arise naturally to the peculiar perceptions of any particular observer'. The emphasis is inevitably placed on the researcher as an instrument of observation. Unfortunately (or fortunately) this means that researchers — particularly participant-observers — are always subject to the influence of their own personality and the personality of others.

'Getting along' with a group may be a problematic thing. Enough becomes enough when your research is clouded by the compromises you have to make in order to get along with the group.

On reflection, Matt decided that while he did receive permission from administrators, he had not communicated well enough with the teachers at the outset:

One of the major problems was that they didn't know what I was doing there — and I never bothered to tell them in any formal, coherent way. Now if I had made clear what I was doing right at the start, and had provided them with the background necessary to understand my interests, and if they had said at that point, 'Sorry, this isn't for us' — fine. I would have found another school. Because I didn't, I wasted valuable time, but not without learning.

As Matt's vignette points out, sometimes we may spend some time in the field and then realize that it is necessary to change sites.

Not all active participants have such difficulties. Diane, for example, was both teacher and researcher of the children whose play styles she documented. It took careful planning to fulfill both roles and Diane still talks of having to be sure 'which hat I was wearing when'. Diane had the good fortune to work with a supportive and understanding school aide. In addition, she had permission to do videotaping and audiotaping so that she could review daily happenings in the relative peace and quiet of her home. She had explained her project to the children and in time they became so involved that they often swept her along with them to where they thought interesting things were happening on the playground and in their homes.

Francia Mercado planned to do her study in the limited-observer role. She found this role difficult to maintain, and shares some of her concerns about 'intruding' as a participant-observer:

> To observe is an unintrusive role. All my training has been geared to an active, participatory role. I'm an extrovert and I'm very social. Being a Latin, I even communicate with my hands. I must control all these feelings. Here I am sitting with a pad and a pencil. The action is out there and I cannot participate.

Ah! But Francia *is* participating. Heisenberg's work tells us that the very act of observing can alter what is being observed. It follows, then, that even at our most unintrusive, we influence the very phenomenon we are studying. This is true of every research paradigm, quantitative and qualitative. For qualitative researchers the important issues are: (1) that we participate as closely as possible in line with the needs of our study; (2) that we make ourselves as aware as possible of the ripples caused by our participation; (3) that we attempt to counter those ripples that might hinder the participant observer relationship and, hence, the study; and (4) that we describe in the report both what worked and what did not. The researcher's growing self-awareness of this process is discussed in depth in Theme II of Chapter 6, 'The Transactional Nature of the Research Process'.

Beginning Observation with Wide Focus

In the beginning, participant observation can be overwhelming in the very richness and complexity that is being played out. Often how much to observe and then to record perplexes novice participant-observers:

> I'm watching the children! I'm watching the teacher! There are so many things going on at the same time! My head is spinning! What should I write in my log? What should I leave out? And to top it all it's just impossible. The minute I put my head down to write, I'm disconnected from what's happening. And if I tune in to what I hear, I may lose an important thought. They didn't tell me that this would be so apparently chaotic and so unnerving. If I'm the instrument, I need to be sent to the repair shop. (Belén Matías)

Many experts, among them Agar (1980), Lincoln and Guba (1985) and Spradley (1980), propose the sensible idea that qualitative researchers proceed through a series of stages in observing-participating. These stages move from an introductory, general overview with broad focus, to one in which the researcher narrows the focus to very specific aspects of the situation that have called attention to themselves in the ongoing cycle of logging and analyzing the data.

It is true that no one can record everything in the broad focus stage. But then, it is not such a bad idea to go in with the idea of trying. Because this is so, you should plan to observe and write about as much as possible and not waste your time fussing about whether something seems trivial or important. The seemingly most mundane happening may be crucial in hindsight. In any case, it is impossible at the very beginning to judge whether what seems trivial or important is really so in the larger, longer scheme of things. Keep writing. Keep listening and looking.

We have found that it is useful to begin by selecting one task or question at a time. For example, Margaret makes a map of the site. Margot asks herself where she might best sit to achieve an overall view of what is happening. All of us have found it helpful to note public communications about rules and procedures, such as time schedules and signing in, that are apparent from the beginning. Spradley (1980, p. 78) lists nine major dimensions of social situations that might be used in the beginning phase to pose questions and guide observations:

1 Space: the physical place or places;
2 Actor: the people involved;
3 Activity: a set of related acts people do;
4 Object: the physical things that are present;

5 Act: single actions that people do;
6 Event: a set of related activities that people carry out;
7 Time: the sequencing that takes place over time;
8 Goal: the things people are trying to accomplish;
9 Feeling: the emotions felt and expressed.

The Loflands (1984, p. 48) suggest that participant-observers who are known to the people in the setting they want to study, who are in Wolcott's terms privileged observers or active participants, might ask themselves questions such as these all through their field experience:

Who is he?
What does he do?
What do you think she meant by that?
What are they supposed to do?
Why did she do that?
Why is that done?
What happens after _____?
What would happen if _____?
What do you think about _____?
Who is responsible if _____?

These questions and procedures are only some suggestions. You will most probably do well by deciding on some specific task or tasks that make sense in getting started as a participant-observer.

Becoming 'The Other'

Entering a setting with an ethnographic stance demands an attitude that puts us into learning roles. Agar (1980) proposes that we conceptualize ourselves through such metaphors as student, child, or apprentice (pp. 69–70). Many of us find it helpful in the starting phase to take on the student role in our work to 'become the other': to attempt to see life through the eyes of the person we are studying. Melissa Rose writes about her experience of both taking a student role and being with students in 'becoming the other'. She shares some insights and repercussions:

> I have, as music chairman and administrative intern, sat in the back of classrooms and observed teachers, but this was a totally different experience from that of doing qualitative research. As I sat attempting at first to empathize with both the students and teacher, it became more and more difficult over time to relate to the teacher and easier by far to 'become' a student, at least for one period a

week. I could recognize this as the beginnings of 'going native', and I could realize how easily this can occur. More and more, as I watched a poor classroom situation I thought of it not in terms of ways for the teacher to improve, as I would if observing in a supervisory capacity, but rather how like a prisoner I felt!

As a 'temporary student', I felt neither pleasure nor interest toward the activities that were being presented. The students themselves reacted in a variety of ways; the most common were passivity, socializing, or clowning. I, being there with the objective of observing as many details as I could grasp, had the advantage of being able to keep my mind occupied with the task at hand. On several occasions, I found myself thinking, 'Boy, is this dull. I'll be glad when this lesson is over'. Often, I found the adolescent socializing and silliness around me to be far more interesting than what was going on in the front of the room. Small wonder that the students felt the same!

Diane is particularly fond of the apprentice metaphor. She relates how she 'apprenticed' herself to the children she was observing by playing with them and learning to play as they played. In our class work, 'shadowing' is an exercise that helps many people learn to 'become the other'. In shadowing, a researcher obtains permission to be with a participant — one student, one doctor, one hair stylist, one secretary — for several hours as that person goes about life. The researcher observes, takes no notes until afterwards, and interacts just as little as possible. In every way, the researcher attempts to learn what it is to be that person. On pages 202–4 Dorothy Deegan writes of her shadowing experiences on police patrol. Finally, the concept of 'bracketing' given us by phenomenologists (Giorgi, 1985) speaks directly to taking on 'the other'. Bracketing requires that we work to become aware of our own assumptions, feelings, and preconceptions, and then, that we strive to put them aside — to bracket them — in order to be open and receptive to what we are attempting to understand.

Prolonged Engagement

Many of us worry that the events we are witnessing as participant-observers may not be characteristic of what 'really' goes on or may even be put on for our benefit just because we are there:

Here I am, ready to take notes on what is going on in the scenario I have selected. I ask myself, is this behavior typical, or are they playing a part for me? They may be. It can take some time before their behavior is uninhibited by my presence. (Francia Mercado)

Qualitative researchers, of course, are to document what is really happening rather than what is being put on for their benefit. Guba and Lincoln's (1989) suggestions of prolonged engagement and persistent observations point to the most helpful techniques for constructing a view of the context in its natural state. Participant observation demands '. . . sufficient involvement at the site to overcome the effects of misinformation, . . . to uncover constructions, and to facilitate immersing oneself in and understanding the context's culture' (Guba and Lincoln, 1989, p. 237). With the two intertwined activities of prolonged engagement and persistent observation, qualitative researchers work to be accepted and trusted in their roles, to construct deep understandings about what they are studying, and to have some basis for deciding what is important and relevant and what is not.

There really is no short cut and no magic. People who do not devote sufficient time, commitment, and work have been called to task by Ray Rist (1980) for doing 'blitzkrieg ethnography'. Qualitative researchers have to be there with all of our senses, with much of our time, and with a quiet stubborn streak that says, 'There is a way. Maybe we haven't found it yet but with patience and skill, maybe tomorrow.'

For many researchers, prolonged engagement with people creates an emotional attachment that is hard to break. Laura Lee Lustbader spent months with a young schizophrenic female, and she felt that she was in some ways deserting her when the study ended. Teri felt so close to her cops that she considered taking a job with the police force. Both of these incidents are more fully described in Chapter 4. Andrea Mandel hopes to follow the elementary school children she studied right through high school, not simply because she is curious to see how they turn out, but because she likes them.

For some qualitative researchers, long engagement also means learning to be sufficiently neutral so that the research can continue. Ioannis Afthinos relates what he thought was a professional dilemma and how he solved it:

> As a face-to-face researcher, often I was forced to keep a conversation going by talking about something the informants introduced not because I personally or professionally agreed, but because this way I could collect information relevant to my study. For example, I am in total disagreement with my participant's view of civil servants. Nevertheless, I have not mentioned anything about my opinions to Jim because I fear that this might make him unwilling to further cooperate with me.

To be accepted by the group as an ongoing observer, a qualitative researcher may offer to undertake some small tasks, as did Hilary Knatz in Chapter 2, but the ability to observe widely and to have the opportunity to make a few notes must not be co-opted by a willingness to be useful. Making contributions of any sort is usually easier and more natural for researchers who are active participants and privileged observers than those who are limited observers. But ways can be found. One of our friends made a leap into contributing as a limited observer when she contributed a birthday cake for the children in 'her' class.

Inevitably, over the span of participant-observation we get to know and often care about the people we study. Because of this, qualitative researchers need to remind themselves that their job is to describe, not fix, not judge. For those of us in the helping professions, the temptation to go in there and make things better requires great resistance, as Jackie Storm relates:

> My analytical brain got in my way. I kept trying to explain *why* something was the way it was, as opposed to simply describing what was going on. Not only did I want to psychoanalyze the family I was studying, I wanted to play the therapist. Role conflict was definitely a problem. As a researcher I was required to observe and record what was going on, yet I constantly battled the impulse to play counselor, helper, and teacher. I not only wanted to tell the woman in my study how to fix her hair, I wanted to jump in and fix her life!

Prolonged engagement provides many surprises. In fact, the researcher often comes across observations that cast all the previous ones into a new light. One of the great pleasures in the methodology is that not getting what you expect may be exactly what you need. Jackie Storm, whose study was plagued by illnesses and hospitalizations both in her own home and in her subject's family, tells us of an insight that occurred almost too late:

> I felt I was sidetracked by some of the situations that came up as a result of the husband/wife relationship. At one point the couple had a fight and the wife ran away from home. 'Woe is me', I thought, 'this will spoil the whole thing because she's not available to be observed'. I failed to see that her running away was what I should be observing.

Jackie's insight parallels an experience related by William Foote Whyte in his Appendix to *Street Corner Society* (1955). Whyte writes movingly about going bowling on many Saturday nights with the 'corner boys' from the Italian-American slum he called Cornerville. He enjoyed the games so much, he sometimes felt guilty about taking time away from research. One afternoon, however, he was hanging out with the guys and listening to them discuss the team's chances that night as they competed for prize money:

> I recall standing on the corner with the boys while they discussed the coming contest. I listened to Doc, Mike, and Danny making

their predictions as to the order in which the men would finish. At first, this made no particular impression upon me, as my own unexpressed predictions were exactly along the same lines. Then, as the men joked and argued, I suddenly began to question and take a new look at the whole situation. I was convinced that Doc, Mike, and Danny were basically correct in their predictions, and yet why should the scores approximate the structure of the gang? Were these top men simply better natural athletes than the rest?

... I went down to the alleys that night fascinated and just a bit awed by what I was about to witness. Here was the social structure in action right on the bowling alleys. It held the individual members in their places — and I along with them.... As my turn came and I stepped up to bowl, I felt supremely confident that I was going to hit the pins that I was aiming at. I have never felt quite that way before — or since. Here at the bowling alley I was experiencing subjectively the impact of the group structure upon the individual.

... I was convinced that now I had something important: the relationship between individual performance and group structure, even though at this time I still did not see how such observation would fit in with the overall pattern. (pp. 318–19)

Whyte regrets the missed opportunities to keep track of the gang's bowling scores during the preceding months, which he believes would have been a statistical gold mine. But more important than regret is his insight that if the researcher stays sufficiently with a situation, then what is important in the situation will unfold. The meaning of 'prolonged' in 'prolonged engagement' is different for different researchers. We talk more of this when we discuss leaving the field on pp. 91–93.

Concern for Objectivity

A great concern of many beginning participant-observers as well as more seasoned researchers is that of reaching for objectivity, although this process may be understood differently with time and experience.

> I knew I was biased and had to learn how to observe, understand, and not make judgments. (Joanna Landau)

In opposition to what many budding ethnography students believe, observation can never be objective and Joanna will never be judgment-free. This is so because observation comes out of what the observer selects to see and chooses to note. All we can work for is that our vision is not too skewed by our own subjectivities. And that means *work* for most of us. But this work is of a different class from that of striving to reach the impossible goal of pure objectivity. The trouble is that, as participant-observers, it looks as if we are trying to do just that. That is, as qualitative researchers, we must educate and re-educate ourselves to practice detailed observation without reading in our own answers, our own biases. That process entails becoming increasingly more aware of our own 'eyeglasses', our own blinders, so that these do not color unfairly both what we observe and what we detail in writing. With all the striving to observe fairly and with all the self-awareness and introspection this demands, we are still subjective people doing a subjective job.

> We will never be entirely free of our own preferred ways of viewing situations and our own biases. We can, however, be more self-aware. (Gail Levine)

We have found it less rewarding to agonize about becoming perfectly objective than to do something about becoming more objective. One's own introspection in the log can be of immense help. The section about analytic memos (pp. 80–82) considers this in more detail. In addition, the feedback provided when checking with the people who were studied can be used as we attempt to see their perspective rather than imposing our own. Often, the vision of a support group is an important factor:

> ... with the help of my support group I began to learn more and more how to control my emotions in order not to undermine or distort the research process. (Flora Keshishian)

What Was That Question Again? Again

In this section we consider moving from a broad to a more narrow research focus. In Chapter 2 we said that qualitative researchers benefit from choosing topics that hold their interest, even passion. This interest-driven search led me, Ann, to study a microcomputer hacker in his home (1988). Margot searched for and found teenagers labeled homeless at a community center, and Teri recruited policewomen for her research. At that point, our interest and questions were broad:

> What is the experience of being a teenaged computer hacker? What is the life of a teenages labeled homeless? How do policewomen see themselves as professionals?

It was not until we began our participant observation that our ongoing study of the very data we were collecting helped us to pose more specific questions:

What is the meaning for Chuck of playing computer games? How do these youth labeled homeless avoid school? What strategies do the policewomen apply to work successfully in the streets in time of danger?

Spradley (1980) calls the broad overview phase 'The Grand Tour', and the specific focus stage 'The Mini Tour'. These metaphors are congruent with Lincoln and Guba's (1985) conviction that, at first, the researcher approaches the study '. . . not knowing what is not known' (p. 235). Logic would have it, then, that when the reseacher knows what is not known, a mini tour is in order. In Margaret's study of the ways in which young students interact with a text, she was surprised to discover in her grand tour that the students' non-verbal communication might form a vital part of the study:

> It was not until yesterday, after studying my field log, that I began to think about how the children in our book discussion group signalled interest, even passionate involvement, with their body language. They sprawled, they leaned, they wove. They touched each other and me. Are these important indices of interest and group cohesion? A new slant. I'll have to focus on that in the observations to come.

Sometimes, indeed, the maxi tour helps qualitative researchers to make 180-degree changes in selecting their topic and in narrowing their focus:

> As I reread my log entries each week, it became increasingly clear that, because of this setting and my own fascination with people, my topic had changed! I no longer noted, in explicit detail, the computer programing functions being explored and how the students gained insight into how they worked. Instead, I was describing in great detail when students came to class, how they behaved when they entered the room, where they stood, what they said and to whom, and how they were greeted. It was this topic that intrigued and surprised me about this situation, not computer programing.
>
> The goal of any research is to add to our knowledge, to enlighten us. Therefore, it is important to be open to what is interesting and potentially enlightening about the situation being studied, even if it is not what was originally intended. It is important to allow for 'distractions', if they are important ones. I did not develop insights into how students learn computer programing that would add to the knowledge available. I did, however, learn a great deal about how students can be invited to participate in a class. (Marcia Kropf)

The process of narrowing the focus means asking questions, developing in-process answers and asking questions again, and understanding that '. . . both questions and answers must be discovered in the social situation being studied' (Spradley, 1980, p. 32). This cycle, this dance, is at the heart of qualitative research. What is more, sometimes our questions are about the questions the people we are studying ask themselves, tacitly or not, as they go about their lives. This makes the questioning cycle even more complex.

Because qualitative researchers depend on the field to help them ask questions, it is not a good idea to enter the field with questions that are too specific, or too tight, or too slanted. A narrow focus from the beginning may well limit what and how we see. Diane Person writes about how she set out to study life in a library:

> In my nervousness to be sure to observe the 'right' things, I used the American Library Association's guidelines, *Information Power*, as a crutch to say this is what I should be observing rather than concentrating on what I was observing.
>
> I envisioned a straightforward series of observations and interviews. I was certain I knew what I would see, and I never questioned my own assumptions about the process. I could not see why I had to look at all facets of the library program.
>
> My initial focus was narrow, and the more I looked at the specifics, the more the whole picture became fractured, remote, distorted. My actual observation experience was far different from what I had anticipated. I had to shed my long cherished assumptions and broaden my own perspective in order to see what was really happening. I came to the realization that the school library is a microcosm of the larger school system with a distinctive media focus. Now as I finish my series of observations I have a whole new set of questions, but not the answers. And the questions come from me — what I observed with my own eyes, from my own perspective, not from the library teacher I observed.

Diane's genuine account describes but does not do justice to communicating her real struggle to change her stance. It takes a great deal of integrity, skill, and will to change from 'I was certain I knew what I would see' to 'I have a whole new set of questions, but not the answers'. What is more, Diane was able to use her insights about what she missed to move forward rather than to be discouraged and dissuaded:

> When I look back on my period of observation, the things which stand out most in my mind are the things I tried hard to ignore: the girl who wandered about the room by herself picking up thumbtacks — that would have been interesting to pursue from the child's perspective as well as the librarian's; the excitement of children working together and discovering information in an almanac; and, what was the pillowed seating area all about, how did the children perceive it, how did the librarian perceive it, whose idea was it to organize the area? What I learned will stand as a warning for next

time. I also think it will be more fun to go in with an open mind, not my preconceived assumptions, to let the data and the questions emerge from my observations.

The issue of the research question is one in which there is a real difference between quantitative and qualitative work. Because we often inhabit worlds where quantitative paradigms have held sway, the process of allowing questions to emerge and to shape during the data-gathering phase, as exemplified in Diane's latter quotation, may not be well received. In such cases, qualitative researchers may have a problem.

> In my usual fashion I decided not to worry about the research question until the time came. But, from my first day of doctoral study, everyone advised me to select a research problem and questions as soon as possible. I wanted to do that, but I did not know where to begin. So I held out and eventually some people understood my dilemma and helped me plan a research process that was right for me. (Beverly Rosenthal)

This problem is parallel to, and a part of, the problem of the demand for a too tight dissertation proposal, discussed in Chapter 2. More of how to handle this dilemma will be discussed in Chapter 6, Theme II, 'Shouting across the Paradigmatic Rift'.

Interviewing

Qualitative research provides a great many opportunities to talk with people. Some interviews are done 'on the hoof' during participant-observation when the time is available and the spirits are amenable. These interviews are usually quite informal. They often flow from a situation, perhaps at its tag end, and usually occur with less prior planning than formal interviews, except for the planning that has been done in the ongoing field log analysis, to be discussed later in the chapter. Sometimes, in addition, they are the only interviews our participants can and/or want to give. We have had informal interviews in pizza parlors, dentists' offices, nurses' stations, around kitchen tables, on subways, and squeezed into the dress-up corner of a classroom for 2-year-olds.

Other interviews, sometimes called formal, are more planned and usually carried out away from the action, so that there is a chance to talk in peace and in greater depth. Some researchers choose ethnographic interviews as their central data-gathering method and do less far-ranging observation-participation, confining it to the interview situation itself. Whatever the kind and circumstance, interviews are at the heart of doing ethnography because they seek the words of the people we are studying, the richer the better, so that we can understand their situations with increasing clarity.

An interview is '... a purposeful conversation usually between two people (but sometimes involving more) that is directed by one in order to get information' (Bogdan and Biklen, 1982, p. 135). The major purpose of an in-depth ethnographic interview is to learn to see the world from the eyes of the person being interviewed. In striving to come closer to understanding people's meanings, the ethnographic interviewer learns from them as informants and seeks to discover how they organize their behavior. In this approach the researcher asks those who are studied to become the teachers and to instruct her or him in the ways of life they find meaningful (Spradley and McCurdy, 1972, pp. 11–12). Not only do so many of us have to learn how to observe in new ways, we also have to unlearn and relearn what we believe we already know about how to conduct an interview. Sometimes this comes as a severe jolt to people in the human services fields of psychology and guidance who have certainly learned to probe, to listen, to support. Their professional interviews have had distinct purposes that were often not compatible with those of ethnographic interviews, even if some of the techniques were the same.

Beatriz Abreu, who was educated as an occupational therapist, found that her usual interview techniques were not sufficient:

> The other surprise I encountered was that although I have used interviews as an evaluation tool in clinical practice for 23 years, I did not know how to use interviews in this methodology. I found myself being clumsy, asking, not probing, and maybe biasing the answer by the way I phrased the question. I also became nervous when one of the therapists was uncomfortable during the interview. Super cool me lost it at times!

Margot reports that at times she feels frustrated that some people understand ethnographic interviews to be 'unstructured' and other interviews to be 'structured'. This is a misperception. Every interview has a structure. The difference lies in how that structure is negotiated. For some interviews, the structure is predetermined. For others, it is shaped in the process:

> While some believe that the ethnographic interviewee can go in any direction, and that the interviewer is passive, nothing is further from reality. Actually. the interviewer knows the areas that need to be explored and sees to it that this occurs. It is how this is done that defines the difference between an ethnographic interview and others.

The key is that the person interviewed is a full partner in the endeavor and often provides the surprising and useful directions not allowed by other, more researcher-centered interviews.

The tasks of an ethnographic interviewer include providing focus, observing, giving direction, being sensitive to clues given by participants, probing, questioning, listening, amalgamating statements, and generally being as involved as possible. At their most useful, ethnographic interviews are interwoven dances of questions and answers in which the researcher follows as well as leads. Qualitative reseachers have added their own twists to the meaning of 'involved'. (Ely, 1984, pp. 4–5)

There are, of course, many excellent sources on interviewing that have been of help to us (Douglas, 1984; Gordon, 1980; Lazarsfeld, 1972; Lightfoot, 1973; Merton *et al.*, 1956; Mishler, 1986; Spradley, 1979; Whyte, 1960).

Beginning Challenges

Unless the researcher takes advantage of an unexpected opportunity for an interview, qualitative researchers consider ambiance, content, and flow. Dick DeLuca created a series of questions that helped him to plan his interview:

1 What do I know about the interviewee? What *should* I know?
2 How will I gain access? What explanations will I give? What assurances of anonymity?
3 How will I begin my questions? Rule of thumb: start with questions that the interviewee will feel comfortable answering.
4 How will I be able to influence the choice of the physical setting for the interview? Will there be sufficient privacy?
5 How much time should I request?
6 Will I use a tape recorder? Strongly recommended. Obtain permission by describing my efforts to protect confidentiality and anonymity. Mention sharing of transcript, if this is reasonable. Tell this person where to reach me.
7 How will I conclude the interview? What opportunity will I provide for clarification? How do I make arrangements for a follow-up interview?

Attending to the specific circumstances of the interview can be a challenge. For instance, Flora Keshishian found that the place she chose and, more important, her own emotions, interfered with her ability to be a good listener:

I did my first interview of Sam in a restaurant where I felt distracted by various elements: the restaurant itself, where I had never been before, the familiar and unfamiliar faces that walked in and out of the restaurant, and the nature of my conversation with Sam.

... It was the first time that he was telling me about his childhood, his being the 'fat' one in the family, and how this image made him obsessed about being 'thin' and 'beautiful'. As he was telling me about his past I felt myself pulled by the distractions in the environment and realized that I had heard only some of what Sam was telling me. Then, I found that I was too busy trying to imagine how he felt when called 'fat' to follow him, let alone tease a question out of the conversation. When I was able to come back to reality, I was too absorbed by Sam's entertaining body language and humor to be able to 'think as a qualitative researcher'. In fact, it was Sam who reminded me to take notes or ask him some questions.

Patricia Thornton describes what it meant to her life to be responsive to her participant's schedules. In this vignette, she discovers again a vital characteristic of qualitative research:

Pat: When can we meet?
Participant: Well, the only time we have free is 7:30 A.M. on Wednesday. Can we meet then?
Pat: Oh, sure 7:30 is fine. See you then. [Thinking: An interview at 7:30 in the morning! I'd better get up at 5 A.M. just to make sure I'm awake. WHAT HAVE I GOTTEN MYSELF INTO?!]

That was only the beginning. The families I am studying are just not available for meetings at the best times for me, so when they're available, I am — 7:30 A.M. breakfasts and 11:00 P.M. dinners. This contrasts sharply with experimental research where the participants are asked to respond and adapt to pre-established experimental procedures and so, to the researcher's demands. In naturalistic research the tables are turned, so to speak, and the ethnographer adapts to the participants and the social situation that the field demands. Ethnographers don't ask their participants to comply to their situations, they adapt to their participants' situations. After all, how the participants live their lives is what an ethnographer wants to study.

Staying Out — Staying In

Often qualitative researchers must learn when not to speak during an interview in order to let the interviewee talk further. This is all the more difficult when what is said strikes a chord, a chord we wish to share because 'we've been there' and because often we have developed warm ties with the people we are studying. Here is Leslie Rice's story:

> When doing interviews, it was surprising to me when the interviewee said something that struck home. It is at these points I was particularly pleased to have a tape recorder. When a point hits home, it is often hard to concentrate on what is being said. The following is a quote from such an interview.
>
>> ... But when you grow up and you don't know what you want, but you know what you don't want, and what you don't want is what everybody else wants, and you gotta figure out how to ... um, I have no role models. There's no one in my family that I could look up to and say, I want to be like that. They're alcoholics; they're in unhappy marriages; their husbands beat them — no one ... at 35 I finally feel like I'm doing something....
>
> It was hard when something hit home not to suddenly jump in and tell the person being interviewed everything about myself and that I felt exactly the same. Emotions play a big role in this type of research.

Ewa Iracka, who studied several immigrants to the USA and their relationship to media, provides a similar example:

> My ability to remain detached was further impeded by my personal response to my respondents' problems. There were a number of occasions when I began to sympathize with *their* frustration. Again my line of questioning was distracted by the plights of my respondents, and I could not always maintain an exterior of neutrality. I wondered if my reactions to their replies were biasing the interview. Sometimes I would feel lonely because I had to maintain the role of an interviewer and had to suppress my personal feelings. Being a foreign born person myself, I wanted to tell them that I understood what they were feeling because I had had similar experiences. I, too, wanted to be understood and liked. At the time, I thought that expressing these thoughts and feelings would have slanted the interview rendering it useless. Detachment was and is a difficult state for me to maintain.

In her search for detachment, Ewa represents a point of view that is common to many beginning qualitative researchers. But we of this writing team are of the opinion that often an interviewer does no harm and indeed does some good by entering judiciously to let the interviewee know that you 'have been there' and can sympathize. A growing trust is the basis for richer interviews. It is this concept of judicious 'entering' that is both vital and difficult. We do not advise researchers to manipulate the interview flow or to hog the scene. We do want to support and facilitate. Some people know how to do this. Others create diversions so that the 'interview' ends up being a friendly conversation that loses its aim because the researcher has accepted other than research roles. This, in itself, is not the end of the world. The researcher often feels sheepish enough without thinking that all is lost. Usually another appointment can be made for an interview. Who knows? It might be far richer for the detour.

Dorothea Hoffner found it difficult to 'stay out' for a variety of reasons, but chiefly because the interviewee was not a stranger:

> As I sat down to interview my colleague one sunny Thursday afternoon, it seemed only natural to spend some time discussing general school problems, the administration's latest mistakes, the news about our colleagues. We have been close professional friends for a long time, and it was good to relax a bit.
>
> Shortly we moved to more substantive matters about my study concerning his role in the learning center at the college. I asked for his view of what is going particularly well, and not so well. I tried to be ethnographic: 'Tell me more about that'. 'What qualities do you look for in staff?' But as the interview moved along, I was mightily tempted to discuss the problems of the center as colleague to colleague, each offering possible causes and solutions. And when he mentioned advisory meetings, I wanted to know why I had not been invited! Later I found myself objecting to his idea of a grammar mini-course, and to his use of computer editing programs: 'You really mean that? I mean, are the kids learning anything by doing that?' We even discussed the virtues of teaching the research paper — two pages of transcript. Totally irrelevant!
>
> The biggest challenge came when my colleague began to criticize our department chairman and other faculty for their lack of support. My eyes and my head did not know what to do and my 'mmm's' grew very strained. However, I suppose the subject was so obviously dangerous that I managed to keep quiet and ease into another area. So much for interviewing a friendly colleague.

Dorothea's story is another example of the perils of studying 'too close to home'. But we find this an idiosyncratic issue. Sometimes people in similar situations can keep their perspective very well. Probably Dorothea can do that also; another day, another time. In talking with her classmates, Dorothea heard the following story from another student. This woman found it difficult to grapple with the interview not so much because she was familiar with her respondent — she was not — but because the topic itself held too much pain for her:

Staying out is sometimes preferable to being on center. Mary found on center to be a very uncomfortable, awkward place. Her case study was of a 75-year-old woman whose husband was dying. At first, while interviewing, Mary often found herself changing the subject when the topic of the husband's death came up. She found herself using clichés such as 'Don't worry about it now' or 'I'm sure everything will be all right', rather than exploring the issues so close to the woman's heart. As Mary said, 'The very topic of my research became the area I most often avoided'. Finally, getting on center, she found that an open discussion with the woman was very revealing and not so difficult as she had imagined it would be.

Each interview creates its own unique challenge to staying out and on center. It is very hard to feel in control and at the same time be responsive and relaxed. But with each new experience, the ethnographer gains a bit more skill.

About Questioning

Learning about questioning, the rhythm, the form, the impact, is a task that never ends for qualitative researchers. It is particularly central to beginners. Sometimes what one learns is frustrating, poignant, and important to the research as well as other facets of life. Patricia Thornton had prepared some specific questions to ask her participants:

> A number of times I ran into the situation where I had set up interviews with different members of the families I studied and prepared questions before the interviews, only to find that that person couldn't make it, and another person was coming instead. I felt thrown and I think some of my interviews suffered because I was busy trying to regain my equilibrium and switch gears in order to ask appropriate questions for that person, rather than for the scheduled person.
>
> Getting stuck can happen at any point in ethnography, and one of the causes may be that the researcher is trying too hard to do something a certain way and is unsuccessful. Rigidity sets in and nothing changes. At this point the researcher has to move on and let go. I now try to be prepared for anyone and anything.

While we, too, attempt to be prepared, we find that there are always some surprises. To be able to swing with events and to put them to good use may be characteristic of qualitative researchers. It is most often an acquired trait, one that lends itself well to a bit of humor:

> There were times when I used to watch Barbara Walters, the alleged interviewer of all time, and I would think that she was overpaid.

After all, she would merely sit comfortably in a lovely setting and glibly and effortlessly ask poignant questions which would elicit informative and sometimes sensational replies. Anyone can do that.

After having indulged in this communication art form for the first time, I am forced to admit that it is not nearly as easy as Barbara makes it appear. Asking the 'right' questions was supposed to be easy because I had anticipated my respondent's replies. I made a valiant effort to form non-biased, precise questions which would allow the respondent to give me non-biasedly the information I was seeking. Each question was designed to bring forth an 'appropriate' reply in an easy to follow sequence. But alas! My respondents were not aware of my plan and they would give me their own answers instead of the replies which were to accompany my questions. To make matters worse, sometimes the answers would make my next question seem inappropriate or almost absurd. When this occurred, I would feel a sense of panic, and I would stumble and flounder for direction while trying externally to maintain a semblance of composure. (Ewa Iracka)

Ewa struggled with how to get her respondent to talk about the topic. This turned out to be more complicated than she anticipated:

My first interview can be compared to taking a puppy for a walk. In the attempt to make my respondent feel comfortable, I wound up being led everywhere except for where I had intended to go. To be perfectly honest, in reviewing the interview, I'm not even sure what my original intentions were. What evolved was a dialogue more conversational in tone than a 'professional' interview.

Carmen had a tendency to answer my vague questions vaguely. When I tried to clarify the questions, I found myself drifting from the topic and then trying to correct the situation by steering Carmen in another direction. Originally, my interview was to gain insight into the television viewing habits of some foreign-born people. Instead of beginning with this topic, I thought I could work my way toward the subject by asking her what kind of newspapers she reads. I thought I could make a smooth transition from one type of media to another. Unfortunately, my opening questions became more of a digression than an introduction. I began the interview with the question 'Are you reading newspapers?' The next few questions and replies centered around printed news. By the time I reached the questions concerning my topic, ... the subject matter had an anti-climatic impact. Halfway through the interview I knew that we were both lost, and I could not bring us back to terra firma.

When the subject of television was finally introduced, instead of being able to determine the viewing habits of the respondent, we ended up talking about TV programs related to drug abuse. I asked Carmen why she liked this type of show. She replied, 'Because I have a child myself and I'm worried about him. I want to know why people take drugs'. Although there is no definitive way to prove that her replies may have differed had the introduction begun with television viewing, it is possible that the theme of crime and drug addicts was introduced because of the questions regarding newspapers.

Ewa might have learned valuable information if she had followed the lead about drug problems. She chose, however, to remain committed to her original goals. She continues the report of her journey with some valuable thoughts about questioning:

> There were times during the first interview when I found myself getting somewhat frustrated when my question was not understood. Having to rephrase the question not only interrupted my train of thought but also seemed to cause some anxiety in the respondent. This seemed to cause a behavioral change in the respondent's attitude in that she seemed to fear that she was not answering my questions 'correctly'. Now I was faced with the problem of having the respondent trying to please me instead of spontaneously answering the questions.

For her next interview, Ewa felt she had the 'right' questions. She was in for a surprise:

> After studying the first interview, I made notes and arming myself with 'foolproof' tactics, I chose a new respondent and tried again. My next 'victim' was David. David was an interviewer's dream in that he had no inhibitions when it came to talking. As a matter of fact, he was flattered that anyone would think he had something of value to say. He was a source of information just waiting to be tapped — or so I thought at the time.
> I had redrafted my questions so that they could be more easily understood by someone who was not proficient in English. Being aware of the previous pitfall of losing control of the interview, I tried subtly to guide the respondent so that he would not drift from the topic. Unfortunately, I overcompensated and the end result was that I asked leading questions instead of open ones, e.g., 'Do you think that the solutions they give on television are *good* solutions?' At one point during the interview with David, I asked him if he liked TV programs about people. He said he didn't know because he didn't understand programs about people. He continued by stating that he did watch one channel about the problems of some people. My next question was 'What kind of problem?' he stated that he could not remember. I tried to clarify the situation but instead of repeating or rephrasing I asked him directly 'What kind of problem? Personal or with the family?' Needless to say, his answers still did not provide the information which I was trying so desperately to glean.

This business of questioning haunts us all. Maybe we are so used to asking leading, narrow questions in the rest of our lives that we are talking of an almost alien concept for many people. Teachers who are striving to ask better questions know this. It is easier to ask: 'Do you like baseball?' than: 'What do you do for recreation?' In addition, it is harder to ask open questions when they are part of the flow of an interview rather than planned beforehand. Do not despair. Asking questions in open ways and then using probes can be learned:

What did you mean by . . . ?

You said you liked watching the joggers. Tell me a bit more about that, please.

You told me you love table tennis. Why is that so?

Open-ended questioning can unearth valuable information that tight questions do not allow. When a person adds to the practice of new or unused skills that of knowing how to ask and then to keep still in order to listen and observe, that person is well on the way. I keep reminding myself that as a qualitative researcher I am interested in understanding my participant's story, and questioning, listening, and observing are the tools that can help me. Many experts give good advice about questions. Spradley (1980), for example, suggests three broad categories of questions: descriptive, structural, and contrast (p. 123).

One caveat seems in order. While interviewing skills can be learned, this often takes time, recursive study of logs and action, strong will, and the ability to laugh. Ewa ends her article with a metaphor and advice:

> I now realize that obtaining a 'successful' interview is like walking a tightrope without a net while juggling sharp swords. It is far from easy and there is a tremendous amount of pressure and responsibility placed on the interviewer. There should be a balance between designed questions, ad libbing, and not leading the respondent down the 'expected' paths to knowledge. All this while maintaining a calm, relaxed, and confident exterior and keeping the respondent from feeling threatened or coerced. Perhaps I had judged Barbara Walters too harshly after all.

Finally, Dick DeLuca offers his advice on essential interview ingredients:

> The best advice anyone can give is LISTEN, LISTEN — and LISTEN MORE. Granted, you have some specific questions to ask, perhaps five to ten. Knowing which questions to ask, and in what general sequence, should enable you to devote full attention to your

interviewee's responses, and should make it easier to listen carefully to those responses.

Listening should be more than attending to the verbal message. Take care to observe the interviewee's body language — tone, gestures, posture, eye movements. For example, if a question evokes a startled look, you might ask: 'From that look, I assume you didn't expect that question; could you tell me why?' Display your sincere interest by responding at times to the information you are receiving: comments like, 'Yes, I see' or 'Oh, I never thought of that'. Your responses should have the effect of building and maintaining your credibility and rapport with the interviewee.

Be particularly sensitive to responses which appear incomplete, or which raise additional questions. Don't be afraid to probe. 'Could you elaborate on that point?' or 'You've explained the reasons for X, but haven't commented on Y; could you do so now?' might yield good results.

Think of your interview as flexibly structured. While you certainly want adequate answers to a few key questions, don't be rigid. Keep an open mind.

Dick advises people to know a few questions with which to begin. Even though we have emphasized that questions change in process, Margot previously stated that an interviewer must have in mind the areas that need to be probed at the start. From where do such questions and areas arise? One source is, of course, what we already know about the topic. This often provides a beginning frame. Some researchers are inspired by friends, colleagues, and mentors about the topic they are investigating. Most other leads come directly from the qualitative research process as it evolves. In our experience the most important impetus for developing questions is the ongoing writing of the field log, which includes interview transcripts, and the analysis that is part of the cyclic process of doing-thinking-doing. Lofland and Lofland (1984) indicate that optimally an interview rests upon some 'puzzlements' that the researcher has teased out from thinking about what has happened. These authors propose that researchers sort and order their puzzlements, their questions about what does not fit or is not evident, and in the end develop an interview guide. This may work best for people who are well into their project and who plan to do a formal ethnographic interview. But harnessing one's puzzlements works well anytime. This is true also for informal interviews, where the puzzlings often arise from recent observations but may also have shown themselves throughout the process. What is essential in creating questions is that they are consonant with or arise from the ongoing data as the qualitative researcher contemplates them.

When the situation is such that interviews are the major data-gathering techniques, often they serve as pivots for thinking about and highlighting one's learning in the entire research process. This was so for Steve Spitz.

Following is his extended note on methodology about an ethnographic interview study of men who were primary caregivers of their children:

The confidence I brought to conducting this investigation temporarily dissipated at the beginning of the study. The indeterminate nature of this investigation's design increased my anxiety about its execution. How would I approach the research participants? What would my role be? Where would I find willing participants? Would they be good respondents? Would I get appropriate data? I believed that I was skilled at psychological evaluation and psychotherapy. How would this process be different?

As is appropriate to this type of investigation, the answers to these questions emerged as the study unfolded. The interview with the first participant, Barry, went relatively smoothly. I was pleased at how easily he was able to share his experiences with me. In some ways, it was much easier than my role in psychotherapy because I didn't feel as invested in being helpful to the participants as I sometimes do with my patients.

Transcribing the first tapes confirmed my initial impressions. The data appeared to be valuable and appropriate to the study. While the actual process of transcribing was tedious, it was tempered by my impression that I was moving forward with the investigation, getting valuable information, and increasing my familiarity with the growing body of data.

I could sense when the interviews were going well, and I became excited when informative and vibrant interactions occurred. Such interactions confirmed my belief about the value of qualitative, case study research.

During the next few interviews, I was reminded of the never-ending variability among people. Not every participant was as open and articulate as Barry. Ira, for example, was much harder to get to know. He seemed guarded and often provided answers that left me wanting more. I became frustrated, reviewed the transcripts and my journal, and questioned whether I had done a good job when interviewing him.

In the end, it became a matter of doing more interviews with some of the participants as well as adapting the questions and probes to each participant's style. By the third interview, Ira was more relaxed, more trusting and able to speak more freely. My experience with Ira sensitized me to my role as an intimate stranger and heightened my sensitivity to each participant's unique style.

I also began to question what the respondents' motives might have been for participating in the study. Were there any benefits for them? This question was answered for me via feedback I received from the men in the study which I solicited during the interviews as well as during member-checking.

Bob, for example, shared with me that the interviews generated subsequent discussions between him and his wife. Through this combined process, he was able to realize that part of his motivation for being a primary caregiver was his desire to be a better father to his son than his father had been to him. In addition to providing valuable data for my study, I felt that our interaction had helped him to grow.

Steve highlights many important issues that have been mentioned so far. In particular, without 'naming' them, Steve discusses the relationship between the emergent nature of his design and his growth in confidence, the role of transcribing and studying the data in moving the study forward, getting sufficient data from interviewees with differing personal styles, the role of time and experience for both researcher and the researched, and some positive ripples from the interviews in the lives of his participants. Some of these issues will be discussed further in other parts of this book.

Logs

We have placed this section on logs after those about participant observation and interviews because, in our way of doing things, the log is the repository of all the data that have been gathered through these two methods. Because of this, transcripts of interviews and videotapes are naturally a part of our logs. If print materials are collected and can fit conveniently, they are placed in the logs. If print and other materials are too bulky, they are cross-indexed in the log to their storage places. As much as possible, our logs are chronological records of what we learn and our insights about how we learn it.

The writing of the logs often is an expansion from what we call 'field notes', those rapid jottings or whisperings into a tape recorder of details and dialogues that serve as guideposts for fuller description. The log contains the data upon which the analysis is begun and carried forward. It is the home for the substance that we use to tease out meanings and reflect upon them as they evolve. The log is the place where each qualitative researcher faces the self as instrument through a personal dialogue about moments of victory and dis-heartenment, hunches, feelings, insights, assumptions, biases, and ongoing ideas about method.

Different experts may have a variety of names for what the writing team calls the log, and there may be some disagreement about what goes into the log. We, however, must report to you what has proven most useful to us, and that is the metaphor of log as cohesive history.

Joanna Landau writes with some eloquence about the log: that object of hate and love, that receptacle of a researcher's description, vision, view, feelings, insights.

> Ah yes, that log! I am convinced that it is the log that really
> develops the progression from 'knowing' what one is going to learn,
> to feeling a bit like a detective uncovering a complex mystery, to
> finally having some beginning understandings about that which is
> being observed. It is the log which serves as the 'other', that con-
> tinuous opportunity to review and review again the events and the
> understandings. The work is never done, and the ending is arbitrary,
> as it was for me with the end of the course.

The biggest of the big ideas about log generation is that *the log is the
data*. Detail is everything; only that which is recorded in the log is available
for research. Be sure, however, to find some way to distinguish between what
was seen and heard 'out there' and what goes on inside you, the researcher —
what Bogdan and Biklen (1982) call the data about data. You'll see examples
of this on the following pages.

Donna Flynn shows how she went from mentioning an event in the log
to describing the event in a way that would prove fruitful for research:

> A rule in logging is describe, describe, describe, and I kept thinking,
> I can't, I can't, I can't. It was a real problem until I came to realize
> that ethnography subsumes a variety of professional disciplines and
> my particular background in nursing was not a perfect match, espe-
> cially in the area of logging.
>
> Thinking back to Nurses' Training, a great deal of emphasis was
> placed on clear, concise, to the point recording, including one's own
> conclusions. In ethnography, detail is everything, especially the in-
> terviewee's own words, descriptions, and perceptions. My quick
> generalizations were not acceptable. I had to unlearn so that I could
> learn.
>
> Here's what I mean: During our first field observation/informal
> interview, my tendency would have been to log, 'E told me about
> her day as a substitute teacher'.
>
> Instead I had to learn to log: 'E said, "You'll never guess what I
> did yesterday. I subbed for a first grade class, and boy, was I wiped
> out at the end of the day". She explained to me that their regular
> teacher was on maternity leave and would be back in April. She said
> she had lots planned, but didn't get to do much of it because the
> children were restless. I asked her what she did do and she said she
> read them stories. I remarked I bet they liked that. She said she was
> physically and emotionally exhausted from it and couldn't see her-
> self doing that every day'.
>
> All this was logged so that I could retain the flavor of her day
> and how she saw it and felt about it.

Donna's second entry was a great deal more helpful to her than the first. She
can continue to improve the quality of the data by recounting even more of
the event in dialogue form. Go for quotations. Many practitioners find that

they develop a capacity for holding large chunks of dialogue for a short time, and that it is easiest to audiotape them. So keep a tape recorder handy, and, if necessary, go off to a quiet place and preserve what you remember on tape. Margot flees to the rest room to make notes during observation periods whenever it is decently possible.

Beginning the Log

When to begin? We suggest in Chapter 2 that as soon as the first murmurings of an idea begin to stir, start the log. Plans, questions, enthusiasms, doubts, and ruminations are all part of the process. Remember, however, to separate what you observe from your thoughts about it. Margot puts brackets around the latter. Diane uses side bars of different colors. Start planning your entrance story in the log and, as Bernice Reyes recommends, record all your interactions with the gatekeeper.

> Log writing begins before the instant you interact with a gatekeeper, and at that point things become really busy! Every phone call, visit, letter, and conversation made as an effort to gain entrée needs to be documented in the log. It makes sense that any responses or follow-ups should be described in the log too.
>
> Don't expect magic yet. That is, your logs might be pretty flat and stale. On the other hand, you might get a reception to write home about. Whatever your interaction is with elements of the social setting you plan to observe, log it. How you gain access to the social setting is a significant part of your research.

Bernice goes on to offer us six tips on doing the first observations and writing field jottings and logs.

1   Observe deeply on the first visit. Be quiet — silence is golden now — and record your observations seriously. Ask people no questions yet. Be patient and watch the setting unfold itself.

2   If anyone asks you about the nature of your assignment, tell them you are observing how the program, class, job, or person operates as part of a homework assignment. Be honest but not so specific that people begin to 'act' for you.

3   Describe your observations without evaluations. Even if what you see is not agreeable to you, it needs to be described in the log as is. It has helped me to cite my judgments during log analysis, not during the initial description of the setting.

4 Do write about your feelings and the questions you pose as you observe.

5 If your participants seem persistently uncomfortable when they see your notepad, and you cannot convince them of your benign presence, then allay their fears by putting the notepad away. Some researchers take frequent trips to the water fountain, rest room, or their parked cars so they can record some key words and phrases.

6 As soon as possible after leaving the field, find a private place and the time to expand your field jottings into the log narrative and to think about it. Then make yourself some directions for the next observation.

Many researchers report some discomfort at the beginning of log writing. Laura Berns, whose research involved observing how college students used microcomputers as part of their composition class, describes her initial experiences with writing a log. You'll notice that she wrestles with concerns about timeliness and note taking:

I sat down at my Macintosh with relief. At least this part of the case study process — the writing of the log — would be familiar. As a graduate student at NYU I was certainly familiar enough with writing, especially since my program is English Education. So, whatever reservations I might have had about spending yet another morning cloistered with my Macintosh, I was comfortable enough with a writing assignment.

I should have known better, of course. I should have known logs were not the old, familiar academic writing. I took seriously, however, this first observation; if I was really going to use this research method for my dissertation, now was the time to learn how to do it right.

I was a little worried because I had already violated the first commandment: Write up the log the same day so that you don't forget. And now it was tomorrow morning and my mind was a blank about what had happened in the computer lab yesterday afternoon. I had not wanted to take extensive notes then because I didn't want to miss anything; but now I was afraid that I would not be able to make much sense out of my page or so of jotting and scribblings. Fortunately, that fear turned out to be groundless, both that first time and indeed for the rest of the semester; for those few notes were in fact sufficient to jog my memory, to bring back a wealth of detailed data — often more than I could conveniently manage. Later, the comments of fellow students confirmed my experience that a page of notes is sufficient. On the other hand, the comments of those who had tried to write a log without any written cues were less sanguine, as they found this approach a prescription for — well, not really for disaster, but for a thin and vague log entry.

Beginning researchers soon learn that taking notes in the field is essential to log writing. Lofland and Lofland (1984) say:

> . . . the complaint of the novice investigator (or the boast of the profession-
> al) that 'he didn't make any notes because nothing important happened' is
> viewed in this tradition as either naive or arrogant, or both. (p. 46)

Depending upon the circumstances and their roles, some people take notes as cues to develop later logs as Laura described, and some take more expanded, richer notes. For field jottings, students have successfully used legal pads, stenographer's notebooks, 5″ × 8″ cards, even scraps of paper. Although there may be some circumstances when researchers will want to share observations with the people they are observing, and although they explain that they will be taking some notes, generally it is good to be as unobtrusive as possible when writing. Videotaping and audiotaping, excellent ways to record the passing scene, will be discussed more fully later in this chapter.

Log Format and Content

Having established that some field notes are essential, Laura Berns tackles questions of log format and presents what we consider to be most valuable guidelines:

> Recall, then, wasn't the problem. The problem was unexpected —
> having to learn to write in a new genre. For writing a log is not the
> old familiar report of analysis, nor is it the informal journal used to
> think about readings in a course. A case study log has its own set of
> rules to be learned and applied. So, I came to realize as I struggled to
> write my log on that gloomy February morning, I was a novice even
> here.
>   For openers, the format rules are different in a log. You need
> generous margins — a few extra inches on the left and double-
> spacing because, unlike much other writing, a log entry is only
> begun on the day you write it. You will go back to it to put in
> additional marginal comments — your categories, your hunches,
> your later discoveries and clarifications. You might even want to
> leave wide margins on both sides so that you can use one margin for
> informal comments and the other for your systematic analysis. You
> will want to use a sequential pagination, rather than starting the
> numbers over again with each new log entry, since you will be
> referring to the log later in analytic memos and presumably in a final
> report.
>   And, despite the inconvenience, you need to number the lines
> of your log so that when you are sorting out similar items and

are documenting your statements later, you have a specific line reference.

In her developing log, Laura applied the principle 'once in, never out'. When you wish to add or change your lines, do so in the margin or in a later note. If you revise your ideas later, write an entry that demonstrates when, why, and how your ideas changed or expanded. For users of some word processing programs, automatic line numbering is a standard feature. For typists, or those who must use longhand, Laura offers additional advice:

> Other students in the class used efficient systems. Several classmates who typed their logs on a standard typewriter did so directly onto numbered sheets, whereas a computer-user made a single empty but numbered page and then used it as a template as she photocopied each page of the log.
> In addition to the format, this new genre has other distinctive requirements; but, fortunately, many of them make the writing more rapid, and more fun than the typical labored academic project. For one thing, there is not the need to find information — no search through dusty tomes in the library, no complex citations from esoteric texts; for you have from the observations and interviews themselves more than enough information. For another, there is no need to agonize over the best order, as you can whiz along, putting first what came first in time and continuing chronologically to the end. In addition, you don't have to be concerned about how many t's in inputting because such polished details are unimportant in a text intended for your eyes only — or, anyway, only for those of a sympathetic few.

Line numbering, though sometimes frustrating, is worth the effort. Not only will researchers be able efficiently to cross reference their logs as their analysis develops, but line numbering also provides a way to cite material when developing the case. You might look again at Margot's discussion of Allie Parrish's story (Chapter 2, pp. 26–29) to see how the line numbering abetted her reasoning. Harriet Parnes provides the following sample log pages, pp. 76–77. These illustrate both how the rules for log format described by Laura were applied, and how Harriet distinguishes between description and her comments about the description.

In addition to Harriet's observational notes, she uses two ways to make comments: in the text itself, set off by parentheses, and in the margin. Bogdan and Biklen (1982) call the reflective jottings of the researcher 'observer's comments' or OC. Researcher reflections may be about analysis; for example, in the margin on p. 77:19–21; 22–24 Harriet is suggesting some tentative analytical categories. The development of these is discussed later in this chapter. Observer's comments may be about method; see p. 76:15–21 for an example. They may be about ethical dilemmas and conflicts; on p. 77:40–43 Harriet talks of some ways in which she might avoid role conflict during her study. Reflections may also be about the observer's frame of mind; see 'I felt like choking' (line 45). Last, observer comments may be points of clarification in which the researcher corrects some previous conclusion or sees things in a different light.

These categories of observer comments are suggested by Bogdan and Biklen (1982, pp. 87–8). Other authors suggest coding descriptive methodological and theoretical comments. Find the ones that suit you. Make up your own if that seems best. But do 'talk' to yourself in the observational section of your field log and in the analytic memo where you will; for example, develop categories, make connections, and move towards answering your questions (see pp. 80–82). What's more, do 'talk to your talk' increasingly as you review field logs, your comments, and your analytic memos. As the research proceeds, you may well make more and different observer comments about your previous observer comments.

Considering the many ingredients of a log, Laura Berns commiserates with us about the amount of time ethnographers spend in log generation.

> Writers in this genre need some consolation. For, as you may have already discovered, short observations turn into long logs — without much regard for what you the writer may have intended. I routinely found that an hour of observation generated ten or more pages of log, an experience shared by many others in the course. So, you might as well know, the writing isn't so rapid that you can spend the afternoon observing and expect to write up the log before the theater.
>
> Some advice-givers promise that the length of logs relative to the hours of observation would grow shorter as the researcher became more focused. I kept waiting for this welcome relief, as did the fellow students I questioned, but quite in vain. Perhaps this awaited transformation happens to researchers sometime after the first semester in the field, or perhaps their families just get tired of having pizza every night for dinner. In the meantime, I found myself crossing the street to avoid conversations with any instructor or student in the computer course because a pleasant five-minute chat meant adding five more pages to my log.

Laura, as a beginning ethnographer, expresses a panic about trying to put everything into the log. Debbie Goldberg echoes Laura's sentiments:

> I just wrote for two hours straight. During the observation I described every action and activity that I saw and the truth is I didn't miss a nuance. I surely know what everyone said and did. I believe I can recount each episode, each trauma, and each interaction of the

From June ~~████~~   Part of the 6/8 entry

Command

!!!

oc

*teacher
control
recall, rote*

oc:
methodology

*teacher
control*

*Had they done
this with the
Sub? This
might go beyond
rote — or it
might not*

*I don't know
now how
accurately
she related
lengths to
her
drawing*

1 At 1:40 Mrs. T started teaching the math lesson. "What I
2 want you to do is take out your rulers." Some move-
3 ment in the class as children went to get rulers.
4 If a child did not have a ruler, he or she had to
5 stand up. Two students did not have what the teacher
6 thought was an acceptable excuse (I should have listed
7 the excuses) and they had to put their heads down on
8 their desks. Mrs. T had been absent when the sub-
9 stitute had taught about perimeter. "Who can tell me
10 what perimeter is?" One student suggested, "The
11 length of the outline of the sides of a shape." The
12 teacher immediately turned to a non-volunteer and
13 said, "What do you think it is?" "Measuring the sides
14 of a shape and adding the sides to get an answer,"
15 was the response. (I think it would be useful for
16 me to draw a quick seating sketch during the pro-
17 posed study so that I can code each student by po-
18 sition and I would know who said what. If class
19 position turns out not to be a good method, then I
20 will have to learn names quickly or come up with some
21 plan for coding students.) The teacher said, "That
22 sounds good. I'll write it on the board. You just
23 sit there." At this moment, Trick was very eager
24 about this lesson. This is what the teacher put on the
25 board: Perimeter — sides of a shape
26
27
28
29   2 in.
            P of this square?
30
31 Someone said the perimeter was 8 inches. The teacher
32 asked why. Someone said because all the sides of a
33 square are the same. The teacher then asked, "How
34 about the perimeter of this shape?" She asked them
35 how they would find the perimeter.
36
37
38
39
40
41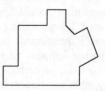
42
43
44
45
46
47 One student asked, "Are all the sides supposed to be
48 the same?" Mrs. T. said, "You tell me." Another
49 child said, "Measure each side," The teacher went to
50 the diagram and added numbers to the figure.

*Had they found perimeters of
irregularly shaped figures before? beyond recall?*

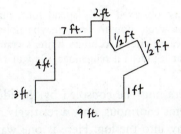

1
2
3
4
5
6
7
8
9
10
11
Review of 12
old skills 13
in a new 14
application 15
16
|17
oC |18
|19
Command 20
control 21
22
encouraging 23
activity 24
25
26
oC |27
|28
29
30
31
teacher 32
prepared 33
┌34
|35
|36
|37
oC |38
|39
|40
|41
|42
└43
teacher 44
errors oC 45
46
47
48
49
50

Meanwhile, Mrs. T. asked one child to look up
perimeter in the dictionary. Notice that the teacher
omitted several lengths from her diagram. This was
never noticed or corrected. She had the class practice mental arithmetic by adding the lengths aloud as
a group. (I had the thought that it was a nice
touch to have them working with whole numbers and
fractions.) The teacher did not pick up on the students'
comments about all the sides having the same lengths
or that they could measure the sides. (This felt
somehow incomplete and unanswered to me.) She then
said, "Without a sound, find something unusual in the
room — not a book or a desk. Take paper, a ruler,
and go to a measuring spot and find the perimeter."
Before the children were actually sent on this ex-
pedition (Was it done for my benefit? I wondered, or
would she have ordinarily have them do this?) a child
read the definition of perimeter from the
dictionary. I didn't pay much attention to it, but I
should have because something must have been mentioned about the perimeter of a circle. The teacher
looked at me and mouthed this question: "What is
that?" I mouthed circumference. (Now, what makes
this pilot very different from the proposed study
is this special relationship we have: though she may
change some of her classroom behaviors because I
am in the room, she is obviously very comfortable
with me and not in the least embarrassed to ask me
for help or admit she doesn't know something. Of
course, next year the teacher and I will have already
agreed on a different definition of my role in the
classroom — as a learner, not as teacher.) The teacher
now added to the dictionary definition: "Area
around an object." I felt like choking!

Harriet's Log — Excerpt of 6/8

people I just observed. Why spend four, maybe six hours typing what I just wrote down? True, maybe nobody else can read my writing because after two hours writer's cramp sets in. But even if it's not that legible, I'll remember. Or will I?

Qualitative researchers must be consoled by the idea that, even though the amount to record seems enormous, only a relatively small piece of what is out there will find its way into the log. Here is one way to think about reality. let's say you are an observer in a classroom. The first level of reality — 100 per cent — is everything that is out there: the physical environment plus the teachers and students — what they say, do, and think. Next comes what you see and hear — 30 per cent?, 40 per cent?, 50 per cent? When focusing on one interchange, many other things pass by unnoticed. And remember, some of what is out there, like people's thoughts, can only be approached through an interview. Then, as you write your log, you will record only what you can of what you saw and heard. While this hard-earned, tiny slice of reality may seem insignificant and discouraging, repeated observations will help you discover the important aspects of the circumstances you observe. I cannot emphasize enough the contributions of such ongoing observations. In my own case, I developed from a person who at first fixated on what I may have missed to one who trusts that important events will most probably show themselves if I observe persistently enough.

Laura's panicked avoidance of people, however, is as understandable as it is humorous; however, not everything that is seen and heard will go into the log. Laura goes on to clarify how log writing is different from writing a personal diary:

> The log differs from a personal diary. It is true that I am the sole reader of my log, at least theoretically. Yet the log is a far more public, accessible document than a journal. At first I found this situation disconcerting because I couldn't decide what I could safely assume and what I had to state explicitly. But I cleared up the muddle a bit by thinking of the 'I' that reads the log as my public, academic self — a rather critical, intellectual self more interested in hard evidence than in vague impressions. And I further cleared it up by thinking of this reader as naive, with knowledge limited to the data in the log, not my 'real' privileged self with diverse sources of information. As an added strategy for determining what this 'reader' would need to know, I found it useful to imagine myself reading the log a year or two later as I was writing my dissertation.

Because a dissertation takes months or years to write, the qualitative researcher should heed Laura's advice to write for a self who is uninformed, even scornful. The log is the right place for hunches and conjectures, but the writer should include all the evidence that weakens or supports these. As Laura affirms, and as we cannot seem to stop repeating, the log *is* the data:

> I also found it useful to keep in mind the second commandment of case study: The log contains the only admissible data. For purposes of reporting, then, if an episode or remark is not in the log, it didn't happen. As a result, my log needed to be full of detailed description of situations, rich in the externals of what was said and done by the participants, not just, as with a diary, with my own impressions and conclusions — brilliant though they might be.

Laura concludes her essay with comments on some of the satisfactions she found in log generation:

> During the observation or interview I was caught up in the process of making sense of events; afterwards, in the writing of the log, I often gained an understanding of events that I had totally missed before. James Britton, guru of English Education, has pointed out this advantage of writing about past experiences, noting that we are then able to be reflective in ways not possible when we were active participants.
>
> In fact, on that gloomy February morning, I was suddenly struck by one of those insights that makes up a bit for the grubbier parts of being a graduate student. I was struck by how dependent I was upon my prior knowledge in making sense of the situation and how inextricably external 'facts' are bound up with interpretation. Eureka! We are peeling the onion, with each layer of interpretation removed only exposing another layer beneath. I may not have run down chilly streets naked, as did Archimedes, but I had my own modest elation.

Laura's two commandments bear highlighting as we conclude this section. First, write your log as soon as possible, and at least within twenty-four hours of the experience. Forgetting begins as soon as the experience ends. It is urgent to turn your field jottings into log. Be firm with yourself about quickly sitting down to write your log. When and if you wait longer, understand and accept this, but strive consciously not to make it a pattern. We know of at least two people who literally had to do their participant observation anew for the want of a richly built log. Second, get as much as possible into your log. At times, a current event may remind you of an earlier event that went unrecorded. Put that memory into your log at the later date, with as many details as you can remember, and cross reference it to the earlier time. Whenever memory overtakes you, get the details into the log.

Erving Goffman (1989) gave this advice:

Write as lushly as you can, as loosely as you can, as long as you put yourself into it, where you say, 'I felt that'.... to be scientific in this area, you've got to start by trusting yourself and writing as fully and as lushly as you can. That's part of the discipline itself, too. (p. 131)

Analytic Memos

In the last sections there were several mentions of analytic memos, sometimes also referred to as researcher memos. These devices serve an important function in moving the methodology and analysis forward. Analytic memos can be thought of as conversations with oneself about what has occurred in the research process, what has been learned, the insights this provides, and the leads these suggest for future action. These memos are written *about* entries in the log, and they themselves become *part* of the log. They may be expansions of the spontaneous 'observer comments' (see Harriet's log, pp. 76–77) that are often woven into the entries. There is no hard and fast rule about when to write an analytic memo. Each researcher must find those points. Margot has decided that it suits her work style to write an analytic memo at least once every three weeks, no matter what has occurred in the research. I, on the other hand, write an analytic memo after each set of three log entries. We do know, however, when too much time has elapsed between memos because then we experiece an input overload and the uneasy realization that we are floundering because we haven't given ourselves the direction we need.

Jim Hinojosa provides one of his analytic memos. This was written during his study about mothers' perceptions of the influence on their family life of occupational and physical therapy home programs for preschool children with cerebral palsy:

Analytic Memo #5

```
1    Date _____
2
3         In order to try and figure out where I am, I have decided
4    to analyze the two interviews I had on 7/27 and 8/20 with
5    regard to the categories I identified in Madge's interview.
6         Category: Special relationship (Jane, 786–7; Madge, 1062–
7    5), probably goes with friendship with a new title. How does
8    the relationship develop? What do they expect from it? I must
9    face the fact that I am more frustrated by Jane than by Madge.
10        Category: Advise and instruct I need to distinguish this
11   category more clearly. Does suggestion = advice? (Madge,
12   1607–11, Jane, 1249–60).
13        A major trend appears to be a lack of spontaneous interac-
14   tion between the child with cerebral palsy and the mother
15   (Jane, 230–41, 801–10, 911–24, 1523–52; Madge, 34–60, 261–
```

1 79, 518–30). Mothers have to learn how to care and must think
2 through how to do things. At this age, the mother of more
3 physically able children might be allowing the children to ex-
4 perience their world more independently, exploring and learn-
5 ing about the world from an upright position with their ability
6 to walk.

7   These two mothers, who are very concerned about their
8 children's ability to learn about their worlds, seem to need
9 therapist input in order to structure the learning experiences.
10 They report that their contact with therapists is in order that
11 they learn (Jane, 1001–42; Madge, 836–53).

12   Mothers learn how to hold, feed (Madge, 180–3; Jane,
13 54–70), and to facilitate their child's development. The therap-
14 ist role seems to be to teach, advise, instruct, and explain. Each
15 mother seems to benefit from observing the therapist interact
16 with her child (Madge, 192–4; Jane, 303–10). Both mothers felt
17 that participation in the child's program was important. Madge
18 felt that participation involved active involvement with the
19 therapist while Jane seems to consider 'home treatment' as
20 involvement (Madge, 81–93; Jane, 410–18).

21   Madge was dealing with monitoring what the child was
22 getting and overseeing every aspect of the child's program
23 (Madge, 434–36).

24   Both mothers allowed their children to engage in activities
25 that they know their therapists do not approve of (Madge,
26 320–31, 568–82, 634–41; Jane, 433–42, 764–73). Why? ...
27 Unlike I expected, the mothers seem rather pleased about it.

28   Time seems to be important. Time to get the child to
29 therapy, time to do the therapy, time to get other things done.
30 Question: What is the implication of this on other things
31 relative to family life? ... I'll try to focus on this during my
32 next interview-observation.

Jim's memo echoes the fact that he wrote it primarily for himself, not others. Note the idiosyncratic style and brief wording, for example, on p. 80:31–32. Such shortcuts are quite understandable to the author. Jim speculates both about his emergent category analysis (p. 80:6–9, 10–11) and some possible trends in the data (p. 80:13–15). These he supports in some detail. However, it is clear that he is still open and tentative in his musings (see the word 'appears' on p. 80:13, 'seem' and 'seems' on p. 81:8, 14, 15, 19, and 'might' on 3). Notice that when Jim talks of emerging trends, he often cites specific supporting data from both mothers. On lines page 80:8–9 Jim faces some of his own feelings about the participants. While his hunches about data throughout can be considered leads for future interviews and observations, he proposes a specific emerging question and gives himself some research focus for his next session in the field on page 80:28–32.

Jim's work is a good case in point that analytic memos allow room for speculation and integration. They allow us to look back so we can check our beginning assumptions, analysis, and conceptual frame, and they allow us to look forward so that we can create direction for our work.

Audiotaping and Videotaping

In addition to all the written material they generate and collect about the situation, many researchers find it useful to document with audiotapes and/or videotapes. Audiotapes add the nuances of a person's voice to the words that print provides. Videotapes show context, people in verbal interaction and such non-verbal elements as the sounds of voices, gestures, facial expressions, light, color, activity, and relative bustle or quiet. In addition, both audiotapes and videotapes allow for analysis through repeated studying, as well as checking against log notes and transcripts about the same events. Many researchers prefer to audiotape their interviews because of the ease of this procedure and its cost effectiveness. Most of our students and all of the writing team have done audiotaping. Most participants have agreed to being audiotaped after they were apprised of the purposes of the activity and their rights to remain anonymous and, at times, to review the transcript. We have found that, after a short while, people relax and seem to be unaware of the tape recorder, but that depends on the tone of the interview. Even though we promise that participants may withdraw from the taping at any time without negative repercussions, not one interviewee has ever done so.

Debbie Goldberg addresses the issues of when to transcribe audiotapes, and how to do it.

> I just finished tape recording my interview. Surely I don't have to type this out. I won't forget the interview. Besides, it's on audiotape. I can play and replay my conversation with my interviewee as many times as I need to, so why spend eight, maybe ten hours transcribing? Typing out an interview is time-consuming and laborious. Instead I could be reading about ethnography, developing analytic questions, or analyzing my data. Certainly these are more important things to do than typing. I have other commitments. If I didn't have to type my field notes or my interview, I could avoid getting up at 3:00 a.m. in order to finish my work.

Despite her doubts, Debbie found, as have other researchers, that transcribing interviews helps to recall the experience, expands the details, and often provides a fresh perspective on the material:

Truthfully, typing helped me to recall details and to relive what happened. 'Tape recorded interviews, when fully transcribed, represent one of the most complete expanded accounts'. (Spradley, 1979, p. 75)

Debbie continues:

> I found that when I wrote out an interview in longhand, I didn't read it as thoroughly as a typed one. It just wasn't as legible. The data are too valuable to be overlooked or perhaps to be misread because of a tired hand. After typing my field notes and my interview, my material was clearly presented, and I coded and analyzed my data more easily. When I needed to photocopy my log, I saved money by typing because the amount of material was compressed. All in all, however, I'm eagerly waiting for one of those machines that print out the spoken word.

Debbie makes the important point that transcripts of audiotaped interviews are also included as part of her log. Further, in order to take advantage of electronic data-organizing packages, word processing is a must.

Richard Stoving recommends videotaping for its 'teleporter-time machine' qualities:

> For the past several weeks, you have been observing the dynamics of a particular elementary classroom. You're moved to wonder why the teacher, Mr Zapp, seems to be so hung up about classroom control. He even has kids standing up when they answer his questions. But in an interview, he described himself as a non-authoritarian teacher.
>
> 'Could it be me?' you ask yourself. 'Am I being fair?' Someone in your support group suggests that perhaps your own evaluation is off base. Time for a little triangulation. You want to see if others see your teacher as you see him, maybe even give him a chance to see himself and to explain his stance to you.
>
> But how? If, in your ethnographer's bag of tricks, you carried around a portable time machine, you could examine this behavior again and again, and if you had a Startrek teleporter, you could move your whole support team into Mr Zapp's class. Cheer up, there is a kind of combination time machine-teleporter available. It is, of course, video.

Francia Mercado longed to become a camera so that she could record 'everything':

> I wish I were a TV camera so I could record all that is happening. Then I reflect that even a camera must be aimed at a specific area of interest, neglecting other areas. A tape recorder preserves verbal

communications but would leave out facial expressions, gestures, posture; and the body language which can be so eloquent would be missing. I begin to understand that I can record not only the action that is taking place, but also what didn't happen; the non-reactions, the things skipped by the players of this particular drama.

Francia's concern for capturing both the verbal and non-verbal messages didn't blind her to the possibility that important things may be happening outside her range, as they do outside that of a camera or microphone.

Belén Matías, who spent more than 1200 hours reviewing 112 videotapes of an early childhood classroom, adds this cautionary note about the time that can be spent in tape analysis:

> I thought it would be wonderful to videotape for a month at the beginning, a month at the middle, and two weeks at the end of school. I would have a rich database. Blessed are the ignorant! As I started the study, I realized the amount of work each single videotape demanded. I had to view it to get the flavor, the flow of things, to do a 'grand tour' à la Spradley. Then I had to study it again to be able to choose the specific classroom events I would select for special attention, the 'mini tour'.
>
> Of course, this is not counting the ten to twelve hours I spent in studying and transcribing just one tape. I wrote down everything, and I mean everything! Every coherent sound I could decipher. I took notes on the non-verbal dynamics/interactions as well as situations where I did not understand the dialogue, but where I could observe the interaction. All this for each twenty-minute videotape.
>
> I did not know this then, but more work was waiting for me as I immersed myself in the analysis. For this I studied the tapes again to check categories and emerging themes. Finally I chose six tapes for micro-analysis. I have mercifully lost count of how many times I reviewed each of them.
>
> One note of caution. Consider carefully how much time you will need to spend in analysis of the taped material. Producing the videotapes is cost efficient in time, dollars, and energy, but the amount of time spent on analysis can be very costly. The project took an extra year because I felt I had to make use of all the data I had collected. Of course, even then I didn't.

Thomas Veltre, a director of documentaries, was struck by the similarities and differences between doing ethnographic research and making documentaries.

> Conceptually, documentary film makers have a variety of approaches. They can be overt advocates of a particular view or position, dispassionate 'fly-on-the-wall' observers of society, inno-

cents in a strange land, or any mixture of the above. Like the ethnographic researcher, they must be conscious of the approach they will be taking before setting out on a new project. Unlike ethnographic researchers, most film makers are not burdened with the responsibility of being 'scientific', of having to present the resulting document as empirical data. This is, of course, a crucial difference.

For both film maker and ethnographic researcher, analysis begins before the very first trip into the field. As the director views the 'rushes' and the researcher reviews the notes and transcripts, each is searching for patterns and ideas which will structure the rest of the project. Every foot of film and every bit of data are examined as soon as they are created. The question is constantly raised about how these will fit in the final product, or what implications they have for the material already gathered.

As much as ethnographers attempt to capture every nuance and inflection of their participant's speech and gestures, they should consider themselves fortunate that they can't record everything. While they are observing or interviewing, they 'filter' out irrelevant data, discriminating between what should be recorded and what must be ignored. If only a movie camera could have such a filter!

For both audiotaping and videotaping, the people whom we are studying need to give their permission. We often do well with a 'dry-run' that gets people acquainted with the equipment. It is useful to select the best vantage point for the main activity you wish to record. If the activity is videotaping, then the camera may be left running quietly on its tripod, though some researchers prefer to use a hand-held camera. Often the participants enjoy a playback after audio and videotaping, depending on the situation and research aims.

Both videotape and audiotape can be used for purposes in addition to collecting data. For example, Margot reviews her audiotaped interviews and selects several pieces to share with her interviewees for further clarification. Margaret played some audiotapes of the sessions in which elementary school students discussed literature so that the children could study and comment on their own group process. Belén Matías shared videotapes of classroom interaction with the teacher so that she would provide her explanations of what occurred in her classroom.

The glory of videotape is that you and as many people as you wish can be looking at the scene as often as you like. This is true also of listening to and studying audiotapes. The misery is that your thoughts and impressions must still be recorded and transcribed into the log so that you can use the data. You can, however, use both sorts of tapes as an excellent way to do triangulation and close analysis. You must decide what is appropriate.

Ongoing Data Analysis

The concept of self-as-instrument may have been exotic at the beginning, and up to the point of analysis most students have felt it as an exciting and compatible vision, a breath of fresh research air. After all, self-as-instrument, rather than having the self dependent on other instruments, connotes personal control and personal responsibility and, therefore, personal creativity. But the start of analysis comes early, with the very first log notation. This is because analysis is part and parcel of the ongoing, intertwined process that powers data collection. For most people, analysis carries feelings somewhat different from assurance. The five of us have found that often the first analyses create a place where reality hits, where doubts, fears, and avoidances begin, where the theory and philosophy of qualitative research are put to a reality test. We have also found that this is a place of great value and rededication and personal joy. When the researcher gets right to it, it is an awesome, even frightening responsibility to bow to the fact that 'self-as-instrument' inevitably means one must create ongoing meaning out of the evolving and evolved data, since raw data alone have little value. But it gives tremendous elation to know it can be done. Thus, the naturalistic researcher must come to rely on his/her own talents, insights, and trustworthiness and, in the end, go public with the reasoning that engendered the results, while accepting with equanimity that other people may make different meaning from the same data.

Joan Giansante discusses the problems associated with getting started on the analysis:

> I am always putting things in order.
>
> On my desk, I have paper clips in one dish, rubber bands in another, and stamps in another. I even have my writing instruments in two jars — pens and pencils in one jar and colored felt markers in another.
>
> When I work as a consultant in corporations, I can easily classify and categorize everybody else's business. Once I was hired to improve a long-winded manual that desperately needed reorganization and editing. After reading the forty-five-page draft, I immediately told the writer, 'You have three different publications here: a brochure to inform management about your service, a user's manual for those who will use your service, and a job manual for your employees'. It seemed so obvious!
>
> Why was I having so much difficulty finding order in the chaos?
>
> The answer seems to have three aspects.
>
> 1 Like the writer I was hired to edit, I was overwhelmed by the data.
> 2 I had great difficulty getting started with analysis. I hesitated

to select a focus, waiting for something to emerge, or hit me over the head. When I settled on three main issues, I could not come up with subcategories. Which brings me to the third aspect of the problem.

3 I skipped a step in the analysis procedure. I tried to go from identifying the main issues to making conclusions about those issues. I had skipped the important step of beginning with descriptive categories.

The categories Joan mentions begin with the smallest, most literal descriptions of the unfolding words and events. Creating categories triggers the construction of a conceptual scheme that suits the data. This scheme helps a researcher to ask questions, to compare across data, to change or drop categories, and to make a hierarchical order of them. At its most useful, the process of establishing categories is a very close, intense conversation between a researcher and the data that has implications for ongoing method, descriptive reporting, and theory building. In the foregoing statements, we have been deeply influenced by the work of Glaser and Strauss (1967) and Strauss (1987). Indeed, apropos of this section, we recommend Anselm Strauss's (1987) detailed, cogent treatise on his sense of the discovery of grounded theory via qualitative analysis. This includes several chapters on coding strategies for a variety of purposes that seem pertinent, whether or not a researcher wants to construct theory.

Establishing categories from qualitative data seems rather like a simultaneous left-brain right-brain exercise. That is, one job is to distill categories and the other is to keep hold of the large picture so that the categories are true to it. Experts (for example, Bogdan and Biklen, 1982; Giorgi, 1989; Goetz and LeCompte, 1984; Lofland and Lofland, 1984; Miles and Huberman, 1984; Tesch, 1990) have explained how they go about establishing categories. The teaching team has worked out its way which amalgamates many of the proposed ideas:

1 Start by reacquainting yourself deeply with what you are about to begin to categorize. Choose one entry in your log. Read and think about those pages several times until you feel you have caught their essence. Don't stint here. The team members do at least four readings for each entry.

2 Next, write some notes in the margins of those pages. 'Free think' your ideas. You might remark on lines that interest you — and why, your question about the text, your insights about your frameworks for observation and interview, and any topics that seem to be cropping up. These notes are useful for the next step, as well as for later when you are working to describe the meaning of your data.

3 Because '. . . nobody can do an analysis without some kind of break-ing into parts' (Giorgi, 1989, p. 48), this is now your job. We've concluded that applying the concept of creating 'meaning units' works well here. This occurs as one reads the narrative and divides it in some way that makes sense. Giorgi (1989) describes that since he is interested in understanding the meaning of experience, every time he notes a change in meaning in the text he puts a slash there, and continues in that manner until he has segmented the entire piece. He says, '. . . I let my spontaneity operate while constructing meaning units; "Something important is happening here", or "There's a change here", or "Something interesting is going on here" ' (p. 49).

4 Now, label your meaning units. That is, in the margin next to each unit, label what that unit is about. Try to use one word, or at least as few words as possible. Use your own labeling words here unless the right label jumps out at you from the text. In this step, make the labels descriptive. Even though they were in their final analysis stage, the labels of Ronna Ziegel and Jim Hinojosa on pp. 146–7 are good examples because the process of creating categories is quite similar at any stage.

5 After you've studied and marked several log entries, make a list of all your labels. Group the ones that seem to fit together and try to find one label that will do for each entire group. Group the ones that don't fit together and let each stand separately. Look for links between labels. Compare. Contrast. Move labels around if that is sensible. Play a bit. Remember, the test for a useful label is that it describes what the meaning unit is about, not that it has occurred many times. Although that happens, a label that occurs once only can be very important to your research.

6 Analyze the next few log entries by applying the labels you've de-cided upon in Step 5. Be careful here not to force labels that don't fit well into meaning units. This indicates that other labels are needed. If so, make some other labels and try them out, yes, from the very beginning to the end of the pages you have already coded once. Do this as many times as you need until you judge that your categories suit the data. Don't try for perfection. Not everything will fit. Try for a sensible organizing scheme. At that point you have succeeded with a valuable qualitative analysis technique. When your labels fit well, they may be considered tentative titles for categories. Understand that sometimes the same meaning units can be an example of more than one category, and, so, can be coded in more than one way. Our categories often overlap.

7 Write analytic memos as you go along. These will help you at this point and in final analysis.

These steps apply particularly to making beginning categories, and I feel it is best not to move too quickly to other meaning constructions. Because of this, the topic is continued in Chapter 5. Two more suggestions may serve. First, if you are having trouble starting the process, take a cue from what we do in class. Margot hands out a transcript — any transcript provided by a person who is not a member of the class — and we construct tentative labels in the ways I have described. It works every time. Find a piece of log narrative, perhaps even a published one, and begin. Second, the section about thinking units on pp. 143–5 may also help you to get started.

The next two quotations are fine examples of how methodology and the creation of categories influence each other in process. Jo Ann Saggese tells how interviewing created difficulties with her categories.

> I began interviewing and analyzing. Things started looking very different. All the observations that fit nicely into categories began to bulge and pucker and made packaging very difficult. For some reason I had a strange notion that if I put my log away, when I finally decided to retrieve it, everything would be analyzed, synthe-sized, and computerized. I tried it. It doesn't work. In the field of occupational therapy, a learning through doing theory exists. Case study exemplifies this theory. I let go of my categories and observed some more. This time my new categories started to make sense.

Marcia Kropf planned to study how students learned computer programming, but as she analyzed her log, she found that what most drew her attention was human interaction:

> My logs began to be filled with the comings and goings of students, the ways in which they were welcomed in the class and asked to participate (or were not), and the ways in which they attempted to participate (or did not). I found myself fascinated by the interactions between these students and the teacher.

Because Marcia stayed in touch with her log through rereading, she was able to identify a new category she tentatively labeled 'interactions' that seemed important to her. This helped her to become a more focused observer in the ensuing sessions. Staying close to the log through repeated rereadings helps the researcher find new directions, refine questions, develop emergent mean-ings, and hone a conceptual scheme.

The timing of discovering useful categories is not the same for everyone. Sometimes a great idea comes along late in analysis, thereby causing a review of all the preceding data in light of the current discovery. For other researchers, the process from descriptive categories to linked categories and finally to establishing overall meaning follows an even progression without major detours. Most of us, however, take a number of detours before we make final meaning. Chapter 5 will continue this discussion by focusing on analysis of data once the researcher has left the field.

Computers as Aids in Analysis

One of the exciting advances in qualitative data analysis is the continuing development of various computer software packages to assist in the tagging and retrieval of data. Although computer programs for text analysis have been around since 1966 (Tesch, 1990), it is only since the mid-1980s that easy-to-use software for the two most common varieties of computers has been widely available. Many word processing packages and database managers have advanced features that allow the user to manipulate data onscreen. Word-Perfect allows the user to create a second document into which text can be moved while the user moves back and forth between the two documents. Other software allows text to be dragged to a 'window' for storage and retrieval. Both methods will speed the laborious process of cut-and-paste, but if the original context is to be preserved, each segment must be identified individually. As of 1990, six packages have been developed by researchers in the social sciences to overcome this limitation: ETHNO, TAP, QUALPRO, The Ethnograph, TEXTBASE ALPHA, and HyperQual. These 'Analysis programs perform only *two basic functions*: They allow you to attach codes to segments of text, and they will, according to your instructions, search through your data for segments that were coded in a certain way, and assemble them' (Tesch, 1990, p. 150).

But wait, you may be breathing too easily. Text analysis packages do not do the analysis for the researcher. The user must still create the categories, do segmenting and coding, and decide what to retrieve and collate. If, however, the researcher is reasonably comfortable with a computer, the analysis packages can remove most of the drudgery from the cut-and-paste process. The main objection to the process, especially from non-computer users, is that the computer and the software put distance between the researcher and the material. Whether or not this happens depends on the researcher's work style, not the computer. People who have used the packages are often amazed that this kind of work, with its thousands of pages of data, could ever have been conducted by hand.

Indeed, because of the ease with which data can be organized and reorganized, the software is much more than an expensive pair of scissors and tape. The savings in time and energy may motivate the researcher to reconsider data that might previously have been put aside or neglected, to place data in more than one category to test new relationships, and, in general, to be more creative. It is our intention merely to alert the beginning researcher to the availability of these packages. For a more detailed examination of these matters, you might consult Renata Tesch's 1990 book, *Qualitative Research: Analysis Types and Software Tools*.

Leaving the Field

> It's time to analyze and present data — and I'm still anxious. Do I have enough data? Do I have the 'right' data? Are my data presented properly? Should I leave the field, or should I stay? How do I know when enough is indeed 'enough?' (Rena Smith)

Knowing when to leave the field is a judgment based on the researcher's sense that substantial amounts of data have been gathered on both the initial questions and the questions that have emerged during the study. Courage, insight, and, for many of us, emotional sturdiness are required to decide that observation has been sufficiently persistent and prolonged; all of us, though, have lived through it, and there is always the comforting thought that we can return to the field if that is necessary.

While this judgment must be faced personally and often alone, there are some criteria for when it is time to leave. Being in the field for a sufficient time should create a feeling of immersion. The researcher should know that he or she can talk for the participants — as the participants — in a legitimate way. If the researcher can't speak for the participants, then more time in the field is necessary. In addition, if there are too many unanswered questions pertaining to the questions asked in process, more time must be spent in the field. Remember, however, that most often there will be more data in the log than can be shared in a research report. Fight the tendency that many of us have to want to include everything in the final report. Useful data can sustain other studies, other articles. Since you are the only expert about your data, your judgment is required to know when your important questions can be answered and, therefore, to know when you have gathered sufficient data. Fight also that old siren song that tells you to stay in the field because it's such fun, because you are needed. Those issues may need to be considered, but they are not sufficient reasons by themselves to stay yet another week, another month:

Leaving the field can also be a time of strong feelings. Who wants to leave doing something that has been so much fun, where people have responded in such a positive fashion? Qualitative researchers have a wonderful time collecting their data. The hard part begins when they have to stop collecting. So when I had to leave the field, there were two feelings. One was the sadness of leaving people who have been fun and interesting and helpful. And the other was the anticipation of the agonizing amount of work that lay ahead. (Leslie Rice)

In deciding when to leave the field, time is relevant, but the significant factor is what is done with that time. A micro-analysis of a series of videotapes may require relatively few hours to tape, but many hours to analyze. When documenting the social interactions among group members, prolonged face-to-face contact is necessary. You are the best judge. So, time alone is not a reliable indicator of when to leave the field. Other elements are also not reliable: 2000 pages in your log, a log too heavy to lift, a log that occupies more than one cardboard carton, forty interviews, exhaustion. Well, if these factors are of no help, what is? Redundancy and a feeling of completion. Lincoln and Guba (1985) tell us that when the data repeat themselves, when the researcher has confidence that themes and examples are repeating instead of extending, it may be time to leave the field. It is time to go when the researcher feels he or she has accomplished what needed to be done (Bogdan and Biklen, 1982). In addition, taking a break and leaving the field can bring unexpected revelations:

I wanted to abandon qualitative methodologies because of inner conflicts. I was able to leave the field for two weeks, and put aside all my work for the study, including the rereading of the logs. After two weeks, the logs beckoned. As I reread what I had written, my doubts began to fade. My log convinced me that qualitative research was for me. (Barbara Gagliardi)

Keeping the Door Open

Qualitative researchers are deeply immersed in the analytical process all through the data-gathering stages, but analytical surprises frequently emerge when the researcher is out of the field and looking again at all the data. It is important, then, to leave the participants in the field with the understanding that the researcher might want to return for another visit, another interview, or a few phone calls. If the researcher has promised to feed back some information, for example, this would be an opportunity to plan that event. Often, the sharing session is an appropriate time to do some final clarifications.

As we have noted, when the research has been a happy experience, the researcher and the participants may be sad about parting company. It's wonderful to make friends, but people generally understand that this is a self-limiting relationship. Sometimes the relationship continues, but in a different way. Laura Lee Lustbader had this to say about her study of a 17-year-old woman labeled schizophrenic:

> My case study for my graduate work is completed now; however, the relationship between Eileen and myself, which is a by-product of the class assignment, is by no means a *fait accompli*. When I wrote my final field notes, I had the overwhelming sense that I was a rat! Here I have a project. I like the project and believe I learned a lot from the doing of it. What happens to Eileen? What does she get out of it? I believe she has a friend. No longer do I need to run to my desk when I finish spending time with her, nor do I have to see her weekly. But, I can see her as she and I wish, and as time permits, to be her friend and sounding board.

Keeping the door open is the key to minimizing any reluctance about leaving the field. We discuss more about returning to the field in Chapter 5.

Establishing Trustworthiness

> Trustworthiness is a big issue; that is, it is big in scope. In fact, it is bigger than I ever imagined. I used to think trustworthiness was pervasive; but after reading Guba and Lincoln, I realize that it is more than pervasive. It's so big that it's bigger than the ethnographic study itself. Not bigger in the sense of how much time it takes. But bigger in the sense of how much it has to be thought about — before, during, and after the ethnographic study is done. (Joan Giansante)

Being trustworthy as a qualitative researcher means at the least that the processes of the research are carried out fairly, that the products represent as closely as possible the experiences of the people who are studied. The entire endeavor must be grounded in ethical principles about how data are collected and analyzed, how one's own assumptions and conclusions are checked, how participants are involved, and how results are communicated. Trustworthiness is, thus, more than a set of procedures. To my mind, it is a personal belief system that shapes the procedures in process.

Because concern for trustworthiness is part of every qualitative research activity, it is present in spirit in every one of our chapters. In two of them, however, trustworthiness is addressed directly. Here, in Chapter 3, we discuss those issues that seem particularly germane to the processes of collecting data and beginning analysis. In Chapter 5, we extend the focus to include final analysis and writing the research report.

No matter what their situation, their past education, or their research experiences, qualitative researchers know that there is considerable concern about trustworthiness, that it comes from many quarters and in many voices, and that it is clothed in some controversy.

The Shock of Recognition

When we first came to consider research during our doctoral studies, all five of us, and we believe most others, came with 'quantitative heads'. We knew that issues about validity and reliability were paramount, and we knew that there were some tried and true ways to establish these. Many of us remember our days in a foundations of research seminar where questions regarding reliability and validity became staples of our weekly critiques of each other's first, stumbling efforts at research design:

How can this be replicated? Is this a representative sample?

What we did not know at the time, even after we first began thinking about qualitative study, was that while issues about reliability and validity apply to both quantitative and qualitative work, they are conceived of and arrived at in different ways. When people inclined toward viewing the world with qualitative lenses recognize this fact and begin to understand the routes to doing acceptable research in that paradigm, it is often an intense and poignant event:

> I felt all those years of struggling to believe — and to get others to believe — that all those sampling procedures, those equations, those different forms of predetermined tests indeed measured whether what I was doing was truly reliable and valid, slip off me like the dead weight I finally accepted they were. Now I could ask questions such as, 'How adequately did I represent what I witnessed?' 'What's the match between my vision and those of the people I studied?'
>
> I didn't fool myself. There was plenty of hard work ahead, harder by far. But let me tell you, I was freed. I was breathing differently. (Margot Ely)

For many of us, the use of different terms for 'validity' and 'reliability' is a deliberate and liberating act. To speak of trustworthiness and its components of credibility, transferability, dependability, and confirmability (Lincoln and Guba, 1985) or of authenticity criteria (Guba and Lincoln, 1989) is to remind ourselves of the issues and processes that must weave their way through and beyond our qualitative research to keep it and us honest and believable. These terms are not just different ways for qualitative researchers to say the same things that positivists say. They indicate real differences, at least to us. Not all qualitative researchers, however, agree, and they continue to use some of the terms of positivist research in their work (Fetterman, 1989; Goetz and LeCompte, 1984; Miles and Huberman, 1984). These people may be doing the rest of us a real service by making a statement in familiar terms to the larger community that qualitative work can be reliable and valid. On the other hand, we have found that the language of positivistic research is not congruent with or adequate to qualitative work, and its use is often a defensive measure that muddies the waters.

To me, the fundamental differences between the naturalistic and positivistic paradigms became most clear in the encounters I had about trustworthiness with other doctoral students and faculty. It was in this arena that research issues went beyond the specifics of a particular piece of research to engender great interest, and heat:

> How do we know?
> What can we know?
> What is worth knowing?

Morgan, as quoted in Lincoln and Guba (1985, pp. 293–9), states: 'Different research perspectives make different kinds of knowledge claims, and the criteria as to what counts as significant knowledge vary from one to another'. In our experience, if one researcher sees 'reality' as single, fixed, and ideally 'objective' and another sees it as multiple, changing, and transactional, the latter position encompasses the former, sees it as one among many possible approaches. The former can encompass only the fixed view. The result is a standoff. This standoff, this clash in points of paradigmatic views, can often show itself in what people consider to be acceptable in their research. What seems important for researchers in any paradigm is to understand thoroughly what needs doing in order for their research to be trustworthy and to work to communicate that as clearly and as non-defensively as possible.

In the Act: Working toward Credibility

The words sound fine. Who could be against Lincoln and Guba's (1985) advice that to increase the chance of doing a credible research job, one that can be believed by the people who were studied as well as by the readers of one's report, a researcher must:

> have prolonged engagement in the field;
> do persistent observation;
> triangulate;
> search for negative cases;
> determine referential adequacy;
> experience peer debriefing;
> check with the people one studied.

It is the doing of these, the actions, however, that establishes credibility. This is not simple or neat. In this section we address the first three of these topics. Chapter 5 considers the rest.

Prolonged and Persistent Observation.   Joan Giansante tells of the value of prolonged engagement and persistent observation to the credibility of her work:

> Prolonged engagement enabled me to ask interview questions that followed up on the decisions I had observed Pam make earlier. After all, it's one thing to say you are going to do something, and quite another to actually do it. My perceptions about the professional demeanor a business must maintain in order to succeed faded over time. And time also played a role in gaining Pam's trust. Because I had enough time, I could devote major portions of the interviews to what Pam wanted to discuss.
>
> Persistent observation forced me to look at the big issues. I tried to clarify what they were and how activities impacted on them. Then I observed them deeply.

And, you ask, how long is prolonged? How much of my life needs to be given to this research? I know two things: this is a meaningful question and there is no one answer. Margaret did her fieldwork over two years, albeit she held a full-time position for the same span. Teri collected data for one and a half years. I did that job in two years. Many of our doctoral students collect data in one semester of six months or less. Prolonged engagement depends so much on your research questions, your data-collection methods, your available time, and the time the research needs. In her experience as mentor to doctoral students, Margot has found that often people give similar time to qualitative and quantitative studies, but they apportion this time in different ways. In her view, qualitative researchers spend more time in the field and in data analysis.

Triangulation.   In previous sections of this chapter, we discussed a number of ways to gather data and several approaches to ongoing data analysis. These are more fully described in Chapter 5. Checking data obtained by a variety of methods is one way of contributing to trustworthiness. Watching for the convergence of at least two pieces of data, for triangulation of findings, can be as suspenseful as it is important.

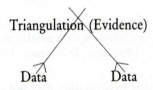

Triangulation (Evidence)

Data   Data

Many experts indicate that triangulation characteristically depends on the convergence of data gathered by different methods, such as observation and interview. We have found that triangulation can occur with data gathered by the same method but gathered over time. This has been true, for example, of observational notes in field logs written over some months. In addition, triangulation can be based on different reports about the same event by two or more researchers who are studying the same phenomenon. Not every log entry requires a search for triangulation. Guba and Lincoln (1989) suggest that researchers seek only to triangulate, to cross check, '... specific data items of a factual nature' (p. 241) and to check insights, results, conclusions, and presentations with the people they studied and with their peer support group. These latter checkings are discussed in Chapter 5.

Patricia Cobb puns about her rather traumatic introduction to the importance of triangulation. She had barely begun to study a colleague's classroom:

> I experienced a sense of being overwhelmed by all the different measures that must be taken into account to continuously establish credibility. During one of my case study classes, Margot talked about an assumption I had made in the field notes in my log about the teacher I was observing. She asked had I established prolonged engagement, done persistent observation, and where was my strangulation? Oops, I mean where was my triangulation to support this assumption.

Suzy Hahn studied the experience of several women of different ages who worked as grocery clerks. Suzy shares what she did to triangulate:

> In reviewing field notes, writing 'thick' descriptions, and composing analytic memos, I checked for triangulation vs. 'seeing what I wanted to see'. I went back to conduct one long and several short interviews to see if the data would repeat. Many did.

While it sounds relatively straightforward, I have found that communication about the idea of triangulation is really rather complex. Some authorities see one clear purpose of that process:

> [Triangulation is] basic in ethnographic research. It is at the heart of ethnographic validity, testing one source against another to strip away alternative explanations and prove a hypothesis. (Fetterman, 1989, p. 89)

Mathison (1988) cautions that triangulation may not only confirm, it may also have a number of other useful purposes:

> In practice, triangulation as a strategy provides a rich and complex picture of some social phenomenon being studied, but rarely does it provide a clear path to a singular view of what is the case.
>
> Because of the predominance of the assumption that triangulation will result in a single valid proposition, we look for the convergence of evidence and miss what I see as the greater value in triangulating. More accurately, there are three outcomes that might result from a triangulation strategy ... convergence, inconsistency, and contradiction. (Mathison, 1988, p. 15)

In introducing this quotation, I used the word 'caution' deliberately. Mathison serves to alert us to the danger of throwing out useful information if we focus too tightly only on the purpose of finding convergent evidence. Inconsistencies and contradictions may help us to refine and revise our framework and findings; but they may be just what they seem: inconsistent and contradictory findings that must stand as they are and be reported as such.

Data that stand out like sore thumbs are sometimes called negative cases. Negative case analysis is the search for evidence that does not fit into our emergent findings and that leads to a re-examination of our findings. This will be discussed in Chapter 5 as a factor in final analysis. However, because this process helps to shape the emerging picture, it also has a place here. Negative case evidence can be extremely helpful in guiding qualitative researchers to '... make data more credible by reducing the number of exceptional cases....' (Lincoln and Guba, 1985, p. 312). It can help qualitative researchers shift their emerging understandings better to describe what they are studying and to be more certain that they have caught some of its essence.

Our colleague, Belén Matías, provides an example of how negative case analysis helped her to reshape her findings:

> In my beginning analysis of field logs and videotapes I had been struck by the number of choices the children had as they entered the classroom. Because of this, I developed a tentative social rule that read: *I [child] am in charge of entrance time.* As I continued to analyze data, this rule held almost to the end, until I realized that

something contradictory had been happening. The teacher had begun ever so slowly to cut into the children's opportunities to make independent choices at entrance by moving teacher-directed academic activities progressively closer to the beginning of the school day. I did not like what I was seeing. I fought to justify and to keep my social rule intact until I had to face the facts of the matter and changed the social rule to: *The teacher can change my entrance routines.* This rule more accurately described what happened in that classroom.

Support Group: The Life Line

Support groups are so vital to every aspect of the 'doing' discussed in this chapter that they deserve special mention here. We described in Chapter 2 how support groups were established and some of the roles they played in the initial qualitative research forays. We return in Chapter 5 to the contributions of support groups during the final research stages. You may have concluded by now that we find support groups indispensable to qualitative researchers. We do. In the team's experience, it has been the support group that has most often been instrumental in helping its members to face possible bias and possibly painful insights with grace and empathy, and in ways that resulted in constructive moves forward. Support groups can consider each member's emerging findings, suggest alternate explanations, and act as auditors of the research process. While that is not all, it is certainly part of the process. There is nothing like being in the same boat and cheering on your fellow paddlers. We know, however, of a number of researchers who do creditable work without the assistance of a support group. Some people prefer this, and we salute them. Most do better in a support group. That has been true for the members of this writing team in our postdoctoral research as well.

Joan Giansante found the support group a comfortable place for airing gripes and frustrations as well as for testing new ideas:

> The support group provided a forum in which I could discuss worries, problems, and frustrations, including those brought on by my computer. It also gave me an opportunity to test out some of my hunches. The discussion about my participant's decision-making process is particularly memorable for me. Other members discussed what intuition meant to them, and consequently broadened my interpretation of it.
>
> Participation in a support group would be a very important consideration if I ever attempted ethnographic research again.

We found that the support group experience served as a model for the beginning researcher's ongoing scholarly work long after the class had finished. Towards the end of the semester, the writing team encouraged class members to begin to establish their continuing support groups. Groups formed themselves on the basis of shared interests, congenial personalities, or geography. Often, the original support groups opted to stay together, although this meant wide travel and attention to a great span of research topics. In our experience, for many people the commonality of applying qualitative methodologies and group cohesiveness have been more important than doing research in a similar topic area. Teachers, artists, nurses, and people from many other academic interests have benefited from each other's vision and help. One of the pleasures in the support group comes from learning about research in other areas.

Support groups need to find their own rhythm, but one good plan is to meet every two to three weeks and to schedule one or two members to present their current work at each meeting. Many people arrange to give their material to the group members during a meeting before the scheduled discussion so that the material can be carefully considered before the next meeting begins. My support group arrived an hour early to find on-the-street parking spots. We then read the current papers in our cars until the spots became legal, and the meeting began. This, of course, was an adaptation to the complications of meeting in downtown Manhattan. The value of reading the material immediately before the meeting was that the content was fresh in everyone's mind. Further, we had a general understanding that we would each accomplish what we could in one hour. Since we were all working feverishly on our own projects, we respected and valued each other's time.

We called ourselves the 'Kitchen Group' because we met in an NYU room that had a stove and a small refrigerator. We lived up to our name by beginning each meeting with a light supper provided by two of us. Inspiration needs nourishment, and we didn't wish to be unkind to inspiration.

A real sense of family developed around that table. It was created by our united effort to fight a common enemy, which was sometimes our committee, sometimes our subjects, sometimes our families, sometimes our own flagging energy; it was created by our joy in each other's progress — we felt we would pull each other through, and we did; and it was created by our growing confidence in ourselves as ethnographers. Eating together was a time for catching up on the news of the week, for relaxing before the last big push of the day — critiquing each other's work — and for celebrating our pleasure in each other's company. Each of us put a little time and effort into making a pleasant meal, and it was easy to see that effort mirrored in the care we gave to each other's writings. Each support group will develop its own rhythms and rituals; dining together is one that ought to be considered.

The members of a support group can help each other in several key ways: offering emotional support, suggesting new points a view, and establishing interim, reachable deadlines. While professors also offer emotional support, committee members cannot often achieve the level of intimacy that colleagues and fellow sufferers manage. It is important that the members of the group respect each other's work, and that most members like each other as well. Groups, though, can work even if not all parties like each other. Members must lift out of the level of personal relationships and focus on the research project itself. One of our colleagues compared the process of doing the dissertation to being on an emotional roller coaster. The support group can help the members smooth out the highs and lows. Members cheer each other on and have a stake in each other's progress. A member can try out new ideas in a supportive, non-judgmental forum; checking a novel idea with your group may be taking a much lower level of risk than trying that same idea on a committee member. Often members will be in different stages of dissertation refinement, and that can be a great comfort to someone who is just beginning the process.

Support group members need to be curious about each other's work. Sometimes a writing jam is relieved because a person in the group takes the outsider's point of view.

Nancy Montgomery did a study of how Jane, one of her freshman writing students, functioned within the structure of her classroom's cooperating writing groups. Nancy shares with us some of the pain and joy of being in a support group that asked her to re-examine her participant's behavior:

> ... my support group helped me get outside myself as the teacher in the class and observe myself more objectively rather than staying inside my own perspective so much. Because of my investment as a participant in what I studied, it was easy to lose my neutral perspective. The support group helped me regain my observer's balance.
>
> If it had not been for the incredibly helpful, insightful, and sometimes upsetting feedback of my group leader and other group members, I might have missed important points for understanding and interpreting my data.

Another critical area of support is establishing deadlines. The Kitchen Group was particularly helpful at breaking down the enormity of the dissertation task into manageable bits. My internal goal changed from 'Write this dissertation in one year' to 'Describe Chuck's relationship with his family for next week'. The first goal paralyzed, the second goal energized. Further, each of us presented the written material orally at each deadline. The very act of saying things out loud is often a way to discover a different point of view, and the comments from the group sometimes challenge, sometimes corroborate the cherished ideas. The group has a way of keeping its members clear and honest. After having discussed the central issues of the dissertation with the group for a year or more, the challenges of the final oral dissertation defense were manageable for me.

If at all possible, find a congenial group of strugglers, share good food and good ideas, and, as David Sternberg (1981) suggests in the title of his book, you will be able to complete your research and survive.

Postscript

In this memo I, Margot, would like to highlight and expand upon three themes that seem crucial to this chapter, indeed to the entire qualitative research endeavor.

Theme 1: Qualitative Research Is Powered by a Group of Disciplined Procedures That Must Be Studied, Practiced, Learned, and Relearned.

While it may seem anticlimactic to talk of this theme at the close of this chapter, I'd like to approach it with a slightly different twist. This theme speaks directly against a myth that is often proposed by people who either (1) have not studied the assumptions and methods of qualitative work, and/or (2) find such research unacceptable to their frame of values. The myth goes something like: 'Qualitative research is soft, unscientific, atheoretical, without substance. It is "touchy-feely" messing about, and at best seeks unsubstantiated opinion rather than facts. Anyone can do it'.

To a qualitative researcher such a myth could not be further from the truth. The myth is anathema to those of us who work with painstaking care: who hone our observational skills, who work as collaborators-in-research with the people whose lives we seek to describe, who engage in increasingly productive ethnographic interview techniques, who surmount the seemingly insurmountable tasks of in-process, recursive analysis, meaning-making, and reporting. While such a myth is anathema, it is also extremely powerful — powerful enough to jolt many advanced graduate students who suspect deep down — or further up — that qualitative study is easier than quantitative, and who find very soon upon engaging in study that qualitative work may be even more complex and difficult than other kinds of research.

What must be faced is that every research paradigm demands disciplined congruent methods. Easier or harder is not the issue when choosing which way to go. The issue lies in people's commitments, their personal styles, what sorts of assumptions they make about research. For qualitative researchers, their commitments include passion to document life in multi-layered, first-hand ways, deep social concern, trust in process, and interest in working with people as well as independently. Qualitative researchers accept in increasingly whole-hearted ways that they themselves create the boundaries of their research and that these evolve in response to what they learn along the way. They delight in the fact that the boundaries of their research plan are begun but not ended before they commence studying. Concomitantly, these researchers depend on their own flexibility and humor in accepting the inevitable and sometimes discomfiting notion that things are not as they seemed when they were planned — even yesterday — and that change may be our only constant.

Some assumptions about research that qualitative researchers abide by are that they can never and should never attempt to remove themselves from what they are studying, that they are interested in documenting as much as possible of the whole of the phenomenon they study rather than its fragmented parts, that they will have more questions as they go along and at the conclusion, that they strive for insight and understanding rather than prediction and control.

These descriptions of some of the stances of qualitative researchers may sound high-handed and unobtainable. That is my problem when I attempt to describe in a linear way what is really a whole, a way of looking at life. Actually, many people who begin to learn about qualitative research experience a flash of understanding, a feeling of rightness. Ann called it a 'shock of recognition' in this chapter. Usually, for these people, anything else can be learned. They are the ones who come to understand, almost from the start, the discipline required of qualitative researchers. In a most human and humane way, they come through.

Theme 2: *Qualitative Research Depends on the Researcher-as-Instrument*

When all is said and done, the actuality of this theme is often both exhilarating and difficult to accept. In presenting the pros and cons of their work, qualitative researchers cannot point to the test, the sampling procedures, the statistical treatment, the outside expert. They can only point to themselves and to how they decided to sample, to treat data, to work with others, to confer with experts, to carry out their research, and to share their findings. This is so because they are their own most important instrument.

The measure of a successful ethnographic interview, for example, rests on the knowledge, sensitivity, and skills of the qualitative researcher. It is that person's skill to 'listen with the third ear', to let the quiet ride, to come in with just the right probe, and to understand and use judiciously the literature in the field that are at issue rather than following prescripted questions in a prescripted order. The sum total of what people are will shape them as qualitative research instruments. These researchers put themselves into the service of their search, analysis, and presentation.

Before all of this becomes too awesome, it's good to remember that, thank heavens, we need not be alone on the journey. This is true even though the researcher-as-instrument is, in a deep sense, responsible for both process and product. Just as instruments can be made better, sharper, more useful, so can researchers-as-instrument.

For the latter, however, it is each person's choice, and no one else's, to work, for example, in a support group, or to consult with a colleague, or to read for inspiration, or to take a rest away from everything smacking of qualitative research. It's a comfort to me to keep learning that there's a possibility that Margot-as-instrument really can get better with age.

Theme 3: Qualitative Research Honors Tacit Knowledge

In one sense, this theme relates to the previous one on researcher-as-instrument, but I feel it deserves its separate place. This statement emphasizes that people know a great deal from their own past and present experiences, from how their vision has been honed, from their evolving insights and hunches. Much of what we know is unspoken, inside us. These same people as qualitative researchers do not attempt to separate themselves from that they know tacitly or, for that matter, openly. Indeed, they use their tacit knowledge in important ways. They listen to their hunches. They attend to the seemingly unrelated sense of direction that pops into their heads at odd moments. They heed their own feelings that this log entry, not that one, carries relevant meaning.

It is essential for qualitative researchers to understand that such hunches, insights, directions do not arise out of nothing and that, often, they are the results generated from meaningful lived experience. What is equally important is that the process of working with such hunches, insights, directions must be one that attempts to lift the tacit from an unspoken to a voiced level; one that can be checked out in many, but not all, cases. Not every hunch is valid; not every insight is borne out by the data. Automaticities, even ones that bear much fruit, such as heeding one's tacit knowledge, are put to the test by qualitative researchers because their paradigm is characterized by a striving for increased reflection and awareness.

I am so often struck in ethnographic interviews by how people seem to depend on tacit knowledge as a road map. 'Why the shadow in his face at just that angle?' 'It felt right'. 'Why three codas for your symphony?' 'Because that's how I saw it!' 'Why the repetitions in this story?' 'I like it that way. It says something to me'. Sometimes, with probes, people give richer explanations, Often not. I wager, though, that in other ways people do examine their own hunches as they move through life, and that this is an essential aspect of their development.

The theme of tacit knowledge nudges at my tacit knowledge to remind me that there is a variety of ways of knowing: complex, not so easily pigeon-holed, important. In that message and its promise, it is a very hopeful theme.

Coda

There are plenty of other possible themes about Chapter 3, all of which are important. But I am aware that once the process of studying any of these ideas is begun, the circles ripple outward to touch all the essentials. It hardly matters where one starts. That's one more fine thing about qualitative work. That is, the undergirding ideas that power this research paradigm are part of the seamless whole.

There is one more message to people who are considering becoming qualitative teachers-as-researchers. Not only the books and courses and lectures teach what needs to be known. The most vital part of that learning is one's self in action: one's self beginning to ask questions, to observe, to share with a support network, to take time, to try something out, to err, to study that again, and to become increasingly courageous and reflective. That's research with a professional kick! We continue this thought in Chapter 6.

Chapter 4

Feeling

Introducing Teri and This Chapter

How do I know what I know? I lean towards the intuitive, the personal, the visualization of 'real life' possibilities rather than the logical deconstruction of ideas. Maddeningly 'female' by social design, I am also competitive, ambitious, and prone to homicidal rashes whenever I hear the terms 'biology' and 'destiny' even remotely equated. It is due to this latter predisposition that I spent years primarily valuing the 'objective', the rational, the analytic, and strove to be successful in a world of logic, relegating my 'gut' to the digestion of food rather than ideas. I eventually entered a PhD program and was faced with the anticipatory unpleasantness of a much-dreaded dissertation. I was thus in a somewhat lugubrious state when I first approached Margot and asked her about a possible methodology to suit my thesis. Never mind that she charmed me with her spontaneity and warmth. And never mind (!) that an undercurrent of playfulness and good humor characterized our meetings. We discussed qualitative methodology, a new-fangled (in my eyes) approach to research that enabled the researcher to be creative, exploring new ideas that could take shape via intuition, vision, and personal experience, *and* to be analytical, so as to imbue that experience with meaning. While initially skeptical, on a deeper level, this research struck me as an excellent amalgam of rational 'smarts' and emotional intelligence. The two no longer appeared to be mutually exclusive or even particularly dichotomous. Suffice it to say: I was hooked.

My dissertation was entitled 'The Experience of Being a Female Police Officer' (1989), and it is from this work that many of the examples in this chapter derive. My primary tool was the in-depth interview, but my total involvement in the police world went much deeper. Over a four-year period I developed a network of acquaintances and friendships with many male and female officers. I went on patrol several times, and attended formal and

107

informal police functions, including retirement parties, weddings, union meetings, and spontaneous get-togethers in police bars. It was for me a novel experience that was exciting and all-encompassing. The process of gathering information in this fashion went beyond the intellectual — my emotions, beliefs, values, and assumptions were continually being exposed, challenged, defined, and refurbished. I began to view qualitative research not only as an excellent tool for investigating the world at large, but as both a passageway and a metaphor for an exploration into self.

As I began to talk to others involved in qualitative research, I learned that complex emotional experiences were common fare. This was, and is, of great interest to me. It is this aspect of qualitative research, the affective component, that I discuss in this chapter.

As qualitative researchers, we have the great good fortune, or perhaps misfortune, depending on one's point of view, to rely on ourselves as the primary research tool. While we may use surveys, questionnaires, or elaborate laboratory equipment to aid us in our research, it is we who are in the field, interviewing, observing, participating in the lives of our research participants. We face the people in our study directly, and must look them squarely in the eye. Occasionally we blink and miss something important. Frequently, however, with time and experience, we develop a sharpened perception and penetrate deeply into the lives we are studying. We note the idiosyncratic and observe the mundane. We attempt to record it all. We are the primary instruments, but we are not cool, automatized instruments. As human beings with warmth and feeling, our pulses resonate with the heartbeat of our research participants. While we try to maintain distance and perspective, we, too, have personal responses to what we see and hear.

What we see and hear may run counter to our experience, beliefs, perhaps even our moral principles. Or we may sympathize, empathize, identify. We may experience love, hate, fear, lust, *angst*. The whole range of emotion is there for the taking. We may discover some dimension of ourselves we like, or be forced to confront certain personal limitations. More than likely, each of us will emerge a slightly different person than the one we were when we began, with not only an increased knowledge of the phenomenon we set out to study, but also increased knowledge of ourselves. As John Forconi wrote, '. . . the aspect of human life you are about to study will most likely be your own'. This chapter describes people's experience of themselves while doing ethnographic research.

I begin this chapter where many of us begin, by discussing the insecurities, anxieties, and fears that accompany a new undertaking. I then examine the emotional connections that we, as researchers, frequently make when we study in-depth the lives of other human beings. Particular attention is paid to situations where the researchers' feelings of affection or personal involvement with research participants become 'too close for comfort'. I next explore the opposite phenomenon, that is, feeling 'too far for comfort' because of dislike, philosophical differences, or any number of negative emotions that threaten to interfere with the development of an in-depth understanding of the people whose lives are being studied. Close attention is given to personal assumptions and biases that contribute to negative feelings that researchers, as human beings, maintain. In sections after that I discuss the emotional components involved with doing research in a familiar setting ('making the familiar unfamiliar') and in an unfamiliar setting ('making the unfamiliar familiar'). Finally, I address the fact that qualitative research makes a number of emotional demands on the researcher, and is clearly not for everyone. You, the reader, are invited in to consider carefully, 'Is qualitative research for you?'

The postscript at the end of the chapter contains Margot's thoughts upon its content.

Facing the Fears

It is typical for the researcher to experience a slew of unanticipated, perhaps chaotic or disorganizing emotions during the course of the research. The sheer novelty of the method may create anxiety for those individuals versed in more traditional quantitative methodologies.

> Today in class we discussed the steps of ethnography — gaining entry, developing rapport, and trust, the flow of data ... it sounds like a foreign language. I imagine myself in the middle of some foreign country thousands of miles away and no one speaks English. I am alone ... with no one to talk to. Am I the only one who feels this way? Does anyone else feel like me? Like their native tongue has disappeared and suddenly there's no one to talk to? What about the 'old' words like mom and apple pie, hypotheses, and statistical power? (Rena Smith)

Feelings of self-doubt and uncertainty have been documented by several qualitative researchers (Hughes, 1960; Lofland and Lofland, 1984, pp. 32–3; Shaffir *et al.*, 1980; Zigarmi and Zigarmi, 1980). Every step of the process can provoke some degree of anxiety. Even a task as clearly defined as contacting a gatekeeper, which in some other universe might be viewed as merely a logistical consideration, has its emotional facets. One might be prepared intellectually. A speech has been rehearsed *ad nauseam*. The phone number of the gatekeeper has been written down in five separate places. The phone is waiting to be used. Regardless, the anxiety of the initial contact may delay the call for days. What if I sound unprofessional? What if I'm being too intrusive? What if they see right through me and discover I don't really know what I'm doing?

Once the researcher has entered into the field, it is common to have moments of unexpected *angst*. Ann Vartanian carefully prepared what looked to be the relatively simple task of asking a 3-year-old child some questions during a brief talk. After her first 'hello', the child immediately responded with, 'I don't like you and I'm going to play that you're not here'. She then ran and hid behind a couch. An unanticipated 'snafu', and Ann experienced a moment of panic. Such moments occur for all of us, and even if the incidents appear trivial or funny in retrospect, at the time they often feel quite important. The ability to embrace them with a sense of humor and presence of mind will help us get through these moments relatively unscathed. It will also provide some of the more interesting anecdotes with which the researcher will undoubtedly amuse colleagues and friends — afterwards! — or develop into one of the 'confessional tales' (Van Maanen, 1988, Ch. 4) which we discuss in Chapter 5 in 'Making the Story'.

Jackie Storm expressed some serious personal fears when embarking on her interviews:

> It brought out all my paranoia. I was plagued with the fear of making a mistake. I thought, 'I'm doing it wrong. I'm missing something. I'm asking the wrong questions'.

I also felt a great deal of anxiety when I began the interview process because I felt very ignorant of the police world that I was investigating. I was afraid that if I appeared overly naive or asked questions that derived from simplistic television stereotypes, the female police officers would not take me seriously and would slough me off with superficial 'by the book' responses. While this may have happened occasionally, by and large the women were available and candid and spoke in depth once rapport was developed. Of course, what I imagined would have been one of my worst nightmares occurred during one of my initial interviews. While describing her sense of alienation from civilians, an interviewee looked me dead in the eye and stated with not a little contempt, 'Hell, I'm sure you can't understand half of what I'm saying.' Confronted on my most sensitive point, knot in pit of stomach, I replied, 'Perhaps not, but I'd like to hear it and learn from you — that's what this project is all about'. That appeared to stave off her immediate sense of alienation, and the interview continued smoothly. It was not as frightening an experience as I anticipated, but such challenges kept my adrenalin flowing throughout the interview process.

Lofland and Lofland (1984) write about certain anxieties that researchers experience during interviews and participant-observation and talk about the stresses of deception and fears of disclosure (p. 32). They make the point that even when people know they are being studied, they probably have only a very limited understanding about what the researcher is doing. The authors raise possible mental questions researchers might put to themselves:

> Did 'X' remember that I was a researcher when she told me that? And if not, when she does remember, will she be angry or upset?

> Is this person I'm interviewing, who seems to be getting restless, about to ask me more about my research aims than I really want to tell right now?

> Is the caretaker of this group I'm studying going to notice that my research interests have shifted since I received permission to do the research, and if he does, will he still approve?

When Lyn Lofland was observing public waiting rooms, she was always vaguely fearful that someone would challenge her continued and repeated presence. On only one occasion was she discovered — in an airport — and even though the official who discovered she was doing research had no objection to her remaining, she was so uncomfortable that she left almost at once and never returned (Lofland and Lofland, 1984, p. 33).

While analyzing and writing about data, inexperienced and seasoned researchers alike may feel the fear of committing ideas to paper, or any number of anxieties that can contribute to writer's block. I was overwhelmed by the sheer size of my log — 1700 pages of interview transcripts alone. Picking and choosing, deciding which ideas to elaborate upon and which to discard, these are difficult decisions. While one may have a support group and others with whom to check the data, ultimately these decisions belong to the researcher alone. The responsibility of making them may be anxiety-provoking and even create a sense of loneliness. Once the research is completed, there is, of course, the gratification that the product is one's own creation. The pathway leading to that finale, however, is not always without its emotional pebbles and potholes.

One of the students in our class, Jackie Storm, spoke early on about how necessary it is to accept the inevitability of emotional insecurities when conducting qualitative research, for first-timers and old-timers alike:

> Learn to live with your fears and insecurities. They are part of the process. Make a note of your paranoia. Write it down in your log; use it as a source of information. You are here to observe what is going on, and your own personal thoughts and feelings are one part of the total picture. To deny our feelings would be to shut out one large chunk of reality.

Confronting fears means facing insecurity, terror of gatekeepers, interview and field malaise — and the list continues. Are students and practitioners of qualitative research particularly xenophobic or faint-of-heart? I doubt it. I strongly suspect that such anxiety exists in doing other kinds of research as well. But qualitative researchers in particular are encouraged to be aware of feelings, biases and personal peccadilloes and to scrutinize closely. We are highly conscious of our personal relationship to our research. Because of this, we must acknowledge and accept the emotional aspect as part and parcel of the method. In the larger sense, we strive to harness this aspect to become more aware, more able, more insightful.

Emotional Connections

> In a case study research, the researcher needs to cross into the subject's personal life to experience what it is like to be the other person.... Researchers whose self-awareness tells them that they are uncomfortable with closeness should not use case study methodology. They must ask, 'How comfortable am I with intimacy and closeness?' (Barbara Gagliardi)

It is natural to develop feelings toward one's research participants. Much of qualitative research involves prolonged engagement in the lives of other human beings, going beyond the superficial mask of public impression and entering a highly personal realm of private thoughts, secret passions. The researcher who is a keen observer and astute interviewer will inevitably be privy to many of the generally undisclosed vulnerabilities, heartaches, fantasies, and joys of the participants. It makes sense, then, that emotional responses such as closeness, identification, sympathy, and warmth would be spontaneously elicited in the researcher. This was a disconcerting experience for many of the students in our class, and one with which they needed to grapple. These students expected research to be a wholly intellectual endeavor, a cognitive kingdom where emotional detachment reigns supreme. They had accepted 'the canonization of objectivity and detachment of prevailing convention' (Munhall, 1988). Some were embarrassed to admit that they had any feelings at all for their participants; emotions were de facto unscientific, contaminating, taboo.

It is the belief of the authors of this book that feelings of intimacy and warmth toward one's research participants are not only natural but in general represent a positive phenomenon. The task of successfully stepping into the shoes of another person is greatly facilitated by feelings of sympathy, compassion, and what Carl Rogers termed unconditional acceptance (Meador and Rogers, 1979) for that person. It is clear, however, that one must attempt to strike a balance between the development of empathy and the pursuit of a distanced, non-judgmental stance. Much has been written (Bogdan and Biklen, 1982; Bogdan and Taylor, 1975; Cowles, 1988; Glazer, 1980) on this subject. Glazer comments:

> A researcher must become deeply involved with his material and allow it to absorb him while remaining emotionally vital enough to step back and perceive the contours of the data. It is a rigorous, affective exercise demanding emotional reserves and critical perceptiveness. (p. 29)

Glazer refers to the concept of 'compassionate analysis, in which the researcher's emotions are intertwined with those studied' (p. 31). This phenomenon, 'in combination with a researcher's determination to understand, often results in rare analytical insights' (p. 31). The authors of this book agree with the goal of attempting to balance 'compassionate analysis' with the 'determination to understand'. The process of striking such a balance can be difficult, however. Many researchers, and that includes us, occasionally feel too intimate or develop an exaggerated sense of kinship with our research participants. On the other hand, many times we feel distanced, dismayed, and even repulsed by our research participants. Both of these stances not only threaten to contaminate the findings, but to interfere with the researchers' personal lives as well. To feel close to, or even a bit removed from, a participant can be used to advantage; to feel too close for comfort, or too far, can be a dismaying experience. The next two sections take up those two sides of the same coin.

Too Close for Comfort

> I was interviewing a homosexual man about his lifestyle. While mentioning the importance of 'beauty' in his life, Sam added that he often thought that the reason he did not have a lover was because he was not good looking enough to attract a man. I was very touched by this statement for two reasons. First, Sam looked and sounded very sincere, which made me empathize with him. Second, his statement seemed very familiar. It was as if he were speaking my mind. I, too, had often felt that I was not beautiful enough to be loved by a man. Feeling sad and sorry for Sam, I tried to protect his feelings or somehow make him feel better. So I looked at him and told him that he was not alone in feeling the way he did; that others felt the same way at different periods in their lives. But what I really had in mind was: 'Don't worry, Sam. I'm in the same boat'. Needless to say, by sympathizing and identifying with Sam, my mind was transported to the times when *I* had felt like Sam did. Given that my mind could not be at two places simultaneously, chances are that I missed parts of Sam's comments in the meantime. (Flora Keshishian)

Flora's identification with her research participant's sense of not being 'beautiful enough' may have interfered with her ability to be a good listener, and may have ultimately distorted the data. Fortunately, she had the perceptiveness and courage to divulge these issues to her support group. She was able to explore these concerns and minimize their interference with the data. The emotional experience of working through these issues was intense. During the discussion of her feelings, the entire support group identified with her concerns about not being attractive to others. This led to an illuminating conversation about personal fears and detoured to related issues about the insecurities we were all experiencing concerning whether our research participants liked us. What began as a detour became a source of liberation. Having aired our anxieties, several of us felt freer to relate to participants more openly and directly. Sharing 'shameful' secrets often renders them benign, especially when trusted others are discovered to be carrying around the same secrets. It was not a major revelation to discover that we all had feelings. Rather, the revelation came in the common assumption that it was terribly *wrong* to have such feelings. We had gone to tremendous lengths to deny those emotions rather than acknowledge them and work them through.

During our research, some of us discovered that we had become so identified with our projects that it began to intrude significantly on our personal lives. I will cite an example from personal experience. The concept of 'going native' has been discussed in the literature (e.g., Lofland and Lofland, 1984, pp. 34–5). I found that the more involved I became with my research, the more I began to create a parallel existence, albeit without realizing it at the time. Prior to my research, my stereotypes of police officers were fairly harsh — cops were brutal, unintelligent, heavy drinking, and macho. They did not inhabit a world with which I wanted to be the least connected. During my research, as I became more involved with their world and they began to 'humanize' in my mind, they no longer resembled these worst caricatures. They also became less distant and exotic. I became less fascinated and more comfortable with them. Their world became for me a regular one, a way to make a living, like any other. In fact, one woman officer called me 'an honorary cop', and the husband of a friend made me a card-carrying member of the union.

My involvement took on other forms also. At a certain point in the interviews, many women officers were expressing the theme of loneliness. During that time I wrote a letter to a friend of mine in which I stated:

> For some people, dissertation brings up anxiety, panic, a sense of being found out as a fraud. For me, too, to some extent. But it has *really* brought up wellsprings of incredible loneliness such as I have never felt. Day in, day out, isolated, not connected to anyone in a meaningful fashion.

Now that was not entirely true. I had friends and family, a dissertation support group, and a committee, all of whom I could go to for comfort and support. What was really happening, I believe, is that I was co-opting the experience of these women. Like medical students' disease, I was taking their symptoms and making them my own. Further, I decided at the time that the way to assuage the loneliness and to connect with people was to get a job. I had stopped working for a while to work full-time on my dissertation. What job did I apply for? A psychologist at the police department! It seemed to make perfect sense to me. I knew the population and was comfortable with them. The next few months of applying for the job were spent in interviews, sending transcripts, having references checked and cross-checked, and knowing that former employers were being contacted. After several months, I was offered the job.

· Lo and behold, by that time I was no longer involved in the theme of loneliness, and consequently I myself was not feeling all that lonely or disconnected. I began to question: why are you joining this system? I was literally jolted out of bed one morning with a case of cold sweats accompanied by the indisputable realization: 'It's not your world!' Subsequently, I turned down the job. Most of my friends and family were puzzled. Why did I turn down the job after having put all this time and energy into the application procedure? To me it was clear. I knew that I had to separate myself and my life from the life of my research participants. I had entered their world and lost sight of my own.

Another dilemma created by feeling extremely close to one's research participants is that the researcher may discover facets of the persons being studied that the researcher would prefer not to see, facets that must be dealt with nonetheless. I felt this when I saw that some of the women police officers whom I had grown to like were overtly, unapologetically racist. Ann expressed the dismay and sadness she felt upon discovering the tedium that predominated her research participant's emotional life:

> One of the sad discoveries of my study with Chuck was that fighting boredom was a central feature of his life. Chuck bored easily, and the computer, video games, and barf parties were some of his weapons in his war on boredom.
>
> One incident in this war occurred when Chuck was on a computer hobbyist bulletin boards, which allowed him to disguise, if he wished, any or all attributes about himself. One of the entertainments Chuck created for himself was to become a female stepsister he named Tina. Tina was a hot number — all leather and lace, with mascara down to her nose; her look, according to Chuck, was 'I'm ready for action'. Chuck interacted with many people on the board as Tina. He went so far as to set up 'dates with guys', for which Tina would not appear. Chuck knew things had gone too far,

however, when one young man arrived at his home asking for Tina. He said he had brought his camera for their nude photo session. Tina abruptly left town to ply her trade in some unnamed banana republic. The thrill for Chuck came from the sense of being the author of a play. He said that Tina was his creation, and he enjoyed manipulating people's responses to her.

Chuck lived in an upper-middle SES home. He was in a program for the gifted and talented. He attended some of the best private schools in the community. His parents were active in school and community activities that involved their children. Yet his life was boring to him. Chuck was not a poverty child, he was not disadvantaged in ways I could fathom, yet during the study he seemed cut adrift, rootless. He appeared to spend much time distracting himself from the burden of creating a meaningful existence. The great characteristic of Chuck's life during the study was its pervasive emptiness. The institutions organized to help children find direction in life had failed him. Chuck, when I last spoke with him, had not found a center that would hold.

It was very difficult for me to acknowledge this in writing. The trust shared with Chuck and his family, and the affection I have for the young man himself, made it painful to commit this reality to print. It was only through the help of my support group and my faculty advisor that I was able to say what I knew.

In the last two examples, both Ann and I liked our participants and were disturbed by what we saw as their negative sides or limitations. Simply put, we did not like our findings, and we both had trouble committing these findings to paper for different reasons. Ann did not wish to see Chuck's unhappiness because it created pain for her, and she worked hard, psychologically, to deny that whole part of his experience. My dilemma was slightly different. While I readily acknowledged the racism I saw in some of my interviewees, I questioned whether I would be betraying the trust of those women who had poured out their hearts so candidly if I were to disclose this facet of their experience on paper. On the other hand, I seriously wondered if it were my job to be the guardian of the darker sides, such as I interpreted them, that were spoken into the tape recorder, discussed 'on the record'. I struggled relentlessly with my impulse to portray the women consistently in the most flattering light possible. The battle to describe the women's total experiences, without advocating for them, was an extremely difficult one. To present honestly their experience, in all its facets, became an act of courage.

Many of our students had experiences similar to Ann's and mine. They discussed these issues in their support groups. Ann and I both talked at length with our support groups and our dissertation committees. I showed transcripts of the interviews to my group and committee to get independent confirmation of the data. I shared the transcripts with the relevant interviewees to see if they wanted to add or subtract anything. When they expressed satisfaction that the transcripts were accurate, I began the process of examining my own exaggerated or misplaced fears. I saw how I was projecting my own value system onto these women. I also discovered that I was idealizing my participants, and not only wanted to protect their image to others but my own illusions as well.

A related conflict — that of feeling overprotective of the privacy of research participants — may also become particularly apparent when a researcher feels very close to the participants. Even when strict ethical standards are maintained, the researcher may have difficulty judging the appropriate place to draw the line between reporting fully and deeply, and invading privacy. This conflict can become especially evident on occasions when an interviewee reveals very intimate or sensitive information. During my interviews with female officers, several women disclosed deeply personal experiences, such as being involved in extramarital affairs, or having been raped or abused as a child. These disclosures frequently shed light on their experience of being police officers by supplying the 'missing piece' as to why they chose this career over all others. However, the spontaneity and lack of guile with which some of these women revealed such intimate details frequently made me suspect that they did not realize how much they were exposing — defenses down, trust established. I wondered whether they would really wish this to become public property, regardless of the fact that it was discussed 'on the record'. I was also fully conscious of my belief that their candor was at least partially due to the rapport I had worked so strenuously to develop with them. This carefully cultivated rapport, the painstakingly executed efforts to help interviewees feel 'natural' and to overcome the potentially stultifying effect of the ever-present tape recorder, began to feel like a cynical manipulation. 'Don't censor', I would request *ad infinitum*. Eventually, they wouldn't, and I was taken aback by the amount and depth of their disclosures. I also felt like a heel. I would wonder if I were taking advantage of a basic human loneliness, the desire to 'confess' to a relative stranger, the wish for absolution. I was powerless to absolve, though I began to want to, experiencing paradoxical but simultaneous feelings of grandiosity and impotence. My role became that of intimate acquaintance. I wanted to jump in and soothe wounds, but I needed to step back and observe. I found this conflict to be very powerful and very disturbing, and discussed it at length not only with professional colleagues, but with personal friends. I, too, needed to self-disclose and be absolved.

In her article on doing qualitative research on sensitive topics, Kathleen Cowles (1988, p. 163) discusses her experience of interviewing family survivors of murder victims. She addresses the many strong emotions she felt, such as *angst*, self-doubts, and tremendous sadness. Her coping strategies included expressing some of these emotions to the interviewees and having a network of trusted colleagues with whom she could debrief. Along with recording emotions in one's field log, these have been found to be effective means of dealing with intense, close personal feelings toward one's participants. Cowles comments that while she prepared by immersing herself in the literature in order to anticipate the emotions of her participants, no amount of preparation could have fully readied her to embrace the quality and intensity of each individual experience.

Another price to pay when one feels very close to research participants is the difficulty of separating from them. Leaving the field after a prescribed time or certain number of interviews may make research sense, but it may also feel like an artificial, sometimes cruel, cutting off. I experienced separation anxiety when parting from several of my research participants. Frequently, I handled it by suggesting we get together for lunch at a future date, but, as may be expected, that most often did not materialize. I did sometimes meet on a social basis with some participants after my research was finished, but it became clear that our lives were extremely different and we eventually drifted apart. Stretching out the relationship was in part a way for me to avoid dealing with my own pangs of separation as well as a way to cope with my ambivalent feelings about having 'used' for research purposes people whom I had grown to like. In my mind, I had confused the boundaries between professional and personal relationships. Saying goodbye felt akin to throwing away new friends, and this was difficult to do. The women themselves appeared to have a clear sense of the professional nature of our relationship and seemed to be satisfied at its completion, with an occasional follow-up telephone call. I eventually grew more comfortable with 'clean breaks'.

Diane experienced the pain of separation from a research participant with whom she had grown to feel quite close:

> I had been told before Woody entered second grade that he re-
> quested me because he heard I hugged. So presto, right there, instant
> bias! Then I had a home visit with him one Saturday, a routine visit
> which I do with all my students. One visit, however, was not
> enough for Woody, and he began to call me at home. He was
> persistent and he got through when others found me impossible to
> reach by phone. He had much to tell me and there was no ending
> the conversation if I didn't invent a reason to get off. I decided to
> visit him again and his mother approved. Thus, we began our
> Saturday odysseys.
>
> Woody's house was an estate of great magnitude. His parents
> were not there when I was. He seemed to be alone most of the time.
> Where were the children to play with? When did he interact with
> other human beings? Was he lonely? I was lonely being with him
> there. There was a live-in maid who frequently brought me tea to

drink and junk food for Woody. He was bony and pallid in appearance. Did he get the right kinds of food to eat? I worried. I wasn't his mother, but I wanted to be at times.

We spent most of our time together in the miles of wooded areas beyond the main house. We explored. He showed me his inventions in the woods which he conceived in rich detail and tall-tale style. There was the 'dog grave' near a creek, the 'cabin' where a foundation had been laid and then abandoned, the giants stalked him, and he entwined many cultural facts with fantasies about places he had visited around the world. The 'you know what?' was endless as we wandered beyond the boundaries of his estate. I was highly anxious about trespassing and ticks. But I listened intently to his stories and believed in his wood creatures.

Back at the mansion we spent time in his darkened bedroom where three six-foot wooden soldiers stood by his bed and on each side of his computer. Whenever Woody's eyes happened to land there, it seemed that all other activities were cancelled and the creatures in his computer games took over with Woody yanking and pushing his joy stick.

At such moments I felt a bit jealous that I could not hold his attention as readily as the computer characters he was busy knocking over. I felt lonely. Now Woody had playmates, robot ones, and I yearned to give him real ones. Was it my own needs calling out? Loneliness from my own childhood? Was Woody the little brother I had loved as a child? I often pondered such thoughts when Woody was deep into a new score on his computer screen.

The computer games came and went and he grabbed my hand to explore the many rooms in the huge house, even locked rooms. He shared and I cared in roles that went beyond the researcher/ teacher.

The research on children's play styles was completed. The school year ended and I had to let go. This was a year ago. I still miss him.

It is a common experience that we, our students, and other researchers have had to wrestle with feelings of identification and overidentification with our participants. Learning to define and create boundaries between 'close' and 'too close' is often difficult. Learning to disengage emotionally when necessary can be even more difficult. We found that discussing these issues openly, among sympathetic colleagues, is a highly effective way of coping with such emotions.

Too Far for Comfort

The previous section focused on researchers' experiences of closeness with their participants. Researchers do not always feel positive emotions toward their participants, however. They may dislike, disrespect, pity, or even be repulsed by the people they study or situations they encounter in the course of their work. Rather than being too close for comfort, in these situations it might be said that the researcher is too far for comfort.

Iris Kaplan observed a tennis instructor about whom she stated:

> Bill is entertaining. He is funny. He makes the kids laugh. He seems to 'talk at' the kids. He seems to crave an audience. He seems to want to be funny. He looks at me often during class to see my reactions. I feel sorry for him.

Iris appears to have experienced her research participant as vaguely pathetic. Julie Wollman-Bonilla observed a teacher in a classroom setting and soon came to agree with the opinions of the students that the teacher 'is a witch'. Melissa Rose, who also observed a classroom setting, began to feel like 'a prisoner' trapped by a teacher whose teaching style was woefully tedious. And Laura Wilson became incensed at a music professor she observed whose pedagogical style was authoritarian and one-sided:

> The metaphor for this class became the missionary converting the pagans ... control and lack of freedom to explore. All decisions were handed down from above.... I was angry! ... I was *forced* to listen to a lot of Kurt Weill. I felt as though I was part of a captive audience and could not move. I probably like Weill even less now than I did before.

These beginning researchers sometimes found it difficult not to act on such negative feelings. Julie Wollman-Bonilla felt that the teacher she observed so greatly undermined the children's confidence and self-respect that on at least one occasion she shared her disagreement about the teacher's tactics with one of the students. Julie realized that this was a mistake, however, because it signalled her willingness to be co-opted by the students. She stated that:

> I realized it would make them question their trust in me. If, for example, I took a student's side in one instance, how could that student feel safe that I would not take the teacher's side another time and betray his or her confidence?

Not only would she be undermining trust in the long run, but as she stated further, 'I realized that ... the quality of my data depended on my commitment to description, not change'.

The impulse to take sides is a natural one. Barring compelling circumstances such as averting gross emotional or physical harm, however, it is not acceptable to most of us to enter into the field to attempt to influence research participants. A neutral stance is preferable during data collection, although it is often an effort to rise above our own non-neutrality. However, the decision to take invasive action usually depends on the context of the situation, so it would be impossible to make an across-the-board rule here.

To dislike excessively or feel alienated from a research participant can potentially distort one's data as much as if one overidentified with the participants. Nonetheless, it is a very common experience. Indeed, because negative emotions arose so frequently in our work and in that of others, we examined how researchers handled such situations. We found that for several support groups, a particularly useful strategy was to look at many aspects of the disliked person's personality, search for motives for the offensive behavior, and examine the context in which the person functioned. While the process did not guarantee answers, it generally resulted in helping people to conceptualize a multi-dimensional person, and enabled them to be more open to the many aspects of that person's experience. In the process, the support group members discovered and were able to liberate certain of their own suppressed emotions that had previously interfered with the development of sympathy or rapport for their research participants.

Another common finding upon examining the phenomenon of negative emotions was that our research participants were acting in some way counter to their own values. In fact, this is often true whether or not we like the participants. In the previous vignettes about our work, both Ann and I became acutely aware that we were disturbed by certain of our findings because we were making judgments based on our personal and philosophical biases. Biases are impossible to escape; we all have them. It is our responsibility as qualitative researchers to attempt to understand and come to terms with them as honestly and completely as we can, so as not to distort the data.

Self-Awareness

Once a little girl was sitting and drawing with some crayons. Her father happened by and asked her what she was drawing. 'I am drawing a picture of God', she announced. 'God?' said her father in wonder and a bit of disbelief. 'You know what God looks like?' 'Sure', replied the girl as she held up her drawing. 'That's what God looks like!'

Was that picture of God a reality to that little girl? You bet it was. If an ethnographer were to study a child's understanding of God, he or she would have to see God through the eyes of children like that little girl, despite any personal theology or lack thereof. (Steve Rosman)

Learning to see through the eyes of others in order to understand and accurately describe their experience is a very complex task. A useful concept here might be that of 'empathic understanding' (Meador and Rogers, 1979), which Carl Rogers employed in therapy settings to describe the process of understanding a client's phenomenal world. He stated:

> Understanding the phenomenal world of the client requires more of the therapist than merely understanding the client's words. The therapist attempts to 'get into the shoes' of his client, to 'get under his skin.' He not only listens to the client's words, but he immerses himself in his world. (p. 152)

Achieving empathic understanding is crucial for the therapist who wants to comprehend the client's experience with a minimum of distortion or bias. Likewise, in ethnographic research, the investigator wants to understand the minds and hearts of the research participants in as total and unadulterated a way as possible. To do so, s/he must attempt to recognize personal prejudices, stereotypes, myths, assumptions, and other thoughts or feelings that may cloud or distort the perception of other people's experiences. I do not believe that we lose subjectivity, for human perception is by nature and definition subjective. I do believe that by recognizing and acknowledging our own myths and prejudices, we can more effectively put them in their place. I also believe that greater self-knowledge can help us to separate our thoughts and feelings from those of our research participants, to be less judgmental, and to appreciate experiences that deviate greatly from our own. Confronting oneself and one's biases was one of the most difficult and thought-provoking aspects of being a qualitative researcher for many students. Here follows a small sampling of their experience:

> I am a storyteller. For several weeks I observed the story hour of a nearby library. The librarian who conducted these story hours conveyed the stories by holding a book at arm's length, open toward the children, and reading from the book. She would glance at the book and gather a line or two of its text in her mind and turn to the children and recite what she remembered. This approach galled me no end. As a storyteller, I have worked hard to learn the stories I tell so that I can present them with a bit of drama and movement. Now here I was observing a person whose style represented the antithesis of my own. Yet, my task as an ethnographer was to be the instrument which recorded what happened during the story hours I observed.... I had to confront my biases and personal feelings so as to put them aside. (Steve Rosman)

> I had to learn a lot about myself and figure out how much I was interfering with my research. Was I really seeing how my colleague

taught, or was I reflecting on my own teaching? I had to learn to use and rely on my good instincts and throw out, or at least attempt to eliminate, my bad ones. Just as I found out what I liked and didn't like in life (while healing from an illness), my study helped me see what I liked and didn't like about teaching and about myself as a teacher. My study became a ... barometer. (Ronna Ziegel)

I had ideas about what good nursing is as opposed to bad and, finally, I have very definite ideas about what is right and wrong, ethical and unethical nursing practice. Again, how could I possibly presume to be an unbiased researcher? Thankfully, I didn't. I knew I was biased and had to learn how to observe, understand, and not make judgments. My questions changed constantly and I learned that I was not in the field to 'prove' anything. (Joanna Landau)

I had to unload myself of a lot of unwanted 'baggage', as it were, during the course of this study — emotions I was dragging around from my past, my own preferred ways of viewing situations, and my own biases. (Gail Levine)

There is no easy or surefire way to dispel bias. Confronting one's own 'hiding ghosts', as Barbara Gagliardi stated, can be a difficult and painful process. Recording feelings, including biases, in the log is extremely helpful for many qualitative researchers. One may choose to keep that part private, as in a diary. However, if a person can share those aspects of the log with others, those others may throw light on the matter in new and useful ways. Steve Rosman articulates the process in his following advice:

... assess the biases and presumptions you bring to the subject(s) of your observation. Use the log to raise these matters to the level of awareness. In addition to recording your observations of the phenomenon in question, be honest and be thorough in the investigation of your feelings. Include copious notes about your emotional reactions.... Additionally ... there are times when it is useful to test one's thinking against the probing inquiry of a disinterested peer. We humans sometimes take our own opinions for fact and, every now and then, need the perspective of another to refocus our attention.

An example of this came from Flora Keshishian who refused to go into a gay bookstore with her homosexual participant because she did not want others to assume she was a lesbian. It was only when she shared this part of her log with her support group that she began to discover her ambivalence about her research participant's life-style and how she may have communicated that to him as well. As a consequence of her discussion of these issues in the support group, she was not only able to bring a heightened awareness and a more subtle understanding to many of her final themes, but she had learned something meaningful about herself in the process.

Deborah Lamb said that perhaps 'all research is me-search'. Me-search, including one's personal biases, is certainly a part of the ethnographer's pursuit of knowledge.

Making the Familiar Unfamiliar

Many people do ethnographic research in settings with which they are familiar, as became clear in the previous vignettes on bias: teachers often study classrooms, nurses do research in hospitals, storytellers observe librarians. In some ways, familiarity with one's setting can be an advantage. As Joanna Landau said:

> Studying the familiar can be a boon rather than a liability since the 'insider' expertise, provided it is continually validated in the field, can really move the work along. Having past experience to guide the flow is extremely helpful.

Familiarity with the subject at hand — the subculture, the jargon, the unwritten codes of behavior — may enable a researcher to delve deeply into the research without having to do all of the preliminary work, such as learning a new lingo, becoming acquainted with the norms, and developing a level of comfort within the environment being studied. There is a certain degree of intimidation upon entering uncharted terrain — I certainly felt it as a total newcomer into the world of police precincts, police bars, street patrol — that may be largely avoided in this way. Avoiding excess intimidation is an advantage not to be dismissed easily, especially when the research process itself might be new and relatively awe-inspiring.

However, there are certain issues that arise from familiarity with the subject of which the researcher must be aware. An important, subtle issue concerns a researcher's presumption of understanding. This was brought home to me in quite a vivid way during my own research experience. After interviewing a number of female police officers of vastly different backgrounds from my own, I set up an appointment with an officer who, like myself, is Jewish. I was thrilled! At last someone with whom I shared a common background. We both sprinkled our conversation with Yiddish expressions, made Jewish jokes, discussed our mutual preference for seltzer water over other sodas. I felt I understood her and I understood how unusual her decision to become a police officer was, given her background. It was only when I asked, half-jokingly, 'So how did a nice Jewish girl like you become a police officer?' that she began to talk about her personal and family history — growing up in a working-class urban area as one of two white children in an otherwise all-black school; the daughter of a civil servant who, contrary to the stereotype of Jewish parents, put little premium on education for their children; a brother who enlisted in the army. This was nothing at all like my suburban upbringing where, among other things, higher education was assumed and the military avoided at all costs. In my erroneous presumption of similarity in all things Jewish, I nearly missed an incredibly interesting, colorful, and individual story. Moreover, I almost neglected to explore her value system, her sense of herself in the world.

As Joanna Landau mentioned above, 'insider' expertise must be validated. Knowledge of others' hearts, minds, and experience simply cannot be assumed, regardless of familiarity, or perhaps especially when one is familiar with their subcultural landscape. When dealing with familiar terrain, self-exploration is crucial for the qualitative researcher. 'Am I talking about them or am I talking about me?' The question must be asked time and again.

Another issue related to making the familiar unfamiliar concerns those deeply held values, expectations, ethics, and biases that are being newly discovered by the researcher during the process of exploring the field. This issue was touched upon in the previous vignettes on personal biases in which the student researchers were acutely aware that they had certain values that they needed to acknowledge and continually explore so as not to impose them on their research participants or otherwise distort the findings. One might hold certain values near and dear and expect others, such as research participants, to do the same. When others do not, the experience might be jolting. Margot tells the following story about her study of boredom in an urban high school.

> I saw so much boredom in this school that it stunned me. Day in and day out, period after period, it seemed that classroom life was characterized best by boredom. It seems that this is a learned social phenomenon, and I felt students had to be angry at what was being ground out each minute of each day in classrooms there. So I thought I'd tackle it frontally by interviewing some of the students I know in that school. They had been good informants before, were generous to a fault with me, although we were different in age, race, experiences, and job possibilities. I asked fifteen people what about being in school was interesting, and I went from there, valiantly probing responses to get as rounded a picture as possible. And of course once one starts asking about interests, one gets other pictures. The pictures I got of interest, non-interest, and boredom were shocking, not so much for content, which was shocking enough and sad, but because it was not at all what I had 'known' it would be. I was pushed to see the familiar from an unfamiliar perspective.

The students did not seem to be at all as interested as I was in the topic. I thought they'd be bursting to talk to a friendly ear about being bored, but they seemed to be passive. I had expected students to express anger, disgust, outrage regarding what was to me the obvious grey pap that filled their school lives. They expressed no great anger. Certainly not outrage. Instead, most indicated that their boredom was their fault. 'If I could get it, I wouldn't be turned off'. Students did not indicate that it was their teacher's job to be less boring. 'Teacher's ain't here to be interesting. Teachers be here to drill facts in my head'. They described a variety of strategies they used when they were bored: 'First I try to get it. Then sometimes I think of something else'. 'I look to fool around, man. It's no use anyway.' They blamed, gently, the school and the larger society, but not the teachers or specific teaching or curriculum. 'It isn't her fault. She tries. Everything in this lousy school is unfair'. They described teaching methods, but did not relate them to their boredom. 'We copy from the board all day. We get tests we don't even have studied for. I don't know what the teacher talk about'. To a person their solutions were passive and self-punitive. 'You just gotta sit an' take it'. And, 'I'll leave, that's all, I'll leave. I'm no good in school'.

It was at first a distinct shock to me not to get my familiar, expected replies about boredom. But then I received another, more valuable, but much more unsettling insight — that of the victims blaming themselves by internalizing convenient, biased, authoritarian, and dis-educational messages. Here the act of making the familiar unfamiliar resulted both in my heightened insight and my heightened sorrow.

The findings when studying a familiar setting are frequently not what one expects. This was part of Margot's experience in the above vignette, as well as the common experience of many students in our class. As Leslie Rice reported, one researcher in her support group:

> ... was observing an adult physical disabilities therapy clinic. He said he was surprised with how much he identified with the patient and how cold he felt the therapists were. This surprised him because he himself is a therapist and he had not experienced the coldness before.

Joanna Landau commented that as she began to observe her place of work from a different vantage point, that of a researcher rather than a nurse, she discovered that she really knew very little about what the staff truly believed. She could no longer take her knowledge of the situation for granted, as 'the subtle truths of that particular environment' were far different from those which her previous understanding had led her to believe. She describes an ironic process:

... the progression from 'knowing' what one is going to learn, to feeling a bit like a detective uncovering a complex mystery, to finally having some beginning understandings about that which is being observed.

The point here is that the familiar, when observed from a different stance or a new perspective, may frequently turn out to be quite unfamiliar. This may have a surreal emotional effect on the researcher:

> ... you are innocent as Alice, faithfully following your curiosity, when suddenly you find yourself tumbling into a world once familiar turned on its head; you walk through the looking glass of your observations and encounter a whole host of strange characters, which come to include yourself. Mirrors, you find, are no longer useful — you are more and less recognizable than ever. Are you awake, or are you dreaming? 'The' truth gives way to a maze of many. (Deborah Lamb)

Being able to see the 'maze of many' truths requires an openness of mind, a willingness to confront one's own beliefs directly, and the strength of character and intellectual honesty to let go of cherished assumptions. This is yet another instance of Deborah Lamb's 'research as "me-search"'.

Making the Unfamiliar Familiar

The need to discard stereotypes, or at least put them into the proper perspective, does not fall within the exclusive domain of those who are doing research in familiar environments. When we enter into research areas for the first time, regardless of our lack of actual experience, we are not devoid of a myriad of images, expectations, and beliefs about those areas. Although I was never directly involved with the police department, I held a slew of stereotypes derived from the media, my political beliefs, the experiences of my friends, and undoubtedly dozens of other sources. As mentioned previously, I had believed that the police, including females, were exemplified by being macho, somewhat impetuous, hard-drinking, loving to break the law in minor ways. After I gained entrée to their world and I began to talk to them in-depth as well as see them in a variety of contexts, a new image began to emerge. I began to hear stories like the following:

> I never forgot this one day, a girlfriend of mine said, 'How was your day?' and I said, 'Let me see, we had a homicide this morning, and we had a baby who was murdered, we had two fires and a couple of robberies, a burglary and two car accidents, it was a pretty busy

day'. I hung up that phone and I tell you, it was like something hit me. Who the frig has a day like that? I mean, I had a dead baby lying in my arms, it was murdered, beaten to death. I had a guy thrown out a window, five-story window, shot four or five times, with maggots crawling all over his body, went into a couple of fires, save a few lives, had a couple of armed robbery victims crying like crazy, people crying on your shoulder, car accident, mangled bodies, this was my day....

... I spent my first year on the job searching dead bodies, because policewomen had to search dead bodies, this was in my time. And I saw dead bodies that I would never in my life forget. The kinds of homicides, the suicides, a patricide, a matricide, infanticide ... and it wasn't the bodies, it was the families around you. The human drama that took place in every single incident. It was like you went into an empty room, you search the body, and nobody gave a shit. This was somebody that was murdered, a child who was beaten to death, it was a mother who was neglected. It was a person who hung herself, suicide, just throwing themselves in front of trains, thinking my children don't want me anymore. You know, that kind of tearing. I used to say, if you ever opened up a cop's chest and found his heart, it would be in shreds.

Well, this certainly wasn't the macho stereotype I was banking on. Once I was shocked out of my complacency, I realized that this theme, the long-term emotional cost of the job on these women was popping up all over the place. The underlying fear and anxiety of the job were becoming apparent. This was especially clear in an interview with one woman whose brother had recently died. The week of our interview, five police officers had also died — two in the line of duty, two suicides, one heart attack. She said:

I don't know where people get the perception that when you become an officer, you become a super-person.... You're still a human being. If you get cut, you're gonna bleed. A lot of people think that officers, because you have on this uniform and a bullet-proof vest and a gun ... it makes you an oddity, different from other people. But you're not! You're still dealing with a human being that suffers. And I think a lot of officers, they try to put on a macho role or 'That doesn't bother me'. But I hurt! I hurt. You see, when I took the badge, it didn't make me bullet-proof.

She cried during this interview, as did several of the women. Sometimes they cried when they were describing what they see on the streets, and sometimes when they talked about the isolation they feel in general — from many male officers who don't accept the women as police officers, and from civilians, especially males, in their experience. They reported that they feel alienated from the outside world, not only because of their experiences, but because, as one woman said, when she tells people what she does for a living, for example at a party, she says, 'You might as well say you eat cobras for a living. People think it's either exotic or abhorrent'. Either way, she describes feeling alienated. Half of the women I interviewed reported that to avoid the discomfort this causes, they lie when asked what they do for a living, saying they are secretaries or word processors or whatever. They seem to put a good deal of thought and energy into trying to remain anonymous.

To deal with all that they need to deal with, the abuse from citizens and some male cops, the grotesque and horrible scenes they witness on the street, I discovered that they have developed a variety of coping mechanisms, such as lying to mask their professional identities, detaching their feelings, or developing raunchy or gallows humor. Moreover, when talking on these topics, these women seem largely aware that they are using coping mechanisms to deal with the streets — that they are consciously trying to ward off hurt. They talked about war stories as catharsis. They know that when they don't vent, they become sick from stress or anger or sorrow. Towards the end of my research, when they told me 'tough cop stories' or did some pretty hard drinking when we were together, they no longer appeared particularly macho or impetuous or interested in daring the law to catch up with them. Rather, they looked to me like human beings whose job it is to deal daily with inhumanity while maintaining their own human face.

It became clear to me during my research that many of my initial questions that had been based on stereotypes, or unknowns, changed. In-depth research can both knock down expectations and bring about new discoveries that were not initially imagined. In either case, it can pierce through superficiality. Laura Lee Lustbader provides a deeply felt tale of having entered into a totally unfamiliar world — the mind of a schizophrenic girl — to do her research — and some of the lessons she learned:

> As a graduate student making my first attempt at qualitative research, it was my choice to do a study of an 18-year-old girl who was recently released from a nine-month hospitalization. Eileen is her name. She had twice tried to kill herself by slitting her wrists, the second time just prior to her high school graduation. Eileen has been diagnosed as schizophrenic. It was my intent to discover what re-entry to home and community would be like for her. Getting to know Eileen was not at all the experience I thought it would be. Looking back, I'm not quite sure what I thought, but I had no experience to pull on to help me. The ease with which I usually come to know others was not present in this case, In fact, it is now four months since I began my case study, and I'd venture to say that what I do know now is that I will never really know who this girl is. However, recognizing some differences in how her mind works has given me some insights into her being (and, into my own). I like her,

yet I am at times frightened by her fantasies. I have had great hopes for her. Yet now I have great doubts about what the future holds.

Getting as far along as I did with Eileen was something akin to a roller coaster ride. I began by telling her what I was involved with in my graduate studies. I explained the case study and told her of the eventuality of an interview situation. I promised her anonymity and honesty. What I failed to understand was that the honesty part, the development of a trust between us, would be the most difficult factor to accomplish. I had read about the importance of establishing and maintaining trust; I had heard about it in class. I was sure, at the onset of the study with Eileen, that this would not be a problem. In fact, I don't think I even gave it much thought. I knew who I was, how I related to others. My own personal respect for ethics, hard work, and honesty were well-grounded. Never before, though, did I have to communicate with such regularity with a schizophrenic individual. What I thought I was so darned sure of became something to work very hard at throughout the study. A simple sentence, a compliment, might be interpreted by her in a whole other way then I had intended. I could see it, feel it — I could sense that I would have to do some work to repave the way and get back to a point of feeling trust. This could take a few sentences of explanation or it could take one or two more meetings to re-establish the groundwork for a trusting relationship.

Each time I met with Eileen, usually for two to four hours, there was a new or different part of her to deal with. What seemed to begin as a relatively 'normal' time together (i.e., simple conversation at home, bowling, dinner) could and oftentimes did turn into an emotion-laden or emotion-barren experience. Her laughter became, at times, depression. Depression became silence. I had to learn to watch for changes in facial expression, posture. I came to recognize that her sweeping body motions indicated more serious, contemplative periods, and chain smoking characterized times of pronounced anxiety.

Along with watching is listening. Changes in tone of voice, the rapidity or slowness of speech — these signaled definite changes in mood, even growing suspicions on her part. There were many times when Eileen would abruptly say, 'I don't want to discuss this anymore', and she'd close down. At first, I reacted by prodding her and cajoling her, as we usually do with people we know. Again, with time as a friend, I came to know when not to talk. So, when Eileen wanted to stop pursuing a topic of conversation, the conversation stopped. It had to be that way. I came to acknowledge and respect that.

Perhaps what I found most difficult was the use of spoken language. I'm an easy talker. The first thing I had to learn to do was to think of my mouth as zipped closed. Too often I could feel the words of suggestions, advice, even criticism knocking against my lips. But ... listen. Just listen. And when I do speak, ask a question — and watch out for how that question is phrased. Misunderstandings of the simplest sentences occurred so frequently at first that I began to doubt what I was saying and how I was saying it. I slowly realized that Eileen often heard something which I had not intended as my message. This had a direct effect on the development of trust between us. Once I saw the problem for what it was, and given the time and willingness of both of us to learn how to be with each other, this problem of understanding intended messages did dissipate and trust no longer was challenged and/or jeopardized during our last few meetings. At least not in a way that required major work for rebuilding.

I found, with Eileen, that time and space have meanings all their own for her. Her use of both is as effective as spoken language. If she were late or early, this had great significance and bearing on how she saw the trust between us. Location proved to be difficult for her from the start and has remained so. This means that whenever we were going to meet, it had to be in one of two places — her home or my own. On the several occasions when I had appointed other places to meet (even something as familiar as the Metropolitan Museum of Art) the meeting never occurred. Eileen got lost, Eileen slept through the meeting time, Eileen took the wrong train. A lesson was there for me each time this happened: do not, under any circumstances, show signs of disappointment or anger. It was absolutely necessary that I learn to keep my feelings in check, that I learn not to be offended — for what was running through Eileen's mind was not intended to offend, disappoint, or anger me. Her fears kept her in a specific place. I had to come to know and understand that those fears are far different from the sort and depth which plague me or most of the people with whom I regularly spend time.

I think the characteristics in me which I really had to draw upon to do a fair job at this case study were patience, openness, and persistence. I learned some things about Eileen that I would never have learned had I not put to check my quickness to talk, interject, and project. Watching my own self so that I could see her better was of the greatest importance. There were times I feared that I was losing my 'self' to this case study. She and it became a top priority, and, in trying to know her mind, I sometimes thought that my grip on my own life was slipping a bit. The temptation to offer advice, to snap out of the listener's mode, was always present; it changed only in matter of degree.

I remember I began this study with a big, personal question to ask of Eileen. It was gnawing at me: How could you do it. . . . How could you, an attractive, smart, lovely 17-year-old girl want to close your eyes and heart? Didn't you at least want to see how tomorrow goes? I know now that Eileen doesn't think that way. I'm not sure exactly how she does think, day to day, but it is not in that way. Endings are not always as sweet as we wish.

It may already be clear to you, our reader, that qualitative research is not the methodology of choice for researchers who wish to remain dispassionate observers, nor for those who view research as an 'objective' endeavor totally divorced from one's personal self. Entering into the minds and hearts of others is by all accounts a powerful experience. Laura was open and flexible enough to observe that Eileen's psychological processes were radically different from what she had assumed they would be, based on her experience of herself and her usual acquaintances. With that observation, she no longer could cling to her initial assumption that an 'attractive, smart, lovely 17-year-old girl' would necessarily envision a future for herself. As a result of her research, Laura grew to understand that her 'truths' may be very different from Eileen's 'truths'. The willingness to recognize certain personal 'truths' as myths, and to abandon them if necessary, takes strength of mind and character and leaves a powerful emotional and intellectual legacy.

Is Qualitative Research for You?

Implicit in this chapter is the assumption that qualitative methodology is not for everyone. It is not the methodology of choice for those who wish their research to be cut-and-dried, bare-boned, or devoid of emotional intensity. Nor is it for those who do not want to become intimately involved with people throughout the course of the research. Who, then, is likely to derive satisfaction from this type of research? What individual characteristics in the researcher are important in order to meet the rigorous demands of this research, as well as to appreciate the unique joys that ensue from the process? To answer, we have looked to ourselves, to our beginning researcher students, and to other experienced researchers in the field.

Flexibility

The overriding characteristic that many qualitative researchers find most crucial is flexibility. Intellectual flexibility is one aspect. We may in fact start out with some ideas of what we will find — it is natural for the human mind to be curious about the future and to anticipate its outcome. But it is incumbent upon qualitative researchers to remain open to the data that emerge from the field. Cognitive rigidity may interfere with seeing many aspects of the data, and may seriously short-circuit the pursuit of further knowledge. Jackie Storm learned this lesson the hard way when she was studying a family of four.

> At one point, the couple had a fight and the wife ran away from home. 'Woe is me', I thought. I became sidetracked by the thought

that she's not available to be observed. I failed to see that her running away was what I should be observing.

As in Jackie's case, it is sometimes very difficult to change plans mid-project when a totally unanticipated event occurs. However, one must learn to be responsive to new data, unexpected data, and, as Jackie experienced, unwelcomed data. Otherwise, one risks imposing one's own perspective, without remaining grounded in the data. As Laura Cohen stated: 'I started out ... with unyielding rigidity and passed through stages of progressive relaxation of my intellectual muscles'. The ability to envision a prism of viewpoints rather than merely one single perspective is crucial if one is to engage successfully in this research methodology which is premised on the notion of multiple realities.

Flexibility of behavior is also extremely important. One is frequently called upon to be spontaneous and to improvise during the research process.

> I have a thorough list of questions that should uncover valuable information about my 3-year-old research participant. 'So, Sarah, what do you like about Grover on Sesame Street?' 'You asked me too many questions. I'm leaving'. (Ann Vartanian)

The situation forced the researcher to rethink her carefully planned interview schedule and follow the lead of the participant, in this case to play behind a couch.

> Researchers must be responsive to ever-changing situations and field demands. Ethnographers don't ask their participants to comply to their situations; they adapt to their participants' situations. After all, how the participants live their lives is what an ethnographer wants to study (Patricia Thornton)

A common experience of researchers is that of being forced to change one's schedule at the last moment to comply with the demands of their participants. This is sometimes due to commonplace logistical complications that are part of everyday existence. It may also be related to the nature of the project itself. During my research, the bane of my existence became the last-minute changes in the women's tours of police duty and the constant emergencies that cropped up as part of police work. Their frequent complaint that their time is not truly their own, due to the nature of their work and the paramilitary structure of the police department, was brought home to me in a very concrete way: I, too, had to work around their relative lack of freedom to plan their lives far in advance. My need to be flexible with my time paralleled theirs. This was something I had not previously considered. I learned a great deal about the virtues of spontaneity during my research.

Humor

The ability to maintain a sense of humor in the face of minor adversity is a tremendous asset for qualitative researchers. During the early stages of her research, Donna Flynn had difficulty framing clear, coherent interview questions. She began her first interview in this way:

> Try answering this introductory interview question: 'I don't really know how to begin this. I would think, I know we talked in terms of a whole life history, maybe if — we got the whole picture there, so I guess we can start at any point of whatever point strikes you or a period of your life. You know, I really don't know, whatever strikes you, how you would want to begin, in talking about your life up to this point?'

Try answering that interview question! As can be seen, anxiety and inexperience can wreak havoc on one's clarity of expression, as illustrated by Donna's initial interview question. Rather than becoming overly concerned, however, the ability to listen to what one has said, to laugh at it, and then seek ways to improve, is a prerequisite to continuing without undue ego-battering or loss of confidence.

Jackie Storm noted that often, what can go wrong, will.

> It all sounds so simple in the book. You observe. You record. You analyze your data. You develop hypotheses. But then reality sets in. You arrive 'in the field' to begin research and the field isn't home. You spend an hour taping a brilliant conversation with one of your observees and when you get home you discover the tape is blank....
>
> Once in an attempt to record a telephone interview, I attached the suction cup to the wrong end of the phone. My own voice came through loud and clear. The voice on the other end of the line was never to be heard again.

Another beginning researcher in our class, Suzy Hahn, reported the time she felt she was being completely inconspicuous while observing a pizza maker at a fast-food restaurant. Suddenly the pizza maker turned around to her and exclaimed, 'Whatsa' da matter, honey? You like a pizza or you lika my face?' She reported that she was completely nonplussed, and not a little embarrassed. Suzy was able to respond to the humor of the situation and retain presence of mind, however, coming away with excellent observational field notes as well as two large slices of pizza.

Students of qualitative research reported countless similar episodes of making mistakes, being caught off-guard, and in general being subjected to a thousand trifling humiliations that, as Rhonda Sternberg noted, 'are all the blunders of trying to be professional and winding up human'. The ability to transform minor adversity into humor is an invaluable resource for the qualitative researcher.

Accepting Ambiguity

It is important that qualitative reseachers be able to tolerate ambiguity. We do not start with a set of fixed hypotheses. We do not know what we will uncover, reveal, or learn. We may begin with some preconceived notions of what we will find based on the literature or past experience, but it is imperative that we be willing to overturn or dismantle such assumptions as the data come to light. Especially in the initial stages of the research, we frequently record events, including verbal interactions, without any idea if they will turn out to be significant or meaningful. There is by necessity a selective element to logging; one cannot possibly write down every single element in the environment that one sees, hears, or otherwise perceives. Decisions need to be made about what to log and what to omit, without knowing which observations will ultimately prove important or relevant. In an interview setting, one must decide which areas of interest should be most deeply probed and which of the many proffered directions would be most profitable to pursue.

There is also the question of interpretation. What level of analysis is appropriate to describe accurately and understand the phenomenon being studied? The researcher must be willing to commit to certain interpretations of data even if he or she perceives other possibilities. During the process, interpretations may change — one may end up seeing a wholly different phenomenon than one imagined. It might be said that one does not know what one will find until one has found it. In addition, not all ambiguities will dissipate. The qualitative researcher must be able to tolerate this uncertainty. Some students found that the lack of a clearly defined, superimposed focus and direction presented difficulty.

> Before I began this project I knew in principle that reality is multi-layered and open to interpretation. I don't think I appreciated the tension that multiplicity can create for an observer ... when you discard conventional frameworks, when you open your range of attention, the focus blurs and it is difficult to see what you are looking at. (Steve Cullinan)

Those researchers who have difficulty tolerating a fairly high degree of ambiguity, or, as Steve called it, a blurred focus, would most likely be happier using another research methodology. Deborah Lamb summed up what might be considered the attitude most compatible with qualitative research:

> Prepare to lose your way,
> prepare to be unprepared, and enjoy it.

Empathy

The ability to empathize, to look at, and understand the world from another person's point of view is necessary for qualitative researchers. To do this, one must sometimes confront one's own beliefs and re-examine them or put them aside long enough to incorporate someone else's perspective. Or, on the contrary, someone may articulate beliefs that the researcher holds but does not wish to reveal to the public, such as prejudices. One must be willing to acknowledge these feelings to oneself so as not to deny, overcompensate, or in any number of other ways distort the data. Carmen Diaz stated, 'It isn't enough to know yourself; you have to be able to feel free enough to see yourself in other people'. To see oneself in others, and to accept that self, is a crucial ingredient in the character of a productive qualitative researcher.

Accepting One's Emotions

The final trait that will be mentioned here is the willingness and ability to tolerate strong emotions, including emotions that have been previously discussed in this chapter such as anxiety, intimacy and closeness, occasional antipathy, and the sadness of separation. It is an advantage to be able to view emotion as a source of strength and to be open to mining one's emotions for their intellectual lessons.

Postscript

> While the dual sides of our research coin — cognition and affect —
> are integral to each chapter in this book, and are thus discussed
> throughout, the direct focus here on feelings has given us permission
> to be as personal, close, and affect-laden as we can communicate
> with words on paper. For this reason, Margot's analytic memo
> considers only one topic — studying oneself.
> Making the familiar unfamiliar usually demands serious work.

But it takes on an entirely different realm of difficulty when the familiar person one is studying is oneself. Indeed, some of our professional colleagues in qualitative research insist that the self may not study the self. Just too tricky, they say; too fraught with possible problems, with eye trouble, with I trouble. Some even maintain a ban on any qualitative study in which the researcher is involved in any way at all in what is being studied. This reasoning would have done away with Diane's study since she was the teacher of the children whose play styles she documented at school and at home. It certainly would have put an end to the plan for Margaret's study because she was the librarian-teacher who interacted with children over two years to describe the process of moving toward transactional teaching and learning strategies. It would shut down a great deal of collaborative research in schools and hospitals in which people study their own situations. These situations, of course, include themselves. It would wreak havoc with Guba and Lincoln's (1989) fourth-generation paradigm of evaluation research since that, too, is based on informed, cooperative study by everyone involved.

So, it is possible to study oneself in interaction, and it has been done. But that is only part of the issue, not the whole. Being a studier of oneself — apart from studying oneself as the researcher — is sometimes excruciatingly difficult, sometimes impossible. Some of that has to do with developing extraordinary vision — that of seeing out of and reporting from double lenses — researcher/researchee — often simultaneously. Some of that has to do with facing the pain of seeing what we would wish not to see.

I have found that making the choice of whether to study oneself is an intensely personal task. But there are some key ingredients to consider. One essential ingredient is awareness of what one might be getting into. That awareness must be accompanied by acceptance of the unique responsibilities that studying oneself entails. Some of our students, for example, have been surprised, nay shocked, to discover that if they wish to study their situations, they are obliged to focus on what they are doing. This, of course, means that they write, reflect on, and analyze data about themselves along with the data about others. Sometimes the unique responsibilities of studying oneself entail such mundane tasks as setting up dual schedules — one for the researcher part, one for the professional part — and swapping lunchroom or ward duty with a kindred soul. Another essential ingredient is the personality of the possible researcher-of-self. The section of this chapter titled 'Is Qualitative Research for You?' may have some special relevance in this regard. In the end, I believe it is most important to know enough about oneself: to know what happens characteristically when you are challenged, or upset, or satisfied; to know the level of personal imperfection and doubt and unfinished business with which you can live; to know what brings feelings of accomplishment. With such considerations, a person can make a decision — with the proviso, of course, that life often brings surprises that can turn around any decision.

Chapter 5

Interpreting

Introducing Diane and This Chapter

I came to Margot's class as a team facilitator with great enthusiasm. Having just finished my dissertation on children's styles during play, my heart was bursting. I had done it! The ethnographic process had worked for me, and I was anxious to spread this gospel. When students began to express their doubts about the ethnographic experience, I would be ready to step in as the all-knowing one. Not exactly humble thinking on my part, but I had not yet reached the point where I realized that qualitative research is a vast and never-ending experience. Once you discover it, you begin to view almost every situation more intensely.

My background had no doubt contributed heavily to an omniscient attitude. I had been a professional actress for more than ten years, and being someone else was part of such a profession. When I discovered that I preferred a children's audience to an adult audience, I realized that it was time to end my frequently unemployed life-style in the theater and go into teaching — a decision I have never regretted. I still have an audience, but I have found, too, that being in the audience as a 'kid-watcher' of my students is most rewarding. Certainly it has sharpened my skills in qualitative research. Teachers can be natural researchers when they reflect on what has happened in their classrooms from the view of students. Keeping a personal journal is part of the teacher-researcher's process.

So it was that I brought my theatrical, elementary school, and doctoral research with me to Margot's class to begin teaching there. I did not know at that time how much I would become the learner, not the teacher.

In this chapter I focus on the ways in which process is transformed into final product. This is when the researcher works to find a way to structure and communicate what was learned. For most of us, this effort illuminates and extends our understanding of the phenomena we are studying. It often reveals, as well, areas where further study is needed.

You, the reader, understand that there are many approaches to the analysis of qualitative data and many ways in which findings can be presented. In selecting those analytical procedures to describe and discuss, we used these criteria.

1 We write about those methods of analysis that, in our experience, have been employed most often.
2 We write about those methods of analysis that can be described rather than solely inferred.
3 We focus on those characteristics of analysis that are common to many qualitative research approaches.

This last criterion is elaborated upon in the postscript at the end of this chapter (pp. 176–8).

The Final Analysis of Data

To analyze is to find some way or ways to tease out what we consider to be essential meaning in the raw data; to reduce and reorganize and combine so that the readers share the researcher's findings in the most economical, interesting fashion. The product of analysis is a creation that speaks to the heart of what was learned.

In Chapter 3 we emphasized that qualitative research involves almost continuous and certainly progressive data analysis from the very beginning of data collection. This process of analysis guides the researcher to focus and refocus observational and/or interview lenses, to phrase and rephrase research questions, to establish and check emergent hunches, trends, insights, ideas, to face oneself as research instrument. The final phase of data analysis is somewhat different, however. It takes place when the researcher has left the field and sits alone. This is the time to begin to tackle the question that lurked in the back of so many of our minds all along the way, as we wrote copious field notes, yet another analytic memo, transcribed various interviews, and collected every bit of social evidence that the study demanded: 'What do I do with all of this?'

It is time to start taming the chaos.

Getting Started

Here one sits, surrounded with stacks of typed and marked field notes, computer printouts, videotapes, analytic memos, scattered and unidentified notes, a file of well-organized index cards, cut and pasted legal-sized papers, and on and on. And here one sits alone. Van Maanen (1988), in *Tales of the Field*, writes of 'that still point in our studies when we have returned from the field and sit before the blank page that must inevitably carry the story of what we have presumably learned' (p. xii). Joan Giansante had this to say about how she felt at that point:

> I was overwhelmed by data. To reverse the common saying, I couldn't see the trees for the forest — much less the branches. There was just one big forest in front of me.

What now? Some of us may experience internal chaos that we then translate into concern about external chaos. At least this is the way I rationalized my possibly neurotic obsession to check, scrub, and polish every corner of shelves and floors in the room in which I worked at the time. I was not alone in this pursuit. Ann tells us she took a toothbrush and bleach to the moldy grouting around her bathroom tiles before she could face final analysis. Others shared such impulses to organize the chaos as a way of avoiding the work. Jim Hinojosa stated:

> Upon leaving the field, I was confronted with the final interpretative aspect of my research pilot study. The challenge was handled with skillfully organized avoidance. I had the cleanest apartment in New York City, ironed shirts, several lists of 'Things that needed to be done', and even a balanced checkbook. Why the avoidance behaviors? Why does it seem so difficult to complete something you have been doing? These are a few of the questions that entered my mind as I attempted and avoided the task of data interpretation.

While they mention novice writers Bogdan and Biklen (1982) could just as well have been speaking of beginning interpreters of data when they said.

> Novice writers are big procrastinators. They find countless reasons not to get started. Even when they finally get themselves seated at their desks, they always seem to find diversions: make the coffee, sharpen the pencil, go to the bathroom, thumb through the literature, sometimes even get up and return to the field. (p. 172)

Perhaps the predicament for many lies in the particular point at which they find themselves; a point before they know what they will know later. Strauss (1987) sees some light at the end of that tunnel for all of us:

> The analytic mode ... is perfectly learnable by any competent social researcher.... It takes no special genius to do that analysis effectively.

> True, when students are first learning it, they often listen in awe to their
> teacher-researcher and mutter about his or her genius at this kind of work,
> but despair of their own capacities for doing it. They never could! ...
> Inevitably, students get over this phase ... as they gain increasing compe-
> tence as well as confidence in that competence. Of course they do not
> believe they can do it until their first major piece of research — usually a
> thesis — has actually been completed.
>
> But let us not dwell on students. The point is that this mode of
> qualitative analysis is entirely feasible. (p. xiii)

I still tend to clean and put things away before I analyze or write. So don't
worry, dear reader, getting ready to work is something we all go through,
each in our own idiosyncratic way.

In addition to that basic act of settling down to work in the first place,
many people have come to realize that there are different approaches, or
styles, to planning and carrying out the work. Lofland and Lofland (1984,
p. 140) identify the 'steady plodders' who work a little each day, methodically
and laboriously building up their analysis, and the 'grand sweepers' who write
very little text at first, but rather work out the entire report in detail in the
form of outlines and organized notes. Others of us, Margaret and Margot for
two, prefer at times to work on chunks of the job, separate and as yet
unrelated, because they draw interest at that point. For those of you who are
doing this for the first time, you may have found how best to begin your final
analysis and writing. If not, you will. Take comfort in the fact that there are
many ways to do this and that, inevitably, it is a personal decision. Perhaps
the next sections will help you in making some choices.

Approaches to Analysis

Long before a researcher comes to this point, some decisions have been made
about data analysis. Many of these decisions spring from the particular vision
of qualitative research that powers the study (Tesch, 1990), since understanding and applying any particular qualitative approach means understanding and
applying those analytical procedures that are congruent with it. It does not
seem likely, for example, for a phenomenologist to apply intensive semantic
analysis as the major analytical tool. It does seem likely for a sociolinguist to
do that.

We come to qualitative research with whatever understanding of analysis
we bring from previous work. We also come with the conventions of our
respective disciplines and professions, the advice of our mentors, and the

models we have internalized from whatever we may have read. We view our data through the lenses we have at our disposal at any given time. Often, as we continue to work with other researchers and to read and study, we develop a grasp of a wider and more varied array of options for analysis. Goetz and LeCompte (1984) describe the more commonly used approaches and place them on scales ranging, for example, from the more inductive to the more deductive. Tesch (1990) elegantly presents and discusses major types of qualitative analysis.

Whatever your approach to analysis, it seems fair to say that you, the researcher, are in charge of making meaning, of making sense of your data. No one else can do that job since you are so intimately bound up with shaping your study and with understanding what you studied. In this sense, all qualitative data analysis is idiosyncratic. To accept that you are at the helm is often frightening at first and comforting at last. It can be any of several shades of overwhelming, as well as liberating and powerful.

Some researchers begin their final analysis with the help of 'thinking units' proposed by experts. Some researchers posit that only they can create analytic schemes from their data to apply to their data. Some begin with a set of categories they distilled from the literature or past research experience and compare their data to that. Some researchers are of a view that although they create their own systems of analysis, it is also sensible to apply other people's analytical schemes if their data are amenable to that. The following sections contain examples of all of these approaches.

Applying Thinking Units

Many researchers appreciate the input of experts who have 'been there many times before' in helping them to get started on final analysis. Authorities in the field offer a variety of guidelines to help qualitative researchers shape their data. Toward that aim, Lofland and Lofland (1984) provide a system of what they call 'thinking units'. We conceptualize these thinking units as broadly framed sorting files. Not every researcher will choose to apply thinking units. They may be useful for researchers who begin final analysis having created rather spotty categories previously, or those who, at this point, feel they have such a volume of data that they need to begin to make order all over again. If thinking units are applied, a researcher can create specific categories and subcategories that are germane to the study at hand by a more detailed scrutiny and reorganization of the data in each thinking unit 'file'. Establishing categories is discussed first in Chapter 3 and in the following section.

Lofland and Lofland indicate that 'There is no definitive list of such units, but several are traditional' (p. 71). They offer the following thinking unit framework:

meanings   groups
practices   organizations
episodes   settlements
encounters   social worlds
roles   life-styles
relationships

These thinking units are quite congruent with Lofland and Lofland's sociologically based studies. It seems reasonable, for example, that if one were documenting the social networking for the care of their children of unmarried teenage mothers, this framework would serve admirably for a beginning sorting system. Researchers from different academic traditions may create other thinking units that can be useful to them in organizing and categorizing for final analysis. Strauss (1987) suggests the following:

conditions
interactions among the actors
strategies and tactics
consequences. (pp. 27–8)

The thinking units included so far are of such a level of abstraction that they can be used by many researchers. Some researchers create their thinking units more in line with the specifics of their studies. Goetz and LeCompte (1984) provide several such sets of categories (pp. 179–84) along with useful examples of analyses and descriptions of procedures (pp. 190–6 and through Chapter 6).

Marsha Diamond developed the following initial thinking units in her study about writing in one classroom:

Classroom Life
Writing — When, Where, Who, How
Interactions:
    Teacher/Students
    Students/Students
    Student Alone
Products
Other

Margot constructed the following frame in the beginning stages of analysis of her study about young adults who seemed to be beating the odds of poverty:

School Experiences
Out-of-School Experiences
Significant Others
Coping Strategies
Personal Philosophy
Future Plans
Other

If you do use thinking units to begin final analysis, we urge you to add one more to any scheme you decide upon, including a scheme you create yourself. We call that thinking unit 'Open'. As long as this unit is included, it serves to remind us that data often contain surprises, even at the thinking unit stage, that few schemes, except the most general, are all-inclusive, and that qualitative researchers depend upon shaping-in-process.

Establishing Categories

Although people organize their final data in a variety of ways, one method that has suited many of us is to establish a set of categories that arise from and make sense of our specific data. This section assumes that you as researcher have done some work on creating categories during the data collection process. This may have happened in various ways. You may have written marginal comments, analytic memos, and analytical thoughts in the field log narrative itself. You may have created categories in your field log narrative as we described in Chapter 3. Further, as a first step in final analysis, you may have done a thinking unit sorting such as we described in the previous section. In essence, when analyzing a field log for categories, our starting questions are, 'What is the smallest meaningful chunk of log narrative that I will call a category?' 'What concept does it imply?' 'What categories will help me to organize the essential aspects of what is written here?' Creating categories, subcategories, and discovering their links brings a researcher into intimate reacquaintance with the data. There is nothing like a line-by-line or phrase-by-phrase lens to accomplish that end.

There is no escape. Making categories means reading, thinking, trying out tentative categories, changing them when others do a better job, checking them until the very last piece of meaningful information is categorized and, even at that point, being open to revising the categories. This holds true for all the ways your data may be stored — from handwritten field log pages to computer text analysis programs.

Ronna Ziegel provided us with wonderful information about the process of creating and recreating categories at the beginning of her final analysis for her study of humor in the classroom:

> I went through all my logs and began to mark for categories. I used M for mood, A for atmosphere, H for humor, S for sarcasm, GT for good teacher, and BL for body language. In order to do this, I ended going through my log several times.
>
> As I pulled everything together to try to find meaning, I realized that my categories were not quite right. What I had arbitrarily marked mood might be atmosphere. What was the line between humor and sarcasm? In fact, didn't the humor and the sarcasm create mood and atmosphere to the point that separating them was problematic? I realized, at the eleventh hour of this assignment, that I had to go back and form new categories. I would have to re-mark all my logs. My tally of 57 references to mood, 29 to atmosphere. 22 for good teacher (a really ridiculous category at second glance), 23 references to humor, 12 to sarcasm, and 9 to body language were pretty useless. It sounded good. It sounded as if I did it right, but what did it all mean?
>
> I cued into the atmosphere of the class and what Moe did to create and perpetuate it. My categories all have something to do with that. If I were doing this as a major study, I would go back into the field and gather tons more data, but it would be geared to some smaller and more specific issue like how this teacher uses humor to amuse his students and himself, to control situations, and to hide behind.

Here is how Jim Hinojosa went about it. His study was about the communication between physical therapists and their clients:

> My final data analysis began with a very systematic reorganizations of materials. Having everything together in one three-ring notebook, I began by rereading the entire log, commenting both on my comments and the observations themselves. I noted specific examples of communication and tried to construct a general overview of the entire picture. My analytic memos and observation comments served as a guide to what I was looking for. While reading, I made a list of categories. Some of these were: client seeking information (CI), therapist providing information (TI), therapist distancing communications (TD), humor-therapist (TA), humor-client (CH), therapist warming climate (TW), therapist cooling climate (TC), therapist providing misinformation (TM). After I established my categories, I organized them into groups that seemed to go together such as 'information' and 'tone of communications'.

Jim's topics and then categories served him well in later guiding the presentation of his final report. Jim's case provides an example of a process that moved from producing more specific to more general organizers.

Some people color code emerging categories. The only problem with that is that you will most probably change your categories along the way and have to reinvent and reapply your color scheme. Others find it most helpful to use brief phrases or terms for their emerging categories, or letters, and to apply these as they go on. When a category changes, they change its label.

So far we have described a category-making process that depends solely upon the knowledge, insight, and imagination of the person who has collected the data. Some of us are adamant that this is the method of choice for them; Margot, Ann, and Teri fall into this group. That is not to say that there are no stated or tacit guidelines to help such people in creating final categories. The entire research experience up to this point helps to provide such guidelines, and of no small importance to this endeavor are the research questions that have been honed in process. The point is that people who depend most heavily in the final analysis on themselves as instrument do not come without direction — quite the opposite.

Creating Organizing Systems for Analysis and Applying Existing Systems

Some qualitative researchers find it useful to try out existing analytical schemes on their data for a variety of reasons. As part of her final analyses, Margaret adapted Hilda Taba *et al.*'s (1965) system to document children's levels of thinking as they worked in small groups to discuss a book they had read. Marsha Diamond studied life around writing in one middle elementary grade classroom. After she analyzed her field logs in progress, she decided that it would help in the understanding of people's interactions with writing to look more closely at questions that teacher and students asked in various classroom contexts. Marsha applied the Gallagher-Aschner (1974) system. Both Margaret and Marsha are examples of researchers who organize and present their data in a variety of ways, each one of which lends an additional facet to the overall findings. Some researchers come to analysis with schemes from the literature that they wish to apply. Others may feel pressed to use certain organizing schemes because they believe that this is the thing to do or because they have been advised by their mentors to do so.

In planning my dissertation research, I had made an intensive study of the literature about children's play. As a result, I distilled a set of play-style categories. These became my beginning system, and it worked quite well through my field trial. Over the course of the study, however, I added six more categories because the data called for that. It is essential to be open to changing a system or scheme even when, or particularly if, it holds well. If it does, we may be extending existing theory. If it does not, we may be suggesting some of our own.

The experiences of Belén Matías bring to light another twist to the business of selecting an organizing system at the beginning of the study. This one didn't work out:

> I thought all was well and smooth. I had found two systems for the study of directive communication. It seemed to me that their combination was just about perfect. One was a three-category system for classifying directives in a classroom. The other system was composed of categories of adult directives. In writing my dissertation proposal, some friendly spirit whispered in my ear that I had better have a fall-back plan in case the systems didn't work out. I knew they would, of course, but I added that I would create analytical categories if this became necessary. Necessary! Little did I realize what I was in for.
>
> Right from the beginning I became aware that the two systems would not work. Briefly said, I was learning so much about the intricacies, the complexities of children's and teachers' directives and the richness with which they were being played out in the varied classroom contexts, that I knew the two systems would never allow me to do justice to my findings.
>
> I set out to make my own scheme. And what a scheme! I tried to capture the communicative flow of directives, their intent, effect, who communicated and who received each directive, whether the directive was verbal or non-verbal, its function, its curricular source, and complex descriptions of clashes of frames of reference. I tried to capture everything that was needed. The price? I labored with a huge analytical scheme in which the original two systems played minor parts. My eyes gave out as I repeatedly watched the same video segment for hours. The VCR protested from thousands of stoppings and startings and my hand was in real pain from writing furiously. My tables became increasingly complex as I presented and related the data. And I, in turn, became increasingly annoyed that the seemingly simple column totals did not communicate the work that produced them.
>
> I am only grateful that this micro-analysis was but one way in which I did final analysis. I doubt I could have lasted.

We know she would have lasted, but Belén's final lines bear more emphasis. In order to bring her multi-faceted findings to life, Belén employed three major analytical approaches: the creation of broader contextualized descriptions of directives in one school setting, more focused micro-analysis of videotaped interactions, and distillations of social rules as thematic statements. Some of these approaches would be considered more inductive than others, but each made its contribution to painting the picture. Final research reports are often amalgams of several ways to present data. Some of these are described in the following sections.

The piece that follows by Steve Cullinan highlights the fact that it is not always easy and self-evident to decide to apply other people's analytical schemes or to create your own:

In my study of small group discussions I had available any one of at least six analytic approaches to the transcripts: analyses of roles, role interactions, themes, topics, syntax, and larger patterns of discourse. Each could conceivably have yielded the kind of insight that I felt was possible. However, I was not satisfied with any of them. What seemed most intriguing about the talk was what the students were trying to do collectively. Each analytic perspective reflects a part of that phenomenon but misses the creative and active construction of group talk. Perhaps if I had known more about how to employ these strategies, it would have been easier to frame my objective and discover an underlying order that produced the conversation that occurred. But group processes don't conform very convincingly to familiar one-dimensional explanations.

Unfortunately, the study doesn't become any easier when you discard conventional frameworks. When you open your range of attention, the focus blurs and it is difficult to see (and remember) what you are looking at. For a time, I considered inventing my own analytic tool through a metaphor that might hold all of the influences together in the same context. I considered selecting passages of transcripts that showed the conversation converging upon and perhaps exposing an issue of mutual concern. This effort jointly to achieve focus and understanding results from social, psychological, and linguistic collaboration. I would call this process 'knotting' to suggest that a problem had been isolated and mutually engaged over many conversational turns and finally fought over to the point that it could no longer be probed without a conclusion(s) being drawn. As interesting as it sounded, the analytic metaphor didn't work much better than the conventional approaches since it committed me to explaining more than the evidence would allow. I simply couldn't find credible instances of the pattern.

It seems that there has to be something of a compromise between idiosyncratic and conventional perception. My swing back to the conventions left me with categories that are homemade but also relatively obvious. They allow me at least to point in the direction of the phenomenon that I want to study. Having now read these transcripts probably fifteen times each, I still see forms of interaction that I should have seen earlier. So I know there is much more to be found. But I recognize also that this is a start in what would be a much more complex struggle of finding lenses, losing them, and finding them again.

Finally, in our experience, one of the joys that qualitative inquiry affords individual researchers is in the leeway to create and choose organizing systems that make sense to each. We like the fact that there is no formula.

Developing Themes

Up to this point we have discussed the making of categories as tools to help us organize our data. Categories, however, can serve another function, and that is to help us tease out the meaning of our findings as we consider the supporting evidence in each category and as we determine how categories may be linked. This section about themes and the next one about vignettes/ constructs describes how categories served researchers in broader meaning-making and in how the results were communicated.

One widely used approach to final analysis is the search for themes. A theme can be defined as a statement of meaning that (1) runs through all or most of the pertinent data, or (2) one in the minority that carries heavy emotional or factual impact (Ely, 1984). It can be thought of as the researcher's inferred statement that highlights explicit or implied attitudes toward life, behavior, or understandings of a person, persons, or culture. Many of us first became aware of the concept of theme as students of literature. Here we became accustomed to analyzing the 'culture' of a novel by looking for the underlying ideas about human existence with which it is concerned. When expressing the themes of literary works, we often use phrases or even single words: *The Hobbit* is a 'quest' story; it celebrates the strengths and values and decencies of ordinary people. In qualitative analysis it is customary to express themes in the form of a statement.

Margot used a thematic analysis to present her findings gleaned from ethnographic interviews of young people from a culture of poverty who appeared to be 'making it' in *Beating the Odds*, (1984). Here is her description of the process:

> I am heavily influenced by the work of Bussis, Chittenden, Amarel, and Carini (1978) in how I develop themes. In brief outline, this is the process I apply:
>
> 1 Study and re-study the raw data to develop detailed, intimate knowledge.
> 2 Note initial impressions.
> 3 List tentative categories.
> 4 Refine categories by examining the results of steps 2 and 3 and returning to the entire database of step 1.
> 5 Group data under the still-tentative categories and revise categories if needed.

6 Select verbatim narrative to link the raw data to the categories.
7 Study results of step 6 and revise if needed.
8 Write theme statements for each participant from my best attempt to speak from her/his point of view by linking data in and across categories.
9 Integrate findings about each person.
10 Compare findings for commonalities or patterns, differences, and unique happenings.

Quite frequently in qualitative work the categories that were created to organize data help the researcher to discover themes by highlighting some relation between them. This is certainly true in my case. For example, in the study, out of the many categories I established, were these three:

José's relationship to mother (Relm).
José's planning strategies (Pl).
José's financial goals (Fin).

After studying the supporting data for these categories, I wrote the following themes as if José were talking:

My mother supports me and helps me to clarify plans for the future.

I sometimes give up immediate positive experiences for what I feel I must do to establish later financial security.

These themes, among others, held strongly for the data about José.
Could I have established the themes without first building a set of categories? Some people might do that. But I feel most grounded in the data when I progress from category to theme. Could other researchers have discovered different categories and themes from the same data? Yes. And this would probably happen. The important process here is to be able to explain one's reasoning for whatever one created. On the other side of the picture, however, is the fact that I am often stunned by how similar the analytic categories and themes are when an entire group of people — a class — is given the same field log pages to analyze. That speaks to an aspect of the topic of trustworthiness, to be discussed later.

Teri writes about finding her themes in the following ways:

My system of creating themes might be considered a 'bottom up' system. I first divided my transcripts into categories. For example, whenever interviewees would discuss interactions with fellow officers, I would put in the code word 'relationships' on the side margin. With the help of a computer program, I then put all the material coded with the word 'relationships' into a separate file. 'Relationships' became a category. I initially had 31 such categories. When the categories were examined for overlap, redundancy, and significance, they were compressed into seven final categories that were judged to encompass the material sufficiently.

Within each category, I reviewed the data for statements that were particularly revealing or expressive or somehow stood out as potential themes. I listed each such statement on a separate index card. (I color coded my index cards — for each different category I had a different combination of colors for the ink and the card.) I grouped together statements that were similar or related. For example, one woman stated,

> We were so visible — we had to outperform; we weren't supposed to make mistakes; we were not supposed to fail.

Another woman stated,

> The propaganda value of one woman screwing up is incredible — by that night the whole borough will know and ... reinforce the suspicion that you're no good.

These two quotes were written on one index card, along with several similar ones sprinkled throughout the transcripts. I wrote the heading on the top of the card, 'Because I'm so visible, I feel heightened pressure not to screw up'. I wrote such statements in first person in order to capture the phenomenological quality — these themes describe women's experience of being police officers — of the research. I discovered that the majority of women had made a related statement, and based on the context in which the statement was made, I assessed that they felt strongly about it. I had defined major themes as those that apply to more than half of the interviewees. I therefore defined this statement as a major theme about 'Relationships'.

Belén Matías analyzed teacher and student directives in a Puerto Rican pre-school setting that seemed to be at work in 'getting things done' in that particular classroom. Here are a few of the thematic social rules that she derived from the data in her categories. They are presented as though they were spoken by the children:

> We must bid for a turn to speak one at a time and listen to others quietly during a presentation of a material or while the teacher gives instructions.

> When the teacher asks questions during circle time, more than one can answer at the same time.

> Most often I am in charge of what I do in the time of entrance/transition to work.

The presentation of each of the social rules was bolstered by data from videotaped and in-person observations as well as information from teacher interviews over one year.

Developing Vignettes/Constructs

During the writing of my dissertation (1986) about the play styles of four kindergartners I developed vignettes about each child. I called these vignettes 'constructs'.

> A construct is an inferred soliloquy based on the content of repeated observation and an interpretive composite of one child's seemingly characteristic thought and behavior. The construct contains statements which are considered central to the way the child perceives his or her experience during a play period. (p. 22)

I used a construct to introduce the readers to the child and to foreshadow trends in the information about each child that followed next. This is Chris's introductory construct:

> I'm looking at these black droppings of this caterpillar I brought into school. I've been doing this for about twenty minutes, and I suppose there are other things going on in the classroom, but I haven't noticed. I'm really intensely into doing this and I guess I haven't moved much. Some people might say the droppings mean the bug went to the bathroom, but I've decided they are eggs, and I might flick one in your eye! I could even make them tiny bullets in my stick gun! What do you think of that? In fact, I think I'll speed across the room to the class wagon, which is mine most of the time, and set up my gun. A lot of kids follow me, and I'll let them see the droppings. I want them to feel them, too. Boy, they feel mushy. After that I'm off on my own to watch for enemies from my wagon. I'm smiling, but those kids bother me sometimes.
>
> When I get home from school, I like to go off on my own and really work at making all the stuff around my house into things I can use for building and fighting. It's okay sometimes to have kids around while I'm doing this. I like Alice, in fact I love her. She's a girl and she does girl things, but she's impressed with the neat things I do. Mrs Garner is pretty impressed too, but she's harder to shock than my mom. I told Mrs Garner I would blow her butt off! Funny, huh?! I did something even better. I took my pants off right in front of her. Boy, I'll bet she was shocked! Course there's Jill, my sister, and Alice's sister Nicola. They get me crazy. I have to get crazy to get my way in things I'm doing. Nicola is really stupid even if she is Alice's sister. When I do things my way, I feel terrific. My dad is a good person to do things with; he's like me and he understands.

The following vignette was developed by Margot from her category files in a study of a project to serve teenagers considered homeless, or in danger of being so, jobless, and probable high school dropouts.

Introducing Trina: My Life Is So Dangerous

I'm real shy and I can't speak right. What's that word? Oh, yes! I stutter. I just feel so strange, like everybody else knows what's happening. Maybe it's because I just came from Haiti a few months back. Maybe it's because I got a big problem with my mother and I can't seem to pay much attention to anything else.

I'm seventeen and I could have stayed in Haiti. Why did she act like she wanted me to come?

My mother don't like me to stay into her house, I don't know why. She only likes my little brother and she doesn't like half of us (8 children). She's just mean. Especially to me. My mother, she wants to put me out.

When I got to New York I went to Catholic school for a few weeks and then to a public school. The day my brother Joe brought me to this high school, I had a problem ... with my mother and Amy [Project Supervisor] brought me here to the project office. That was a couple of weeks ago and it's a good thing too. Amy and Dan [Project Supervisor] try to help me out. Sometimes if I'm hungry, he [Dan] feeds me. He give me the money to my Aunt and that's because my mother don't feed me. He wanted me to get a letter from my mother. A letter to put me in my own house, to live by myself. And my mother did not want to give it to me.

I come down to talk with Dan every day. He always pays attention to us. To the students. But I still have trouble in classes. These kids bother me in my class.... I don't want to leave this school too. I want to finish school here. I've got a lot of credits to go. Dan will help. I hope other people can help me with school.

Sometimes I dream of what I'll be when I grow up. I want to be a fashion model. But, you have to go to a training for that and you've got to have money too, to get any. I don't know how I'll get the money. I used to work but now I can't.

You want to know what I'm going to do with my life? I don't know. My life is so dangerous. (Ely, 1989, pp. 59–60)

You may have noticed that often these themes, social rules, and vignettes/constructs are stated in the first person. When possible, they include the actual words of the participant(s). Otherwise, they are distilled from the data in as close a likeness as possible of the participant's mode of expression. The intention is to present in miniature the essence of what the researcher has seen and heard over time. Not every researcher opts to use first person, although we are of the mind that this brings readers closer to the people who were studied. That is a personal choice. In the final chapter, you will notice that Margaret uses thematic statements in third person to introduce the topics she discusses.

It stands to reason that themes, social rules, and constructs/vignettes do not stand alone. They are devices that are established through analysis and offered to provide meaning, cohesion, and color to the presentation. They serve also to counter the danger of overabstracting by anchoring the findings firmly in the field that gave rise to them. Other presentation devices that have been developed from the analysis of qualitative researchers are discussed as part of making the story (pp. 167–75).

Including Numbers

One bane of my qualitative researcher existence is the assumption held by some that this research must be number-free; that it is not appropriate to distill numbers, and certainly not appropriate to apply statistical treatment. Ostensibly, this assumption is laid to rest by the availability of at least one volume about qualitative data analysis that involves among other aspects, those authors' versions of how numerical data from qualitative research may be compiled, treated, and presented (Miles and Huberman, 1984). So, why this assumption?

The answer may lie in several possibilities — for a start. First, some people seem to believe that the difference between positivist and naturalistic research lies in the absence of numerical data in the work of the latter persuasion. This group includes some beginning doctoral students. A second possibility that may give rise to the assumption is the fact that many qualitative reports do not include visible numbers.

> Many researchers who write case studies use qualitative data because they believe them to be richer, more insightful, and more flexible than quantitative data. They believe that the meaning of an event is more likely to be caught in the qualitative net than on the quantitative hook (US General Accounting Office, 1987, p. 55)

Many researchers, however, do include numbers. For example, in my study on children's play styles, I judged it informative to include a rather complex table that presented numerical results about each style category as observed over time. I presented frequency counts in order to compare quantitative loadings in play-style categories, as well as consistencies/inconsistencies over observations and contexts. These data were also used to produce a quantitative play-style category profile for each child and for the entire group. While I chose not to do further statistical treatment, the numerical data about play style and contexts were such that I might well have done so had I considered it useful in the spirit of my work. Researchers who do semantic analysis often present more complex statistical treatments. While they may at times include numbers, 'Phenomenology, hermeneutics, psychological case studies, anthropology, critical sociology, and linguistics all have long traditions of non-numerical research' (Tesch, 1987, p. 3).

On perhaps a more important level, every category, every theme, every finding, whatever its form, arises from the fact that it exists in the data and as such can be counted even though the researcher may choose not to do so. For example, in this book we hold that a theme may be established (1) because it appeared many times and/or for the majority of people who were studied, or (2) it appeared once or a very few times but carried important analytical impact. (Margot is known to say that she has to be slapped hard only once to know something meaningful has happened.) Other researchers present only majority themes. In both cases, themes arise because the support for them is evident to the analyzer. The responsibility of a qualitative researcher in the final report is to bring public spotlight on her/his decision-making process in establishing findings. When this holds, readers have the information with which to judge for themselves whether the findings are reasonable.

Return to Trustworthiness

We pondered at some length where to place this section. Discussions of the 'quality control' of qualitative research traditionally occur toward the end of books and articles on research methodologies. It is difficult to choose the correct place for talking about trustworthiness because, as we emphasized in previous chapters, a qualitative researcher pays continuous, recursive, and, we dare say, excruciating attention to being trustworthy. This concern begins before the first word is written and does not end until the research is completed. The quest is to make the research project credible, produce results that can be trusted, and establish findings that are, to use Lincoln and Guba's phrase, 'worth paying attention to' (1985, p. 290). We have, as you see, negotiated a solution by presenting issues about trustworthiness in two places: in Chapter 3 and here.

The topics in this section deal with aspects of trustworthiness that seem particularly pertinent during the final stages of a research project. Here, as throughout the book, we focus on the facets of establishing credibility because, to us, this is the bedrock of trustworthiness.

Back to the Field

You've just left the field! Why, then, this section about returning? Because, in the final analysis process, so many people experience the need to check again, to ask another question, to jump back in for a very specific purpose. Sometimes the reason to return to the field lies in an anomaly in the data. Sometimes just a bit more information is needed. Sometimes it seems vital to check an observation with the person who was observed. Sometimes it is the nagging thought that one was not as fair as possible in collecting data. Here Beverly Rosenthal, who did a pilot study on the impact of computers on writing in a classroom, tells why she decided to return to the field after she thought she was through:

> Trustworthiness became an even greater issue when it came time to analyze the data and report the findings. My concern was that perhaps I had overemphasized the negative and had not seen enough of the positive aspects of the implementation. I was struggling for a balanced and fair perspective.
>
> The observations confirmed as well as conflicted with my personal experiences, and with my reading and research experiences. For example, I had uncritically accepted the notion that the networked computers would automatically and conveniently facilitate peer response. The literature, course announcements, the program director, and the computer coordinator presented enthusiastic claims for the technology. However, after observing several classes, it became apparent, much to my consternation, that there was a discrepancy between the expected uses and outcomes and the real uses and outcomes of implementing the technology.
>
> I had not considered that in reality the use of the networked computers was fraught with difficulties. I was compelled to find out more. I returned to a critical examination of the literature on computers and composition, the factors affecting composition instruction and innovation and organizational change theory. I also spent some time critically reflecting upon myself as researcher. Was it consternation or interest I should have been expressing when I found the discrepancy between the expected and real?
>
> When I returned to the field, this reflection helped me to discover some possible factors that related to the discrepancies: lack of specific instructional and implementation guidelines, inadequate software, incomplete installation of necessary hardware, no teacher training in the technology, high turnover of teachers, no full-time faculty devoted to teaching the course, no evaluation procedures, inadequate student training, inadequate access to the technology for both student and instructor, and inadequate resources allocated to the program. Returning to the field was not only satisfying but a relief.

Beverly's account illuminates one fact we all know only too well: the broad and general plans we laid at the start in order to establish credibility will almost certainly be redefined and augmented as the real thing comes along. As with every other phase of qualitative research, so even more here, the researcher struggles with the demands of emergent design. While Beverly's return to the field occurred during her final analysis, this can and often does happen at any time in the research process. It is to her credit, however, that she did not decide to ignore the whispers of her own voice at that particular point near the very end of her work.

When Is Enough Enough?

One criterion for being credible is to engage in collecting data for such duration and in such ways that these are sufficient to help us understand what we set out to study. What 'sufficient' means is often perplexing. Near the completion of my analyses. I began to hyperventilate with fears that I had not collected all the necessary data. I returned to the field briefly to continue observing. In less than a week, I experienced a weary sense of relief, knowing my data were sufficient because they were repeating themselves.

Margot (Ely *et al.*, 1989, pp. 30–1) tells her own story:

> My sabbatical project was to work on a piece of research I titled *Beating the Odds: An Ethnographic Interview Study of Young Adults from the Culture of Poverty*. After a time, I left for an island hideaway laden with the voluminous transcript of the eight interviews that had been carried out. My task was to analyze. Well, I did. I categorized, cut, pasted, reorganized, categorized again, in cycles, while the island breezes blew my little pieces of paper merrily around the room. Yes, I am one of those strange folks who need to cut and paste. I was bewitched! No beach, no time off, no Sunday brunches, just trying to make sense. After two and a half months I arrived at some analytical insights that seemed reasonable. Well, almost. I went about with this terrible feeling that maybe I had missed something. Suppose I had not asked the right questions? Suppose I should have probed more? Less? Suppose the people were putting me on? Suppose they were so stunned by the lengths of the transcripts I had shared with them that they carelessly agreed that what was there was the story as they lived it?
>
> After worrying about this for some days, I packed up my by now even more huge pile of notes, papers, and files and flew back home. I got in touch with the eight people and did a lengthy follow-up interview with each. Again, I spent months analyzing, cutting, pasting. Same results! Not one new category. Not one new theme. A few more examples.
>
> What to learn from all this? I don't quite know. Perhaps to be a bit more confident when I follow what I consider decent methodology? But then again, suppose some really new, terrific findings had come from the second round? Perhaps to exult that the findings were so similar? Perhaps to be leery about just that? Perhaps to learn to let go, in the knowledge that ethnographic research often means letting go to come back? Certainly, I now see things in a different light when I work with doctoral students who grapple with the demons of 'When is enough enough?'

It seems that every qualitative researcher fights those demons. Some of us cling hopefully to the criterion of redundancy; of trusting that when data repeat themselves, it is time to stop. But then, there is always the spectre of another interesting person to interview, another observation that may unearth shatteringly different and useful information, another event to experience that will just clinch things beautifully. May you fight your demons successfully. Let us know please.

Sometimes, returning to the field has less to do with establishing credibility than with providing a very seductive strategy to avoid what we feel is that awesome final analysis and write-up. Some of us return to the field once too often, and we know it. Others labor mightily to fulfill the impossible dream of 'getting it all'. Somewhere between 'barely sufficient' and 'any number of cycles of the recursive qualitative research process' lies that place where enough may not be all, but enough is enough. Finding that place and then having the confidence and skill to define it and to use it well are key to qualitative researchers. That place can be found.

It is far easier but perhaps more unsettling to know when enough is *not* enough. Essentially, this is a personal conviction which transcends time limits, family concerns, job deadlines, and plans for vacation. I believe we've all been through that also. Even when it looks sufficient to all the relatives who have wondered when you'll ever be finished, even when the support group says to stop, even when your dissertation committee argues that this is it, there are instances, small as they may be, when the researcher knows well that some thing or things need to be done. If this is so, and if you can stand it, do what needs doing. You've come this far and you live with yourself.

Negative Case Analysis

Surely this process is not new at this stage of the game. The search for disconfirming evidence to help us check our in-progress conclusions, to reconceptualize our categories and themes, and/or to point us to minority subthemes, has been part and parcel of the ongoing analysis and collection up to this point. Sometimes, however, unearthing evidence that does not support the emerging findings and deciding how to handle that situation take on special meaning at final analysis time.

Ruth Alperson shares how her findings about 4-year-old Mary served to broaden her outlook and, in the end, reshape her vision about humor in the final analysis phase:

> I feel that I have focused on Mary here because I have learned most
> about humor, in a way, from her. This is ironic, for I concluded, at

first, that I would probably get very little from Mary that was humorous. What happened, in final analysis, however, was that my very narrow appraisal of what belonged in the category of the humorous became transformed and broadened by what I saw, unexpectedly, within the workings of Mary's various behaviors. Mary finally confounded and corrected my assumptions.

Although I had concluded otherwise, I learned very near the end of my analysis that Mary, who had a nervous demeanor, and who I would characterize as a tense, worried child, had her own brand of humor, which is not particularly funny, but I would term it humor, nonetheless. Kay, the assistant teacher, called Mary's joking 'pathetic', and described one instance of this in her interview with me. Mary was particularly anxious that her babysitter be on time to pick her up from school. Lia was always on time, and very indulgent with Mary, but Mary worried nonetheless. When Lia appeared at the school, Mary liked to 'tease' her. Kay said that one day Mary hid from Lia after Lia had started to leave with her. Lia could not find Mary for a short time, and really became concerned. Mary popped out of her hiding place, laughing heartily. I felt, on hearing this, that Mary was setting up a situation in which she could vicariously experience her own fear of not finding Lia, of being left alone, through Lia. I categorized this act as humorous, as in black comedy, because in Mary's eyes, it seemed she was, ostensibly, playing a joke, and because she laughed so at its conclusion. It seemed like humor used as a defense, or a cover; it was funniness creating its own flip-side, fear in the guise of funny. I wanted to check this out so I went back to observe Marry. This aspect of her humor reappeared with sufficient impact to allow me to have some faith about my insight.

In Ruth's example, her finding served both to challenge an emerging conclusion about Mary and to broaden the meaning of a category. Teri recounts how she discovered a negative case theme and presented it to stand separately, in juxtaposition to a major theme.

In my dissertation on women police officers, I included a category entitled 'Behind the Blue Wall: Professional Relationships within the Precinct'. Within that category, I discussed several themes that pertained to the interviewees' experience of professional relationships between male and female officers. Some of these themes highlighted: the pervasive undercurrent of hostility that women experience as directed towards them when they are promoted or given a good assignment; increased pressure not to make mistakes because of their small percentage in the department and heightened visibility; the conflict they feel between trying to integrate into a man's world while not wanting to become 'one of the boys'.

One theme was very strong for the majority of women. This was, 'I found a home here. It's family'. This theme describes their perception that, despite the obvious ambivalence that characterizes many of their professional relationships with male officers, they feel that they have been accepted into the police family. Interestingly, however, this theme applied to all the women but one. Delores felt strongly that she had never been accepted into the police family. Moreover, she felt that no women were, and that those who felt they had been accepted were deluding themselves:

> You're an anomaly. And there is no real place for you. I think all the girls know it at a certain level.
>
> No matter how much you fit in, *per se*, you don't — it's superficial. Even the girls that think they fit in, they don't.
>
> Some of the men are decent human beings — intelligent, articulate, with something to bring to your daily professional life. But the vast majority aren't. So you're constantly out of synch.

Her acute sensitivity to sexism in the police force, with a strong sense of self-worth and perception that she was never duly credited for her performance, created for her an overriding bitterness and loneliness that has colored the whole tenor of her police experience. She was the only woman I interviewed who clearly felt her career choice was a grave mistake. She alone stated she would never do it agin. She counted the days towards retirement.

In-depth analysis of Delores' interviews revealed that her experience provides an exception to the theme, 'I found a home here. It's family'. I therefore constructed a second theme that would describe her unique experience, and include it here as an example of the result of negative case analysis.

Some researchers (Goetz and LeCompte, 1984) distinguish between negative case — an exception to the emerging rule — and discrepant case — a variation of the emerging rule. A negative case refutes a construct while a discrepant case refines a construct (pp. 188–9). In this light, Teri's example is about a negative case and Ruth's is about a discrepant one. Most often in our work, the line between negative and discrepant blurs. We worry less about what to name the 'differing instances' than to use them to shape and refine the findings. The essential idea is that qualitative researchers go through an active process of confirmation and are willing to change their minds about findings when the data so dictate.

Peer Involvement in the Research Process

Peers can play several vital roles in helping each other to be credible. We have discussed the formation and function of peer support groups in Chapter 2, and their important contributions during the research process in Chapter 3.

Here we present some ideas about peer involvement during the final stage of the process.

Peer Support Groups. Lincoln and Guba (1985) suggest peer debriefing as one technique for maintaining credibility:

> ... the process helps keep the inquirer 'honest', exposing him or her to searching questions by an experienced protagonist doing his or her best to play the devil's advocate. (p. 308)

With much less emphasis on playing devil's advocate, we call the vehicle of that process peer support groups. In our experience, support groups have been extremely important in helping people establish and maintain credibility. Belén Matías shares one way in which her support group served to force her to face the need to check her findings with data from yet another source:

> I had promised in my proposal that my major data would come from a micro-analysis of some classroom communication events. Actually, I did everything but that. The observational data were so fascinating, so magnetic that I was drawn — not against my will — to describing classroom life first in very broad strokes. Next I established and supported a series of social rules from and with the data. These gave me ground to make some tentative generalizations about the wielding of power in that classroom. I was planning to write three case studies to illustrate how the social rules worked themselves out in the school lives of individual children when a member of my support group put an end to that. 'What if the results of your micro-analysis go against the statements your social rules are making? Suppose you can't write the case studies in the way you now envision? I think you need to get those micro-analysis data now!' I saw the sense to that and what's more, I feel that without my support group I would have plowed ahead with my own plan, much to my disadvantage.

In my own dissertation fieldwork, I did not have a support group. It was a lonely experience not to share with peers the extraordinary happenings I had documented. I had to find other ways to check my insights about the children who had provided me with such rich details. Particularly in the final stages, my doctoral committee came the closest to being a support group, but a doctoral committee is quite different from a group of peers who are going through the same thing. I missed that.

Nancy Biederman sees similarities in the ways professional support systems serve therapists and ethnographers:

> As a therapist, it is imperative to achieve the equivalent of Guba and Lincoln's trustworthiness. How do you check yourself as an accu-

rate instrument in the understanding and exploration of someone else's reality? In much the same way that ethnographers do. I have been in individual and/or group supervision consistently throughout my practice. It is here that one triangulates — checks feelings and perceptions, gets feedback and fresh perspectives. Support groups and meetings with experienced ethnographers can function in much the same way. Clients, too, can be a source of verification.

Several experiences in my support group, and meetings with Margot, very much remind me of the supervisory process. Both kinds of work are in many ways introspective and solitary. It felt tremendously helpful and reassuring to get other people's perspectives and support. I remember feeling frustrated and despairing about my project and, after discussing it, taking heart and feeling hopeful. This was also very true, especially in my first years as a therapist, in the supervisory process.

Nancy's contribution highlights the fact that some qualitative research processes are akin to those in many human service professions. Could this help to explain why those of us who wrote this book feel so related to the qualitative paradigm?

We have found the peer support network exceedingly useful in establishing credibility. It is necessary, however, to remember that a group can be just as blind as the researcher alone, unless the members strive to counter that. Janis (1973) writes about this in his provocative look at 'groupthink' during what he labels some of our historical fiascos (p. 407); those of the Bay of Pigs invasion, Pearl Harbor and escalation in Vietnam. Janis reminds us that a group may value uniformity more than variety. Indeed, group members may find it much easier to agree, to be nice, than to make possibly upsetting waves or to take different stands. Members of some groups strive more for social acceptance than they do to grapple with the tasks for which the group was formed.

This danger sounded, this team has found qualitative research support groups to be amazingly and refreshingly helpful, supportive, forthright, and dedicated. Support groups have differed when it was easier not to do so, but the ways in which they have differed and faced other difficult moments with each other have been constructive down the line. One of the most potent reasons for such cohesiveness has been the dedication of the members to help each other produce the most substantial and credible work possible and to do this both through their own eyes and through the imagined eyes of others who would read and assess the final product.

Peer-Checking. A few qualitative researchers believe that one aspect of being credible is to obtain statistical agreement about some of their findings with at least one other person. Often this person is a member of the peer support group or a colleague on the job. The process is called establishing inter-rater reliability, a phrase that is borrowed from the traditional research paradigm. All five of us have established inter-rater reliability at various points in our research careers. We do not do so now.

When I was conducting my ethnographic study, I had not quite loosened my bonds with the experimental research community, and was fearful that my research might not be looked upon as acceptable if someone else couldn't duplicate my findings. For this reason, I established inter-rater reliability in my analysis. In this case, this meant that a second observer, the teacher's aide in another classroom, would join me in observing the four children. During four practice observations, this person was instructed in identifying specific play-style features and providing descriptions for each feature observed. Immediately following each practice observation, I met with her to discuss the features that were identified and described by me in the same sessions. We also viewed videotapes together and wrote and compared field notes. Following the training period, I asked this colleague to observe each child for a half-hour once a month and to keep a written record of the observations. As we had done during the training period, we met after each observation and compared the play-styles we identified in our written records. We reached a 98 per cent level of agreement for the four months in which this was done.

Another sort of peer-checking is that which occurs in the support group. One example is that one member shares sections of a field log, asks people to create categories and even themes, and then compared the individual results with those that the researcher had established. If this last process does not result in substantial agreement, it is the researcher's job to seek understanding about the analytical reasoning of the group members and either agree of disagree, accept or not accept the ideas proffered.

It is probably evident that I find this last example of checking emerging results most sensible in qualitative research. In fact, all five of us on this writing team have given up establishing statistical inter-rater reliability via the training-retraining model because it does not serve our understanding of being credible in naturalistic research. However, we all endorse the idea of checking and honing our findings with a support group.

Within the range of qualitative researchers, there are groups who do not depend on any sort of confirmation by and with others. Those who do reflective phenomenology and heuristic research are two such groups (Tesch, 1990, p. 70). They hold the position that analysis is their idiosyncratic creation which can only be internally confirmed by them, and if they do a good job of communicating their reasoning, perhaps their results can be understood and even supported by others. This is a good example of the fact that the epistemological underpinnings of one's research shape every part of the method, and that includes how one establishes and reports the findings.

Member-Checking

There is no question but that we are wholehearted about another aspect of being credible: checking our interpretations periodically with the very people we are studying. This is called member-checking by Lincoln and Guba (1985), and it is, in their view, at the heart of establishing credibility:

> Credibility is a trustworthiness criterion that is satisfied when source respondents [like people who provided the information] agree to honor the reconstructions; that fact should also satisfy the consumer. (p. 329)

During the final months of my study I interviewed parents, siblings, and other teachers of the children I studied. As part of this process, I also shared some of my emerging findings about each child's play-style for their consideration. I felt I was at this time closer to recognizing the consistent patterns of each child's style, and more equipped with knowledge that allowed me to elicit detailed descriptions and comparisons from the informants by introducing explicit examples of what had happened. Obtaining feedback about my findings in these interviews helped me to establish credibility, but it also deepened and substantiated data gathered in other ways.

Because of the nature of my study, I did not verbally check findings with the 5-year-old children whose play styles I documented. However, when it is appropriate, most of our colleagues check directly. Matt Foley shared his findings at several points with the young people whose coping strategies in slum streets were the focus of his study. Don McGuire checked his categories and supporting evidence with his participants, young adults who had attempted suicide during ages 5 through 9. In both of these cases, the people who were studied agreed with the findings and interpretations. In one case, several people gave more descriptive examples for some of the categories. In the other, two young adults provided more detailed specifics for the case study that was written to describe their lives.

Steve Spitz's thesis was about the experience of fathers who were major caregivers to their children. Steve writes:

> As part of member-checking, I sent profiles that had been developed to the participants for their review. Barry received his just prior to Father's Day. He called me to tell me that his profile was the best Father's Day present he had ever received and that he had read it to his entire family. Mark wrote back that he had showed the profile to his wife and parents who found it to be quite moving.

Not every case of member-checking is a constructive event, however. The outcome depends on a variety of factors that include what is studied, what data are provided as feedback for the checking, the relations of the researcher to the people who are studied, and the context in which the checking occurs. Stephan Ball provided a rich description of just such an interplay of factors when he attempted to check with the faculty and administration of a British comprehensive school in which he carried out a sociological study of mixed ability grouping (Burgess, 1984, pp. 65–96). Ball, who had been a participant observer in this school for three years, provided in-progress chapters as well as a final draft to the people who were involved. He found that '... many of the staff had apparently read my chapter solely in terms of what it had to say about them in their subject' (p. 86). Further, he discovered that despite his numerous explanations, the people involved '... clearly had little idea of what sociological research was and the sort of outcomes it might produce' (p. 87). In this case, member-checking was made even more thorny because several administrators were put off by the possibility that the school would somehow be publicly recognized, judged, and found wanting. At that point, he was met with a challenge:

> The head of science continued with queries about the 'scientific' adequacy of my work. He asked what 'measures' I had used and what 'tests of significance' were employed, adding '... well, I think it comes back to what I said originally. Your sample is so tiny that you can't hope to make comments like that'. The remainder of the session consisted of my attempts to explain the epistemological basis of ethnographic research and the conflicts between positivist and interpretive sociologies. The head of science remained quite unconvinced by my arguments and finally dismissed my account as 'honestly, absolute drivel'. (p. 88)

Ball pointed out that at times the political realities are such that arriving at consensus may not be in the real interest of participants. At such times, member-checking may well fail in its ideal purpose and alternate solutions for establishing credibility must be relied upon.

We have had no such troubles with member-checking. Guba and Lincoln (1989) add:

> We should note here that in no research or evaluation project we have ever worked on or conducted has any participant or stakeholder asked to have a direct quotation removed from the final case study — even though it has become clear that others in the setting can identify its 'voice'. Few of our graduate students ever have to remove quotations from their dissertations, either, in the member-check process. (p. 133)

It is entirely possible that member-checking will create problems in some studies. Nevertheless, it seems to us that the effort to check and to discuss must be made. Particularly important is the shared discussion and what this can do to inform and to establish collegiality.

Making the Story

You're ready to tell it. Your job here is to create a text in which the person or persons you have learned about come to life. This means that you have a tremendous responsibility to be true to their meanings. The written presentation is of crucial importance: in a deep sense, what one writes *is* what happened and what was learned. The presentation, not what is held privately in the head and heart of the researcher, is what exists about the research. What one writes can make what was studied tangible, compelling, credible, or flat, uninteresting, questionable.

Nervous? I'm with you. I suddenly have an awful urge to clean the fingerprints I just noticed on the wall above my computer, but delving right into writing is the better action. The first draft is not the final one after all. This is a time of individual and lonely expression. Your support group and other sources of inspiration help, but in the end only you can put it all together and expose the meaning. I lost ten pounds, lived in a single room so I would not be distracted, and thanked God I had the summer off from my elementary teaching in order to give my all to the perilous journey of organizing the chaos, final analysis, and writing.

Little demons came to me, too. I would be working steadily, finally, and up would pop one of my demons with a question: Are you absolutely sure you have the facts as they existed for the children you observed? Other questions: Are you positive that all your data are here in this room? Suppose the house burns down? Why didn't I transfer everything to a computer instead of insisting I couldn't afford one and could depend more on my typewriter? One summer did not bring me to the completion of organizing the chaos, much less the final analyses, but my room remained spotless and I remained contentedly hopeful.

Although writing the completed account is usually discussed as a culminating activity, as we are doing here, there are those who advise researchers to begin written drafts while still in the field just as analysis is begun during these early stages. Wolcott (1988, p. 200) draws on his own experience in suggesting strategies for beginning the narrative:

> It is splendid indeed if one is able to follow the advice to prepare a first draft while fieldwork is still in progress. In attempting to set down in writing what you understand, you become most acutely aware of what you do *not*

understand and can recognize 'gaps' in the data while time remains to make further inquiry. But lacking the time, practice, or perspective required for drafting a full account, one can nonetheless begin to 'think' in chapters, sections, or expanded outlines, and thus keep tuned to the difficult task sometimes dismissed as simply 'writing up one's notes'.

Wolcott goes on to suggest that 'wherever and whenever the task of writing begins ... begin at a relatively easy place'. Most of us and many colleagues have started with a description of our entry into the field and a 'grand tour' (Spradley, 1980) account of our fieldwork as a whole. Margaret, whose observations spanned two school years, used the summer between them to start writing her 'overview' chapter and to work on the presentation of one approach to classroom interactions. So, if we are fortunate, we will begin with chunks of writing already in draft form. But however we begin, it is with the purpose of shaping a complete descriptive account that meshes our fieldwork with the interpretations that have emerged from our analyses.

Finding a Voice

Among our basic tasks in making a story are cultivating personal style and finding a voice. These are choices that we must make as writers and ideally we do so consciously. When we undertake academic writing, however, we often let that choice be made for us. 'Academics-in-training ... adopt what they see around them, the style professional journal articles and books are written in, as an appropriate signal of guild membership' (Becker, 1986, pp. 39–40).

Becker tells the story of one of his doctoral students whose initial drafts of dissertation chapters were written in the academic conventions she considered 'classy', what we sometimes term 'dissertationese'. When Becker pressed her to remove 'redundancy and academic flourish', she wrote in reply:

> While I personally find scholarly writing boring and prefer to spend my time reading novels, academic elitism is a part of every graduate student's socialization. I mean that academic writing is not English but is written in a shorthand that only members of the profession can decipher.... I think it is a way to maintain group boundaries of elitism.... Ideas are supposed to be written in such a fashion that they are difficult for untrained people to understand. This is scholarly writing. And if you want to be a scholar, you need to learn to reproduce this way of writing.

We wish we could give more space to Becker's student and her story in our book. Since that cannot be, we refer all who are concerned with the issues of 'dissertationese', or 'classy' scholarly writing to Becker. Fortunately for us all, we are working at a time when even in academic circles scholars are expressing themselves in clearer, more direct, and personal voices. We recognize also that each one of us may go about actualizing our own voice differently.

Creating a Narrative

The writing of a qualitative research report demands the creation of a narrative. Although concerned specifically with case studies, a United States General Accounting Office booklet (1987) includes the following about the narrative heart of qualitative writing:

> Case studies are usually reported as narratives that read like chronologies of what led up to an event and what happened during and after it.... In this respect, the narrative mode is not a stylistic choice, it is inherent in the purpose of case studies and the nature of their inquiry. (p. 59)

The writing of a narrative is the telling of a tale after all. As such, and with important differences, the process has much in common with all other literary undertakings. Some of the students we worked with were highly conscious of the similarities with fiction. Raimundo Mora was particularly intrigued by the artistic nature of ethnographic writing:

> When I read the most recent novel by Gabriel García Márquez, *Amor en los Tiempos de Colera*, I found that its structure was similar to an ethnographic study. This novel describes a love affair from the point of view of five different characters. Each of these characters belongs to a different geographic and socioeconomic world. Each version of the events reveals a different psychological and social interpretation.

Laura Berns undertook a study of a computer lab. A student of literature, she had a heightened awareness of the process of composing in 'a whole new genre'. Although speaking here of her log, the comparisons she draws are even more relevant to writing the final report.

> As something of a closet novelist, I took delight in the unfolding of this 'story' in a computer lab. A log, though, is clearly a different genre. In writing fiction, the details — the single gold earring, the sigh, the 'Oh, shit!' — are put there intentionally because they contribute to the writer's preconceived notion of character or plot or theme. But this careful selection, this filtering of details to fit a 'theory', is anathema for case study research, which encourages an open mind, an inductive strategy in which data are first collected and only later analyzed for categories, patterns, themes. Yet, even in the

'real' world, we are of necessity always selecting tidbits of data from a vast smorgasbord. I was never able to resolve this difficulty to my satisfaction, with the result that my log seemed at times to be a random assortment of details and at other times to be leading covertly to an implicit 'conclusion'.

In fact, on one gloomy February morning, I was suddenly struck by one of those insights that makes up a bit for the grubbier parts of being a graduate student. I was struck by how dependent I was upon my prior knowledge in making sense of the situation and how inextricably external 'facts' are bound up with interpretation. I was aware of how my interpretation of Bill's saying, 'How do I get it to double-space?' was dependent upon my prior understanding of computers, of the writing course, of learning theories, of human motivation. Indeed, even my 'knowledge' that Bill was a first-year college student enrolled in a computer section of Writing 2 — not an instructor or a freeloading senior writing a paper for Economics 453 — was based upon interpretation.

This relativistic viewpoint was not intellectually novel, as it is a theme that surfaces insidiously in nearly every graduate course I take. I read Bruner's *In Search of Mind* (1983) and stumble over his New Look revelation that there is no 'immaculate perception'. I read literary theory, to find a shared assumption, even among the warring camps of structuralist, deconstructionist, and reader response critics, that the interpretation of a text is dependent upon the reader's prior knowledge. But what was new that February morning as I struggled to write my log was the experiential, pre-verbal revelation of the pervasiveness of interpreting in routine situations.

The point for us to remember, of course, is that the ongoing mental act of interpreting is here consciously harnessed in the service of presenting the context we have studied as fully and richly as possible. If in our logs we have learned to include every detail we can manage, always remembering, as Laura expressed it, that 'we are of necessity selecting tidbits of data', when we compose our final reports we become even more selective. Although our aim is to portray natural settings and phenomena, the writing is crafted. It is a construction by an author.

Description should transport the reader to the scene, convey the pervasive qualities or characteristics of the phenomenon, and evoke the feeling and nature of the ... experience.... The use of [linguistic] devices should create a description so vivid the reader can almost see it and hear it. (Ross, 1988, p. 166)

John Van Maanen (1988) has spotlighted three distinct styles of ethnographic writing which he categorizes as realist tales, confessional tales, and impressionist tales. He characterizes the three forms of tale as follows:

Realist tales ... provide a rather direct, matter-of-fact portrait of a studied culture, unclouded by much concern for how the field worker produced such a portrait.... Confessional tales focus far more on the fieldworker than on the cultures studied.... Impressionist tales are personalized accounts of fleeting moments of fieldwork cast in dramatic form; they therefore carry elements of both realist and confessional writing. (p. 7)

We find that we are most familiar with realist tales, and Van Maanen presents them as the most prevalent and familiar form of ethnographic writing (1988, p. 45). In them, the researcher 'vanishes behind a steady descriptive narrative'. In some realist tales, the narrator adopts the device of allowing various informants to speak for themselves. John Devine did a preliminary study of the experience of Haitian students in an urban high school. Here is how he handled the weaving together of voices he had documented:

> At the most basic level, one must clarify who the 'I' of the resear-
> cher is for each successive narrative or story. This past year, I found
> that at times, the 'I' of the storyteller was myself because it was I
> who had interacted with the Haitian student. At other times, I was
> recounting a tale told me by a Haitian teacher who had in turn
> interacted with a student; in this case, the teacher, my informant,
> was the 'I'. In a third case, it was the principal telling me how he had
> handled a suicide threat, and in a fourth, it was a tutor from the
> university explaining how overjoyed a student was in getting an
> award.

Although this team and our students have all written in the realist mode, most of us find that there are confessional elements woven into our realist tales. This is particularly evident when we write about our reflections upon qualitative methods in the discussion toward the end of the research report.

As this writing team has discussed the role of the 'confessional tale', we have found ourselves uncomfortable with this term. Ann has written to this point in the postscript which appears at the end of this chapter. The term 'autobiographical account' is used by some of the writers in *The Research Process in Educational Settings: Ten Case Studies*, edited by Robert G. Burgess (1984), and we prefer that usage, just as we also concur with certain points made there. Burgess offers the following rationale for having presented a collection of autobiographical accounts of research studies:

> The accounts that have been provided in this book focus upon personal and
> professional issues in the research process as well as technical matters. While
> each account highlights different aspects of the research process, they all point
> towards several broadly similar lessons that can be learned. First, that
> research is a social process and as such is worthy of study in its own right.
> Secondly, that doing research is not merely about techniques of social

investigation but about the ways in which studies begin and are funded, access is obtained, relationships formed, methods used, data recorded, and analyses conducted. Finally, they also indicate the importance of examining the ways in which evidence is accepted, rejected, and received. In these terms, the accounts would seem to have much to offer. (pp. 251–2)

Paul Atkinson (Burgess, 1984), who writes about such issues as handling the 'familiar' and the 'strange' as researchers conduct studies in their own society, concludes by stating:

> ... while we can often learn much from autobiographical confessionals, they should be used to develop more systematic perspectives on the conduct of ethnographic research.
> ... We make some things 'strange' against a background of unexamined assumptions. The value of autobiography and reflection may be in helping us to conjure up and confront ... personal and methodological failings. (p. 182)

We recognize that there are objections in the literature to autobiographical accounts (Burgess, 1984; Van Maanen, 1988). It is not our intent in this book to argue for more or less of these confessional tales. It is our intent to highlight the characteristics of qualitative work. One such is that most researchers in this mode bring to the reader their reasoning as well as their stumbles and reservations about their findings. For these people, this sharing is considered essential. What needs to be understood is that researchers in all paradigms have some joys, some doubts and reservations. Airing these is extremely valuable to understanding results as well as to fashioning future research projects. In our opinion, every report must carry at least some of this 'confessional' element, whatever it is labeled.

Van Maanen (1988) notes that impressionist tales 'are typically enclosed within realist, or perhaps more frequently, confessional tales' (p. 106). Perhaps it is here that our instincts as storytellers take over most strongly. Ellen Klohman describes the powerful pull of this creative urge:

> I should be writing this down. This is important and I'll forget it if I don't describe it. I should be writing and I'm not. This is an important story. It should be told, but I don't know how to start it. There's a novel here or at least a short story. How should it start? Can I possibly get the feel of it — the *angst*, the terror, the joy, the relief. Why can't I think about anything but writing?
> Never let it be said that the 'voice of the turtle' isn't heard by the ethnographer! In fact at times it seems that nothing else can be heard above the din of the ethnography muse urging that every incident, every utterance be captured and recorded. The artistic impulse that lurks just beneath the surface of every ethnographic study is a strong

and demanding force that gives no rest from endless 'important' scenarios that the ethnographer encounters each day.

What advice is there for those newly afflicted with the condition? Accept the creative urge and find out what it can teach is the counsel of some seasoned ethnographers.

> Social scientists probably have a lot to learn from novelists and essayists. They'd best not set themselves apart, but rather try to understand what it is that they can learn from them to improve their own trade. (Bogdan and Biklen, 1982)

Narrative Devices

We discussed the narrative and rhetorical devices of themes, social rules, and constructs/vignettes in the section of this chapter entitled 'The Final Analysis of Data' (pp. 140–56). Usually such formulations begin to take shape, at least in the researcher's mind, or as framework for analysis, long before making the final story. We have found that most researchers combine a number of approaches to presentation. We have also noted that each person brings a particular shade of newness to the writing. It may be in the color, or order of presentation, in a particularly vibrant way of using quotations, or in presenting a new narrative device.

Some other narrative devices that have served in telling the story are these:

- A case, or a story over time about a bounded system such as one person, one event, or one institution that was the focus of study, in order to illuminate important findings about that person or about the entire broader social unit. Oral histories sometimes take this form. Gail Cueto wrote several individual stories over time about the re-entry process of Latino youth offenders after being in prison.
- Composites which are similar to constructs/vignettes but which describe findings that apply to a group of people rather than to any one unique individual. Ann used this device to describe, for example, a group of teachers who changed their view of authority in their classroom.
- Descriptions of 'critical incidents' in the data. These are incidents that carried important meaning about what was being studied and, so, were considered hallmarks of the findings. Margaret used this device in her study about children's reponses to literature.
- Presentation of 'snapshots, moving pictures, and reruns' (Lofland, 1971). I used these devices. The 'snapshot' was a written description that attempted to paint a single picture which captured the totality of

one child's play style. In Chapter 2 we included a snapshot of the beginning of our class. The 'moving picture' was written to illuminate the dominant time-oriented sequences of a child's play style. The 're-run' was written to describe cycles of activity within one child's play.

- Studies in contrasts and contradictions. These are seen by Werner and Schoepfle (1987) as '... The secret of fertile ethnographic insights' (p. 61). Contradictions have been presented in a variety of ways: Debrah Goldberg offered side-by-side vignettes of an 'outsider' and an 'insider' in a kindergarten classroom, each of whom had a vastly different experience there. In that same study, Debbie highlighted the contrasting reports and observed behaviors of other teachers toward these same two children. Gail Cueto related the stories of their re-entry from prison to wider community of a small number of Latino youth by contrasting what these people said and what they did, both in and out of prison. Maryann Downing, Belén Matías, Margaret, and Margot illustrated four versions of the same classroom experience in what they called the Rashomon Syndrome by focusing on contrasts as well as agreements.

Revising

In spite of our best efforts, sometimes our narrative devices can fall flat. It is often frustrating as well as depressing to read one's own text only to know that it does not do justice to the study. Courage! There is always the fact that writing means continual revision:

> Revision is commonly regarded as a central and important part of writing. It may powerfully affect writers' knowledge. Revision enables writers to muddle through and organize what they know in order to find a line of argument, to learn anew, and to discover what was not known before. (Fitzgerald, 1987, p. 480)

Revision may be onerous, but it is a very necessary element in completing the analysis and telling the story. Strauss (1987) adds another twist to the meaning of revision as he relates how the writing process and the research process intertwine, even at this final juncture:

> Ideally all of the integration, or at least its major features, should have been accomplished by the time that actual writing for publication takes place. Yet even when a first draft of a monograph (or the initial articles) is written, understandably, researchers always find themselves discovering something

that tightens up or extends the total analysis. When the first draft is reviewed and revised one or more times — sometimes many more — then
additional integrative details may be added. Even entire integrative steps
may be taken, since further data collecting or at least further coding may be
deemed necessary, not only to add more detail but to add to the final
integration of the analysis. (p. 212)

Indeed, Strauss's 'rules of thumb' for final analysis and writing (pp. 213–14)
have been a valuable resource to many of us. The following advice seems
particularly germane:

> ... you must fight the temptation to be finished, to wash your hands of this
> project once and for all. You are finished, when finished! On the other
> hand, do not go to the other extreme ... and spend years tinkering with the
> product long after it could have withstood public scrutiny, and perhaps long
> after its effective impact might have been made. (Strauss, 1987, p. 214)

Personal Work Strategies

Finally, it benefits each one of us to honor our personal work strategies.
Margot must write in longhand, insists that she solves writing snags while she
sleeps, and writes in spurts until the time when she slaves demonically away,
eighteen hours at a stretch. Ann writes only and directly on her computer,
must sometimes find a place away from her home to write, and works still to
overcome her feeling that she really cannot write, all the while she is writing.
I myself run hot and cold. For example, for this book I was the first person to
write a draft because I knew I'd need numerous revisions. I write copiously
about my travels, while for other purposes I sometimes pull a dramatic
farewell to the whole business, only to return to writing when I've cooled off.

It may help all of us to know that many of our strategies and feelings are
shared. It may also help to take a break.

> It is wise to lay your report aside for a while after having written it: for a
> few days, a week, months, or even a year or more. We all tend to develop a
> mental attitude toward a piece of work we are involved in — a particular
> 'locked-in' view of what we are doing. It may well happen that your attitude
> is a good and insightful one. Then again, it may not. By backing off from a
> piece of writing for a while, forgetting and losing your commitment to what
> you had in mind, you can later come back with a fresh view. (Lofland and
> Lofland, 1984, p. 150)

In terms of dissertation writing, people have found that an exceedingly long
break is not helpful. There are often prices to be paid for such long breaks
like the 'cooling' of one's feel for the data. Try a vacation, not a divorce.

Postscript

This postscript comes from three people, Ann, Diane, and Margot. Each person speaks in her own voice.

Ann

I'd like to share with you why I take exception to Van Maanen's use of the word 'confessional' in his analysis of types of naturalistic writing. My two objections are both on the grounds of the unfortunate connotations of the word. For Catholics, and many others, 'to confess' means to unburden one's soul of transgressions. The confessional is a place for seeking forgiveness from God. Naturalistic writing may relieve some participants of the burden of long-kept secrets, but it is not the intention for the writer to be forgiven, nor is it a forum for forgiveness.

Journalism is another context that suggests inappropriate connotations for the use of this word in naturalistic inquiry. In journalism, confessional writing connotes some of its worst excesses of emotionalism. The 'sob sister' story is one type of journalistic confessional writing, and much of what appears in tabloids, when not accusatory, purports to be confessional in nature.

Perhaps a better term for this sort of naturalistic writing might be 'revelatory'. It is characteristic that qualitative researchers reveal. Revealing one's research thoughts and actions is both an inherent imperative and a strength of the methodology. The public sharing of insights, reasoning, emotions, changes, consistencies — whatever — is done in the service of helping the readers to 'be there' with the researcher, to understand, and to make their own assessments of the research in informal ways. That is a far cry from the commonly understood purposes of confessing.

Diane

I was profoundly engaged in making final meaning of my study; so much so that it took me a while to get the distance I needed to be a bit more clear about what it was that touched me so deeply. I believe it was this: in studying the children, I connected to the child in me, the child I had not forgotten, the child I came to again when another child mirrored my own face of long ago.

Upon becoming aware of this, I took special care in forming categories and developing themes so that it was not the child in me who powered analytical decisions. But it was the child in me who could compare experiences. For example, my story of Chris and his need to gain approval of others while maintaining his independence resonated strongly with my own memories. Chris and I walked similar paths. But it also became clear that the paths were not the same. My study of Chris provided both similarities and contrasts to my own experience. I feel that my understanding of Chris was substantially heightened by actively reflecting on my own life.

If my insights hold for others, then the task of searching for meaning as one writes begins with the crucial task of discovering ourselves, and our understanding of others in the final analytic presentation can only be as profound as the wisdom we possess as we look inward upon ourselves. Forgive me if I preach. Perhaps it was Arthur Jersild in his *When Teachers Face Themselves* (1955) who inspired me in my final reflections, but then I myself experienced that one can profit from trying to catch the meaning of one's own life when one strives to catch the meaning of the lives of others.

As you write, keep yourself actively up front. To be personally passive in ethnographic research may be dangerous to the health of what you are doing.

Margot

In this chapter (p. 145), we mention that we applied three criteria in order to select topics about final analysis. The third criterion states that we focus on those characteristics of analysis that are common to a large number of qualitative research approaches. I believe these commonalities deserve special mention because they are essential to understanding those analytical methods and some other major messages in this book.

In her 1990 work, Tesch discusses the results of analyzing texts on qualitative analysis for common characteristics of analytical principles and procedures (pp. 95–7). While at first no universal characteristics held, when Tesch omitted both extremes — the formal, most quantitatively based types of analysis, and the most obscure, unspecified types — she did develop ten principles and practices that hold true for the remaining types of analysis, from ethnomethodology to phenomenology (in addition, of course, to the usual principles of good scholarship such as honesty and ethical conduct) (p. 95)

In a condensed version, here are the ten common characteristics.

1   Analysis is not the last phase of the research process; it is concurrent with data collection or cyclic. Both analysis and data collection inform each other.
2   The analysis process is systematic, but not rigid. The analysis ends when new data no longer generate new insights.
3   Attending to data includes a reflective activity that results in a set of analytical notes that guide the process.

4 Data are 'segmented', i.e., divided into relevant meaning 'units', yet the connection to the whole is maintained. The analysis always begins with reading all data so as to provide context for the smaller pieces.

5 The data segments are categorized according to an organizational system that is predominantly derived from the data themselves.

6 The main intellectual tool is comparison. The goal is to discern conceptual similarities, to refine the discriminative power of categories and to discover patterns.

7 Categories for sorting segments are tentative and preliminary in the beginning; they remain flexible.

8 Manipulating qualitative data during analysis is an eclectic activity; there is no one right way.

9 The procedures are neither 'scientific' nor 'mechanistic'; qualitative analysis is 'intellectual craftsmanship'. (Mills, 1959)

10 The result of the analysis is some type of higher level synthesis. (Tesch, 1990, pp. 95–97)

Although this list is presented here, in Chapter 5, the essence of these ten items applies to various sections throughout the book. You might examine our chapters in terms of these ten characteristics. For example, where and how do we talk of concurrent data collection and analysis? How do we treat each of the other commonalities?

Here is one good test for this book. How does it measure up?

Chapter 6

Reflecting

Introducing Margaret and This Chapter

Up to this point in this book we have been looking forward to, or looking straight at, the planning and undertaking of a qualitative research project and the writing of a research report. Now we are going to take a backward look at the collected experiences of the 'we' whose voices are heard in these pages.

I feel that a sense of shared experience is especially helpful for researcher like us as we first enter into any new endeavor. Perhaps it is because we are most raw and vulnerable then. Everything is new and unexpected — especially our own unanticipated emotions. I sensed my own beginnings as a qualitative researcher at a particularly lonely time — no colleagues close at hand, no support group. Now I realize that even for researchers with more props, the first times are intense and lonely. I am the only member of this writing team who was not also a member of the teaching team during the gathering of the papers which form the database of this book. This means that the papers have come to me weeks or months after the end of a term, and covered with the comments of both the group facilitators and Margot. As the students wrote of their most meaningful experiences, among the more common teacher comments were 'You're in good company', 'This is not unusual', 'Many have found this to be true', and Margot's familiar 'Me too!' It has been one of our goals throughout this book to extend the circle of shared experience and to affirm the value of the personal and emotional as well as the methodological and cognitive learnings that never cease to accompany our research efforts.

Now, as we look back over what we have written, we seek to lift our affirming 'Me too!' to yet another level. Since this is not only a handbook but also an analysis of the learning experiences of both beginning and more experienced qualitative researchers, it seems natural to follow a familiar format — a discussion of our findings in this final chapter. Doing qualitative research is by nature a reflective and recursive process. The preceding chapters are structured to parallel the steps followed in conducting qualitative research, not exhaustively, but as our students, our colleagues, our outside references, and we ourselves have experienced them. The entire work is thus reflective, personal, and meta-analytic in nature. We are now at the point of reflecting upon the reflections, so to speak — of working within the 'hall of mirrors' (Anzul and Ely, 1988).

In this chapter we have singled out five overarching meta-themes that have emerged from our data and that seem to us to have significance as we follow our dual callings as researchers and professionals. The themes we highlight are:

I   Learning by doing qualitative research can become a powerful process that is often described in vital metaphors.
II   As qualitative researchers, we become aware of ourselves as contingent, interactive, open to change as a way of life.
III The processes of qualitative research also become processes of professional growth.
IV   Qualitative researchers often feel as though they are shouting across a paradigmatic rift.
V   Ethical concerns are woven through every step of qualitative research.

Theme I: Learning by Doing Qualitative Research Can Become a Powerful Process That Is Often Described in Vital Metaphors

As I read through the accumulated student 'articles' for the first time, I was struck by the frequency with which the authors wove in and played with metaphor.

Part of what we have to learn, it seems, is to clear and fine tune our senses so that we can take in the worlds we need to study, something like the way an infant does air for the first time. (Deborah Lamb)

Getting along as far as I did was something akin to a roller coaster ride. (Laura Lee Lustbader)

I felt like Tevye in *Fiddler on the Roof* dealing with major philosophical issues. Tevye raises his hands to the sky and talks to himself. (Sharon Lefkofsky)

Shedding a snake's skin is easier than shedding cherished assumptions. (Diane Person)

I felt like the tortoise at the end of the line, doggedly plodding along. (Yukiko Okada)

My first interview can be compared to taking a puppy for a walk. (Ewa Iracka)

You know that if you run with your head down, you create a very large blind spot for yourself. The blind spot is right in front of you. You never see where you're heading until you're there. If you're lucky, you won't run into any trees along the way. It's amazing how some of us can run through a forest and never see a single tree. I felt somewhat fortunate to have made it through without hitting one headfirst. (John Forconi)

Just when I was getting big enough to 'fit my britches', the suspenders broke ... I began interviewing and meta-analyzing and all the observations that fit nicely into categories began to bulge and pucker. (Jo Ann Saggese)

You walk through the looking glass of your observations, and encounter a whole host of strange characters, which come to include yourself. (Deborah Lamb)

We are peeling the onion, with each layer of interpretation removed only exposing another layer beneath. (Laura Berns)

'Being fair' is letting yourself and the subject of your research unravel like thread off a spool that slips between unsewn spaces. 'Being fair' is taking your hand and piecing the threads together, justifying them whole. (Wendy Hesford)

The surprise seduction of this methodology.... (Beatriz Abreu)

I felt like an archeologist on a very special 'dig'. How slowly and carefully I dug out my 'fragments'! (Belén Matías)

... the pressure to get my dissertation done within a tight time frame has made me feel like my head has a cloud floating above it, my neck has a noose around it, or my ankle is shackled with a ball and chain — take your pick. (Annie Hauck Lawson)

As a teacher, I tend to be quite conscious of students' spontaneous use of metaphor because metaphor-making signifies a high quality of learning. Scholars in the field refer to metaphor as a 'conceptual leap' (Sacks, 1979). The process of making metaphors involves making new meanings or generating new frames of reference within which problems are considered (Schön, 1979). It may also signal a conflict with prior expectations (Swanson, 1978) or a 'creative, pleasurable, or inventive act'. Paul Ricoeur (1979) discusses how working with metaphor is not only a cognitive act, but involves imagination and feeling as well. From this perspective, a high degree of metaphor-making has educational significance. It would appear to indicate that students are actively growing into new knowledge and doing so with a certain passion. In most of the papers, of course, there were the stock metaphors that are part of the idiomatic baggage of American English, and I am not concerned with those here. When the students in the qualitative research classes chose to detail their most meaningful experiences in metaphoric terms, they frequently selected metaphors of immediate personal significance and developed them at some length in ways that were often ingenious, sometimes amusing, and sometimes deeply touching.

For ease in discussing, I have divided the uses of metaphor into three categories, each of which is discussed in a separate section:

1 metaphors that described the learning of qualitative methods or the acquisition of attitudes supportive of these methods;
2 metaphors that portrayed research-as-life/life-as-research; and
3 metaphors that connected with the transformation of the self during the qualitative research process.

Learning Qualitative Methods and Attitudes

> Surprise! Surprise! Surprise! What may come as a surprise is your reaction to qualitative processes. My classmates and I laughed, cried, integrated, refused to believe, and were puzzled by them. (Beatriz Abreu)

Our students, our colleagues, and we have all been educated within the positivist paradigm, and most of us come to the naturalistic paradigm formed by many years of intellectual discipline. We would not choose to work in a new mode if we did not consider it advantageous, but even with eagerness and the best will, we struggle with the difficulties of shedding carefully nurtured and honed habits of work and developing new ones.

Among the most fundamental of these habits and attitudes are those that relate to control. Many of us come to research believing that every step must be planned beforehand, that we must be in total control of 'variables'. As we grow into this new paradigm, we find that we must become unexpectedly flexible as we learn to deal with emergent design, emergent patterns of analysis, emergent everything. For some of us, set structure and a lack of flexibility had been viewed as virtues or at least as necessary vices. For others, the realization that we were less flexible than we thought was one of the surprises we had to face and to conquer.

> I marched out to meet the world of ethnography prepared in starched, crisp form, only to find starch to be the number one cause of *angst*. Ethnography is not a method of research for the rigid (Ann Vartanian)

Then there is one of our favorite comments by John Forconi that we have used in Chapter 4:

> Now you're ready to learn the most important thing you'll ever find throughout your academic career. You are going to learn to become flexible. I mean you, the epitome of rigidity, are about to bend over and literally touch your forehead to the floor and leave your hands on your hips.

Students enroll in courses about the various research methodologies at different points in their individual careers as researchers, some with no experience and no plans, others with developed research proposals. Laura Cohen is representative of students who entered the course with well-developed dissertation proposals and the intention to take from the course only what they needed to carry through their already formulated plans. It came as an initial shock to some of these students when they realized that the course was structured so that they would learn by doing a range of qualitative methods, although in the end most realized, as Laura did, that there was a payoff in the added depth and rigor a variety of data collection methods provided. Laura had wanted to do a series of interviews to discover what happens when people read literature that they find therapeutic. Here is how she describes the first class sessions:

> Margot raised the possibility that we could do a pilot study for our dissertations. I knew I was on my way. I discussed my tentative plans in small groups during the second week of class and met my first obstacle. It seemed that in order to meet class objectives, I would have to do a project that entailed more than just interviewing. After an initial state of panic, I talked things over with my adviser, thought a lot and came up with a setting in which to observe that would be agreeable to all parties.
>
> The next obstacle was gaining entry.... I planned to observe a poetry therapy group at a psychiatric hospital, which required all sorts of official decisions and permissions ... I did my reading assignments and tried not to think of the days that slipped by....
>
> ... One Sunday I took a break from my studies and my family and I went roller skating. We had a great time gliding around the rink. My 6-year-old was a bit unsteady on his wheeled feet and would cling to my hand until he lost his balance and fell, laughing, to the ground. We laughed a lot that day.
>
> My laughter stopped when my son tumbled and brought me down with him. I felt something snap in my back, felt sharp pain that left me gasping, unable to move. It was only a bad muscle pull, the physician said. Stay in bed and rest for a few days until the pain goes away, he said. I did, and it didn't.

Laura was only one of many of us who have had to continue our research projects in spite of personal pain or tragedy or domestic obstacles. Like several others, she used this highly personal aspect of her life to detail her progress as a novice researcher:

> I had weeks of days that slipped by. It was five weeks before I was able to make it back to class. Even then, I spent most of the time standing to avoid sitting, which aggravated my still fragile back muscles.... I was in the field twice weekly for several weeks to make up for days that had slipped away. Doing field visits twice a week meant twice as much time with my word processor. On the plus side, doing field visits more often meant I was forced to live with the data more intensively. I think this helped me focus and analyze more effectively.
>
> There is a saying that if you can't bend, you break. This is never more true than in the process of qualitative research. The answers to questions raised in this method can be, and many times must be, answered in ways which are not predictable at the start of the research. The plan must be a plan to be flexible, to be yielding, both to the method and to the data. I started out this course with unyielding rigidity and passed through stages of progressive relaxation of my intellectual muscles. What I learned is that those muscles can be flexible even if it appears you can't bend.

Laura had developed increased skills in collecting observational data as well as in the art of interviewing to which she had originally expected to be able to confine herself. Because the exigencies of her personal life forced her to observe more intensively than she would have planned, she learned the value of that, too. But above all she learned the value of letting herself go with the process and of trusting it. This is nicely underscored by her use of metaphors.

Another student during another semester had a similar physical problem and described her complex of learning experiences in very similar terms. Ronna Ziegel woke up with a pain in the neck a few days before the course started. This was finally diagnosed two weeks later as a pinched nerve:

> Once I found out what was wrong with me and what I was looking for in my work, a hectic, unfamiliar and uncomfortable regimen began. My hours were filled, on the one hand, with physical therapy at a local hospital, daily swimming at the nearby fitness center, and miles of walking to take the place of the running I used to do. On the other hand, at work, where I am a high school English teacher, I was replacing my much needed coffee break time with hours of observation in the small yellow classroom down the hall where one of my colleagues teaches French.
>
> I'd never lived with pain over an extended period of time and

doing so, like being a researcher, required some management skills. I'd always been the kind of person who bulldozed through things I had to do and always, above all else, maintained control. I wasn't controlling either my pain or my work for a long time and it was not a good feeling. I learned that managing pain meant getting in touch with my body and listening to it. Eliminating pain often meant eliminating situations that made it worse and concentrating on those that made it better. I found what I liked and didn't like in my life by the way my neck felt. It was one hell of a barometer.

There came hours at a time where the pain was dim enough that I didn't have to listen to it. During these times, I was able to listen to other things and my research began to make a bit more sense. My neck, shoulder and back muscles became a little less tangled and so did my logs. There wasn't a light at the end of the tunnel for anything yet, but the paths were well marked. What I was doing was working somewhat, and after a bit more of the same, I knew that I could stop, re-evaluate, and refine my course even more. So I did. I added some interviews for triangulation and a bit more physical activity and carefully chosen exercises for my neck. My logs spoke often to me and showed patterns, reccurring themes, and gave me something to go on. My body smiled at me for the first time in months and it was good.

My invalid state, especially the weeks when I wore a collar, taught me a little about how society views and reacts to the infirm. My researcher hat, which at times felt as uncomfortable and confining as the collar, taught me about how society views and reacts to the strange species that haunts the field. In both situations, I sometimes felt uneasy, conspicuous, and dependent upon the kindness of strangers.

We were struck by the fact that two students, in different semesters, saw in their illness and recovery an analogy to their development as qualitative researchers. Triangulation sometimes comes in surprising ways. These two metaphoric statements highlighted the importance that the ability to be flexible, to accept and capitalize on surprises, comes to have for qualitative researchers.

People selected varied and graphic metaphors to discuss aspects of qualitative methodology. Bernice Reyes structured her paper around subheadings that played on the word 'log':

Log Rhythms and Other Melodies
Suffering from 'Log Lag'
Strolling Down Logger's Lane
Great Balls of Fire — Relating to Your Logs: Only You Can Capture the
   Pure Joy of the Moment When Illumination about Some Aspect of the
   Field Falls upon You.

Some student writers also played with the term 'field'. We have already quoted from Molly Ayhe's 'Please Don't Crash into the Field':

> You must not be fooled by the pastoral-sounding name — field. This naturally conjures up visions of meadows....

And Ewa Iracka described her first attempt at interviewing as

> ... like taking a puppy for a walk.... I now realize that obtaining a 'successful' interview is like walking a tightrope without a net while juggling sharp swords.

Many have written of the growing sense of excitement when categories for analysis begin to emerge after weeks of data collection, transcriptions, and re-reading. What had seemed endless drudgery was suddenly seen to be yielding rich rewards. Mayumi Tsutsui, who came from Japan to participate in a doctoral program in nursing, acknowledged that language problems added to the complexities of learning research methodologies. She wrote of the difficulties and frustrations of conducting interviews and maintaining a log about mothers of babies in a day care center, but ended by saying, 'I feel my observations and log are like a treasure to me'. Belén Matías used a similar metaphor when she said of her analysis, 'I'm really getting excited about this. It's like a discovery, like opening Tutankhamen's tomb. I knew it was all there, but I didn't really know how much I had'.

Life-as-Research/Research-as-Life

Some student researchers wrote of their experience of the process as a whole rather than singling out a discrete aspect. Joe Simplicio entitled his paper 'Lost on a Back Road Called Ethnography', and developed an extended metaphor about traveling on this new road.

> Life is usually a matter of treading the same road to insure that those things which have become ingrained and routine are constantly reinforced. So it is with a career in education. Research to date meant traveling Interstate 101, better known as Scientific Boulevard.

A turn off this road led him eventually to a large field where many people seemed to be busy at work, presided over by a 'learned one'.

> As I walked around I could hear many voices, too many for the small gathering I could see. I approached the learned individual and

asked, 'Where are all those voices coming from?' She answered with
a smile and said, 'From out in the field'. She gestured and it was
only then that I noticed for the first time the large field behind the
buildings. It ran as far as the eye could see in all directions. As I
looked out into the field, I saw many people. Some were sitting
quietly watching, some were speaking with others there, some were
busy writing, some seemed happy while others appeared confused or
frustrated.

I turned back to the learned one and asked again, 'What are
they doing?' 'Why not go into the field yourself and see', was her
reply. I agreed and stepped on to the fresh soil. My footing was
unsure and at first I stumbled and almost lost my balance several
times. I became scared. But, as I continued on, I noticed that this
field was not really chaotic and unorganized as I first had believed.
In fact there was a definite pattern to its existence. I walked and at
first just watched. There was so much to see and yet I understood so
little. Why were there so many people, why were there so few
machines? Soon I began to speak to others myself. My questions at
first were met with answers I did not understand. I was frustrated. It
appeared as though I had to ask my questions in a better way if I
expected answers I could understand. What was the matter with
these people anyway? Soon, though, the process of moving about
the field and asking the right types of questions became easier —
even enjoyable!

I watched, I talked, I listened, and I wrote. It seemed as though
I had only been in the field a short time, but soon I came to see that
I had gathered all kinds of little notes about the interesting people I
had met. 'Now what do I do with these?' I thought to myself. The
answer was not to be found out here in the field. 'I know, I will ask
the learned one', but no, that would mean I would have to leave the
field. Although the field confused me, especially my stop at the
lemonade stand run by a guy known as Mister Multiple Realities, I
was growing to love it. I looked for a way to solve my dilemma. My
answer, though, was the same one Dorothy had sought in the
Wizard of Oz. I had to go elsewhere and find one wiser than I. This
was, of course, the learned one. I walked slowly until I reached the
edge of the field. I turned back one more time and again saw the
busy people in it. This time, though, not all were strangers, some
even waved and smiled. I waved back. I knew that someday I would
return.

I slowly approached the learned one and she seemed to sense
both my sorrows and joys. 'Let me see what you have done', she
said. I held out my marked-up and battered works. She looked over
these (half of which she could not read) and said, 'Fine, now what
will you do?' 'Don't you know?' I asked, with surprise in both my
face and voice. 'Well, it's your work. All I can do is suggest ways to
help'. 'But there must be ONE WAY, ONE METHOD, ONE
TRUTH', I shouted. She smiled and pointed toward the field again.
I now understood.

> Today as I drive up and down Cover Story Street on my way
> back and forth to the field in my car (renamed Coder) I can hear
> that super Highway 101, old Scientific Boulevard, out in the dis-
> tance. It seems to travel so fast. It is for some I am sure, but as for
> me I think my little voice was correct. I'll stay where I am.

Nick Surdo opened his paper with an extended analogy in which he
likens various aspects of collecting qualitative data to a former period in his
life when he worked as a dairy farmer. Another student, Liz Tucker, wrote a
paper entitled 'Basketball and the Ethnographic Team: Playing to Win'.

> I still wonder at the strong connection in my mind between basket-
> ball and ethnographic research. But then, it makes some sense.
> Basketball is a game that employs participant observation and re-
> quires skills such as ball-handling, dribbling, passing, guarding, and
> shooting. These skills are developed through practice and good
> coaching. Natural skills include reach, speed, coordination, and the
> ability to analyze a situation and think quickly. Ethnographic re-
> search is a type of research that is observational in nature and
> employs talking with people also. It requires skills such as people-
> handling, writing, problem-solving, keen insight, and focus. Natural
> skills include depth, timing, coordination and the ability to analyze a
> situation and think carefully.

Several students, particularly those in counseling and psychiatric social
work, found many correspondences as well as contrasts between their professions and aspects of qualitative methodologies. These are not quoted here
because they contribute to Theme III as aspects of professional growth. The
point is that, in many cases, whatever was most central to the writer's life
became the analogue for the ethnographic experience. Not all of these
metaphors 'work'. Some would not hold up under close scrutiny. There are
certainly some I could quarrel with on one issue or another. These examples
are included here to illustrate the power that this learning experience had for
many.

Some of the studies conducted as course work were deeply touching.
Laura Lee Lustbader's struggles with herself as she slowly and painfully
learned to interview a young mental patient have already been discussed in
Chapter 4. To introduce this account, she developed an analogy with the
bittersweet tale of Anna and the King of Siam.

> ... 'getting to know all about you. Getting to like you, getting to
> hope you like me'. Anna and the King of Siam had quite a time
> trying to learn about each other. It was an experience that was
> heart-breaking yet held the potential for achieving great joys in the
> knowledge revealed and shared. It was both fearful and attractive,

intimidating and yet freeing. Two minds, two cultures and histories
— meeting in the persons of one man and one woman. Together, as
well as each alone, they made something wonderful!

The patience, desire, and willingness to learn that were involved
in the developing saga of Anna and the King of Siam are top among
the ingredients necessary when one is about to embark on a journey
as a qualitative researcher. All of us who grew up loving the story of
The King and I recognized that what we were most attracted to was
the strength of character in each personality. Each time the end of
the play is viewed, I sit there, glued to my seat, wishing the final
scene will be different — the King will survive his broken heart, the
conflict of cultures will loom less in the shadows, and he and Anna
shall live on, happily ever after. Endings, however, are not always as
sweet as we wish, and the recognition of time and cultural boundaries is of the essence in knowing that the King must die. There
simply was no other alternative.

Why am I going on so about Anna and the King? It is because
as a graduate student making my first attempt at qualitative research,
I frequently found myself in one quandary or another that reminded
me of their story.

Later Laura refers to the 'roller coaster ride' of the emotions during successive
interviews with this young woman over time as she patiently tried to maintain
a spirit of trust.

Even more intimately involving analogies have been developed by those
who likened their experiences within the naturalistic paradigm to sexual
encounters, marriage or parenthood:

> I feel as if I were married to experimental methodology and through
> this course had a love affair with qualitative methodology. What has
> this done to my marriage? It's too soon to tell.

So wrote Beatriz Abreu, and then went on to explain the insights that
working with qualitative methods had given her:

> I can tell you I took this course because my advisor insisted it would
> expand my thinking. She and I knew how set I was on the quantita-
> tive method. Well, I took the risk: I went along with her suggestion.
> Criticizing and comparing methods were always in my mind. I knew
> this class was an intellectual exercise for me. But it turned out to be
> different. It has been a very powerful emotional experience.
>
> My method for my dissertation research relies on a costly and
> sophisticated tool. I had just finished doing a pilot study and my
> findings showed 'no statistical significance'. My experimental
> methodology professor encouraged me by saying the scores are
> spread differently among normal and abnormal subjects. I
> videotaped my experimental study, and from observation I could

demonstrate the differences — differences that could not be picked up by the sophisticated tool that records cycles-per-second changes! I learned to trust myself and have faith in myself as an imperfect instrument. The process was not easy and, honestly, I still hope to use my high-tech tool if I can. The difference is in how I feel. Now I believe that technological instrumentation is not the only answer in scientific inquiry.

The feelings of surprise and anxiety that accompanied the move into an unfamiliar paradigm were pictured even more graphically by Rena Smith:

> I can't do this ... be 'natural' in post-positivistic, naturalistic methodology. This whole business of me (ME?!) being the instrument, complete with my value-bound inquiry and multiple realities is making me crazy. Where, oh where, is 'control?' What about the 'old' words like mom and apple pie, hypotheses, and statistical power? ... I feel like I've entered some weird erogenous zone that should be written up in *Cosmopolitan*. We spoke about the dangers of being co-opted, how to disguise the name you select, the dangers of 'being too tight?' What is this experience of, ... sex? orgasm?
>
> In starting the case study (read, THE CASE STUDY!), I feel like I did when I had sex the first time. All of a sudden, there's a whole new language to learn and all new feelings to experience, and it surely doesn't feel like I think 'RESEARCH' should feel. Then again, neither did sex — and I sure don't feel comfortable about either subject....
>
> ... Tonight Margot spoke of having faith, that patterns would come if you do enough logs. That's no help. It's like telling someone that you will have an orgasm if you have sex often enough. It doesn't necessarily follow. And I have one more thing to worry about. Will I 'come' to the patterns she's talking about? What if I don't? Am I then dysfunctional?

As can be seen from the sampling of student concerns represented in these pages, concerns about control and its loss and the efforts of the novice researchers, with the urging of their mentors, to be flexible, to be open to change, to trust the process, ran like a thread through many of the writings. Maria del Carmen Diaz likened it to parenthood:

> It was the lack of control over the situation and the people that frightened me. I felt the same way most parents feel the first time their child goes before an audience. But if you are like me and thrive on challenges, enjoy learning about yourself, and enjoy other people, then naturalistic case study is for you. The rewards are as close to the rewards you experience being a parent without the nine months and the eighteen years that follow.

We, the writing team, had already become aware that, for some of the students, their encounters with qualitative methodologies were so powerful that they were at least temporarily thinking in metaphors of life-as-ethnography or ethnography-as-life. Deborah Lamb was married during the mid-semester break. In her final paper she invited us to 'walk in her shoes (they are white satin, very chic!)' as she considered her forays into research through the lens of her recent marriage.

> Some people say all research is me-search. I did not intend to have my sister's death, my mother's bout with cancer, my marriage plans or my own medical history come creeping into my field work; but like the fearfully imagined night creatures looming large as a child's imagination under the bed at night, these things clamored for a place in my study and made themselves at home. The interconnected layers of self-as-researcher and woman becoming a wife emerged in my log and began to structure the project at hand as systematically and elegantly as the tiers of the wedding cake awaiting us at Spring Break....
>
> ... Even in the age of ABD's, divorce, and career changes, to commit yourself to a dissertation or similarly important project is, like marriage, a rite of passage — a journey towards a 'terminal' degree or endpoint, with consequences. Assuming one lives through the process of engagement or entry to the field, a commitment to 'stay for the duration' may arise and mark a transition from one part of life or research to what is to come. In my case, each step I made into the inevitable growing up tasks that were part of this wedding led me further into a domain of authorship and responsibility previously only flirted with. In a parallel way, my interest and enthusiasm for the case study method deepened as the relationships which developed with colleagues and research partners grew. My courage in facing the life-and-death issues I wanted to study ebbed and flowed, just like I had thoughts of running away to Paris by myself many times before the wedding day. Just as I faced my fears of depending on and revealing myself to a mate, my fears of losing him and being responsible equally, so I wrestled with demons in my log and talked of stumbling blocks and uncertainties with my group members and teachers. In searching for new means of accountability and trustworthiness as a researcher, I came to know more intimately my own needs.

Transformation of Self during the Qualitative Process

Although much use of metaphor was spread across all the topics the student researchers chose to discuss, there was a particular concentration in the cluster of papers in which the writers dealt with the personal transformation of self that working within the naturalistic paradigm implied for them. The excerpts in the preceding section also reveal a high degree of self-awareness and insight on the part of the writers. They have tended, however, to focus more on the changes necessary to accept the claims and to work within this unfamiliar methodology. For some of us, and I place myself in their number, a growing understanding of the philosophical bases of the naturalistic research paradigm has accompanied an overall broadening and refining of world view, a redefinition of values, the development of what the Loflands call a 'transcendent' view, so that we can say in their words, 'You are not the person you were when you began' (Lofland and Lofland, 1984, pp. 119–20).

Francia DeBeer and Dalia Sachs worked together on a paper that they titled 'From Caterpillar to Butterfly: Metamorphic Changes that Occur in Naturalistic Research':

> The first change we had to face was the change in our belief system that occurred as we learned the methods and significance of naturalistic studies. During all of our professional/academic education, we were brainwashed into believing that quantitative research was the only respected research in which one should be engaged. We were also focused toward the ideal that research was done by being objective and detached rather than subjective and involved. Second, we needed the ability to recognize the need for and thus to adapt to the ongoing changes with which one is involved in naturalistic research.

Francia and Dalia then enumerated specific points in the research process that required them to adapt to the constantly changing and evolving nature of their projects. Many of these have already been touched on in the excerpts we have quoted above. Toward the close of their paper, they return to their metaphor of metamorphosis, however, and to the difficulties that lie ahead as they opt for not only this methodology but also the 'personal changes' they will have to face.

> We became aware that the changes were occurring on two levels. First, they were intrinsic to the research methods, the planning and the procedures; second, they were impacting on our own perceptions and attitudes toward ourselves. After observing and listening to the people we were concerned with, some of our preconceived ideas had to be discarded and new hunches had to be followed up. At the same time, listening to our taped interviews was a blatant sign that we had to change and modify our techniques.... There is still a long way to go in the cocoon before a beautiful butterfly can emerge.

Others have chosen different metaphors. In the following section, one researcher develops the concept of rebirth. I have chosen to develop further this topic of personal change as a separate theme in the following section in order to move beyond the constriction that working solely with metaphors would impose. As Francia and Dalia pointed out, 'the core, and the *angst*, of naturalistic research is an ever-evolving process of exploring, analyzing, and changing'. It is important to explore this process further as not only beginning but also more experienced researchers have perceived it.

Theme II: As Qualitative Researchers, We Become Aware of Ourselves as Contingent, Interactive, Open to Change as a Way of Life

Transformation was a haunting theme in our students' essays — one that resonated strongly and personally for all of us too. Perhaps this was in part because some of us were fairly fresh from our own first steps as researchers, and we all have a strong sense of ourselves as persons 'in process'. In fact, as we have discussed these ideas, both formally in professional gatherings and informally in conversations, we have been, sometimes surprisingly strongly, confirmed in our realization that becoming a naturalistic researcher is a powerful, transformative process. Our sense is that it is characteristic of established naturalistic researchers to be aware of themselves as continually growing and evolving. Lincoln and Guba, for example, speak of the evolving nature of their own thought in the preface to *Naturalistic Inquiry* (1985):

> This book should not be viewed as a completed product. It is more profitably seen as a snapshot in time of a set of emergent ideas. A historical comparison of our earlier papers and book will reveal that our thinking has undergone many changes, some of them dramatic.... These changes are the inevitable accompaniment of a burgeoning field in which new questions are being raised almost more quickly than the old can be (even partially) answered.
>
> By way of illustration of this continuous press for change, let us cite just one example that currently is engaging our attention. We have for some time argued that inquiry is not and cannot be value free, but the full implications of that assertion have just begun to dawn on us.... It seems clear that our ideas are very much in evolution; it will not be surprising to us to find ourselves saying different (and, we hope, more sophisticated) things a year or two hence. (pp. 9–12)

And lo and behold, four years hence these same authors did indeed talk differently about several important facets of their 1985 stance. What is more, they include these statements in the foreword to their 1989 work, *Fourth Generation Evaluation*:

> We regard our work as simply another construction. We hope the reader will find it reasonably informed and sophisticated but it is certainly far from universal truth. Indeed *there is no universal truth* to which our construction is a more or less good approximation. If we have a moral imperative embodied in our work, it is simply this: that we will continue to make every effort to seek out and take account of every reaction and criticism that we can, and will attempt to deal with them, even if that means completely abandoning our present construction and embracing an utterly different one (which is what we believe is meant by the phrase, 'paradigm revolution'). (p. 16)

Issues surrounding the necessarily value-bound nature of inquiry derive from philosophical implications of the naturalistic paradigm. Lincoln and Guba refer to the gradual evolution of their thought as they work through the implications of this theoretical position. It sounds a familiar note for us that even as they pursue the practical responsibilities of professional life, they continue to think through its philosophical underpinnings. The most far-reaching change that we discern in ourselves and other researchers is the recognition that we have found an intellectual home within a new paradigm, or alternatively, that we have found a research paradigm that is consonant with our personal philosophy. Although fundamental changes may begin to be evident as we take our first steps as researchers, it is only gradually and over some time that the many implications begin to unfold. And I think it is safe to say that at whatever points and in whatever ways philosophy and methodology mesh, there are always further ramifications to explore.

Marlene Barron was one of several students who wrote of their transformation from quantitative to qualitative researcher — in her words, 'from a hard-nosed quantitative researcher to a juvenile ethnographer'. She, in common with others who describe this change, sees herself as someone whose convictions, whose world-view, were shaped by the experimental paradigm. She characterizes her personal paradigm shift as 'internal struggles ... the war was fought over control of my being, my *weltanschauung*'.

> The brightest beam came from Guba and Lincoln. Their arguments and organization spoke to my questions. Their chapter was acutely difficult for me to read and I found myself taking detailed notes which I continue to carry with me in my handbag, the way a child carries a security blanket. I touch them regularly, magically believing that through osmosis their tenuous hold in my personal knowledge base will become strengthened.

In addition to the paradigm change, Marlene grappled with changes in her perception of herself:

> My internal struggles also challenged that part of my self image which believes that I thrive in ambiguous situations and enjoy creating structure out of seeming disarray. I have discovered that believing that change is a positive experience and going through the change process are not always compatible notions.

Marlene detailed the stages she went through as one assignment after another carried her further into the qualitative process:

> I continually resented the time needed to do the endless tasks.... I dragged forward through the assignments.... I plodded toward the textbook beacons.... With all these misgivings, I managed to experience a cognitive and emotional breakthrough doing the interview and accompanying log and analytic memo. I found that I was enjoying the tasks. In fact the categories and themes literally jumped out from the text. It is an exciting feeling to be able to begin to see an event through the eyes of the subject.

The task that brought about Marlene's 'rebirth', however, was the specifically meta-cognitive one — the writing of the final paper in which she reflected on the semester's experience.

> Until I did the interview log and accompanying memo, I felt ill prepared for May 16th, our final session. The various times I faced this paper were experienced as intense contractions forcing me to finish, to get on with my work, to be born. But I didn't want to! I didn't want to finish because I felt I had not yet gone full term. I was still a preemie. I was just not ready to give up twenty-five years of my personal research history after only fourteen frantic weeks.

It has become my personal hobby, when I read accounts of such transformations, to notice what the researcher singles out as an agent of change. In the quotation above by Francia DeBeer and Dalia Sachs, they talk about the effect that listening to the tapes of their interviews had for them. Marlene Barron comments on the experience of writing a meta-analytic paper. Joanna Landau refers to the experience of writing up her log: 'Ah yes, that log.... It is the log that serves as the "other"'. For everyone who writes of change, there is that 'other' that serves as the mirror to reflect back oneself. For me, it was the tape recorder that I used while working with children in literature discussion groups.

I first began taping in order to record some of the fascinating things the children said. I was at that time gradually becoming aware of the area of inquiry rather loosely covered by the umbrella term 'response to literature'. Later I would decide to do research in this area, and still later become aware of qualitative research as an appropriate methodology. But my evolution into a researcher began at that point when another reality than the taken-for-granted mirrored my work back to me. As time went on, transcripts of audiotapes provided a stationary 'other', a reflection of both my own work and my students' responses to literature, that I could go to again and again. As these accumulated over time, they began to reflect off each other. Analysis of one day's class session would illuminate another long past. I truly began to have that sensation of working within a hall of mirrors.

Research as a Transactional Process

In my work, I was becoming increasingly convinced that research, like all other knowing, is a transactional process — the knower and the known both act upon each other. Louise Rosenblatt's (1978) transactional theory of literature provided a theoretical framework for both my teaching and my research. In the fall following the episode just related, in a different school and with different students, I began a two-year period of teaching and data collection for my dissertation study.

As my colleagues and I in the doctoral program undertook our various research projects, we formed a support group and began to share the experiences of those of us who were doing naturalistic research in classrooms. One told of a teacher friend who had invited her to observe in his class for her field trials. Although she sat as unintrusively as possible in a corner and made no comments on any aspects of what she saw, she found that the teacher-friend became increasingly defensive and even argumentative in explaining to her what he had been doing. 'That is because you have introduced the reflective mode into that room', commented Maryann Downing, another member of the support group. She continued:

> No matter how unobtrusive and non-judgmental your presence is, it is heightening his own awareness of what he is doing. He is probably not entirely comfortable with his own teaching, and when he seems to be trying to argue with you, he is really arguing with himself over what he is seeing.

It is my experience that once the reflective mode is introduced, this impulse toward examination and impetus to change is inevitable and inexorable. In fact, once the habit of reflection is introduced into a setting, the setting has already changed, however slightly and subtly. People who have never before articulated their beliefs and customs now are asked to do so, and what may never before have been examined has now become verbally objectified, so that it is at least present for examination. The aspect of this topic I wish to single out for consideration here is the ever-present reality of the transactional process. This is an element that is not always understood. It is at least a two-way process and, like much else in naturalistic research, it is emergent and results usually cannot be predicted.

Sometimes the effect of the research on the participants is unanticipated. Mary A. Porter, in 'The Modification of Method in Researching Postgraduate Education' (1984), tells of her experiences while interviewing part-time graduate students in the sociology departments of British universities. In the course of asking which facilities were open to them, she introduced aspects of their education some of them had never considered:

> During the first round of interviews, one of the questions that students were asked was to what facilities they were entitled in the department. Many of them gave their reply and then asked whether there were facilities of which they were unaware.... Scott and I discovered that in one sociology department, following our visit the students organized and demanded certain facilities to which they decided they were entitled after having talked to us.
>
> In the second round of interviews, we were asked for an updating and elaboration of information given earlier, and there were often in-depth discussions on one topic such as supervision of work. During the course of discussion the interviewees asked for opinions, or specific advice about what they should do. This was more difficult to defer until the end and consideration had to be given to the fact that they sometimes had no other source of advice; that, in itself, is a reason for giving it freely, but it also raises the issue of altering the course of events in the area being studied, a traditionally forbidden action for a researcher.... I was perhaps altering the course of events but there was a commitment to the students which would not allow total detachment from their interests. (pp. 157–8)

Porter's essay is one chapter in *The Research Process in Educational Settings: Ten Case Studies*, edited by Robert H. Burgess. These accounts of their experiences in the field by established researchers have become a part of the database for this chapter. They extend and confirm the experiences documented by students. In that collection, Stephen J. Ball raises many of the issues, methodological and otherwise, that he grappled with as he studied 'Beachside School'. 'I must recognize that my presence stimulated talk, produced response, encouraged concern'. He went on to quote another researcher, T.J. Cottle, who had noted that '... what I observe and record is not only the material experienced by me, it is in part generated by me' (Ball, 1984, pp. 82–3).

Martyn Hammersley (1984) has woven throughout an account of his research and teaching experiences the changes in thinking — social, theoretical, methodological — that accompanied his early career:

The process of research forced me to recognize features of the setting I would previously have ignored or misinterpreted. However, it also made me reconsider the nature of sociology and I began to question much that I had taken for granted hitherto. (p. 51)

Hammersley also describes how his later experiences as a teacher and as a member of a research team led him to refine and revise his thinking. He concludes that:

The most striking feature of my experience of research, as I think emerges clearly from this account, is that it was a voyage of discovery and much of the time was spent at sea. . . . (p. 62)

Hammersley raises the issue of selecting a methodology to fit one's theoretical position. Goetz and LeCompte (1984, pp. 33–62) provide a detailed discussion of levels of theory and how they can be incorporated into research design. At some levels, choice of method is governed by one's theoretical biases. At other, usually more particularized levels, the research findings may also ground, extend, or refute theory. Hammersley's experience, however, like my own, indicates that many of us either do not have a well-developed theoretical position as novice researcher, or, that if we do, it may become modified as we go along. The process of thinking through more deeply the philosophical underpinnings of our enterprise is ongoing, cyclical, and transactional. It is often experienced as the wellspring of personal and professional transformations.

Theme III: The Processes of Qualitative Research Also Become Processes of Professional Growth

In what I have written so far about my own growth as a teacher and as a researcher, I have tried to make the point that the essence of the change process can be traced to the introduction of the reflective mode that allowed me simultaneously to see myself and become aware of alternative ways of thinking and acting. Although I could not have pinned a tag on it when I started, with Margot as a mentor I had taken on the role of what is now commonly referred to as a teacher-researcher. I only gradually became aware that many others were traveling the same path. I had just completed collecting the data for my dissertation when I came across an article by Vivian Gussin Paley (1986) that in many ways described my own situation:

> I was truly curious about my role in the classroom, but there were no researchers ready to set up an incriminating study to show me when — and perhaps why — I consistently veered away from the child's agenda. Then I discovered the tape recorder and knew, after transcribing the first tape, that I could become my own best witness.
>
> The tape recorder, with its unrelenting fidelity, captured the unheard or unfinished murmur, the misunderstood and mystifying context, the disembodied voices asking for clarification and comfort. It also captured the impatience in *my* voice as children struggled for attention, approval, and justice. The tape recordings created for me an overwhelming need to know more about the process of teaching and learning and about my own classroom as a unique society to be studied.
>
> The act of teaching became a daily search for the child's point of view accompanied by the sometimes unwelcome disclosure of my hidden attitudes. The search was what mattered — only later did someone tell me it was research — and it provided an open-ended script from which to observe, interpret, and integrate the living drama of the classroom. (pp. 123–4)

It was fascinating for me to find that someone else's experiences had paralleled my own. It has been even more fascinating to uncover this process at work in the lives of a number of the beginning researchers in our classes. Beyond the data from their articles are our collective experiences of working with not only researchers but fellow professionals in various capacities.

To us the introduction of the reflective mode is the most effective form of professional in-service — far more powerful than programs imposed from above. Every qualitative researcher I know who is active in a professional field has come to new insights about professional practice as a result of the research process. What is more, when this process involves the participants at some deeper levels, the in-service impact is often a dual one, on the researchers and on the participants. A powerful example comes from an article entitled 'The Growth of Teacher Reflection' (1990) The authors, Daniel Walsh, Mary Smith, and Natalie Baturka, describe their '. . . three-and-a-half-year ethnographic study of kindergarten and first grade teachers' involvement in curriculum development and implementation in a rural/suburban Virginia school district'. They write:

> We have been observing in classrooms and interviewing teachers, administrators, and children. We have attended assemblies, PTO meetings, and parent conferences. On rare occasions we have served as substitute teachers. We have used videotape, audiotape, lap-top computers, as well as the more traditional notebook, to collect data.

During the third year of our work, an interesting phenomenon began to occur. Teachers commented that as they talked to us each week they had begun to examine their beliefs by listening to themselves talk. They noted, for example, that talking about retention had caused them to question and revise their beliefs. At the same time, a number of teachers who were active in the district's Early Childhood Steering Committee wanted us to help them start regular discussion groups. These groups — open to all district kindergarten, first- and second-grade teachers, and to other interested people — began in the spring of 1989 and have continued through this fall....

... We have been examining our notes from these discussions and the electronic exchanges in an effort to understand the growth of reflection among experienced teachers. There does indeed seem to be power in numbers, for reflection is viewed by most as a group phenomenon rather than an individual activity. (p. 1)

The researchers in our classes who were also teachers found cause for reflection on their own teaching as they observed other teachers. Melissa Rose was a music teacher and supervisor who attempted to observe a junior school music class from students' perspectives:

Analysis of each week's observation furnished so much food for thought, not only concerning my future work in the field, but for interaction with my own classes as well. Trying to see ourselves as our students might be seeing us is a bit frightening, but nevertheless one of the most enlightening experiences one could have. My study helped me see what I liked and didn't like about teaching and about myself as a teacher.

Nancy Montgomery chose to do a pilot study on 'how students in freshman writing classes worked together in collaborative writing groups'. The student she selected for her case study was a member of her basic writing course. This, of course, raised for Nancy many of the 'too close for comfort issues' we have addressed elsewhere. In her article at the end of the semester she focused on being too much a participant on the participant-observer continuum (see Chapter 3, p. 101). A by-product of this project, however, was a series of challenges and insights into herself as teacher. When Nancy's support group reviewed her logs and the transcripts of her tapes, their first responses were often observations on her teaching rather than her research:

It was hard to take when, on two occasions, my group, after reading sections of my log, showed great surprise that I was letting Jane get away with some of her off-the-wall remarks and unusual behaviors. For example, I said one time that students might be interested in reading more about a certain author and Jane stated, 'And we may not be'. Also once Jane just lit up a cigarette in the middle of class and started smoking. She often came in a bit late and announced her entrance loudly with a 'hello' or 'well, here I am', and she made some strange throat-clearing noises and sighs. Now, I had not seen my responses to this behavior as lax nor had I felt I let Jane 'get away' with anything. The subject was Jane, and yet in my class the subject was bound to be interactions between me and Jane also. When the members of my support group then commented on my style as a teacher, I felt kind of threatened and defensive and certainly nervous. It would have been easy to 'turn them off' and just start justifying my behavior and talk to myself.

However, I had everything to gain by listening openly to their opinions. One of them suggested that perhaps I let Jane get by with more than the usual student because she was quite bright and a great leader in class discussion in a class which happened to be pretty stultifying sometimes. Maybe, this group member proposed, I was negotiating with Jane — giving her more power than usual but using her at the same time as a great help to my teaching this class. Often, the students would not pick up on my questions until Jane took them up. They may have seen commenting on Jane's answer as less threatening than on the teacher's. Hence, my support group helped me get outside myself as the teacher in the class and observe myself more objectively rather than staying inside my own perspective so much.

The following quotations provide two further examples of how teachers reflected on their own practice through their research:

> Observing this professor has given me much to think about. For instance, when I was in the classroom, especially the pre-conservatory setting, how glib was I? I can recall telling students, 'If I can't write perfect dictation from your playing, you are not playing correctly'. How loaded is that statement? Professor X, thank you for your help. It has been enlightening. (Laura Wilson)

> I cued into the atmosphere of that class and what Moe did to create and perpetuate it. My categories all have something to do with that. This seems to be a mirror for me because so much of what I responded to is part of my teaching style, use of humor, and desire for the 'right' kind of atmosphere. Was I watching Moe or myself in that field? (Ronna Ziegel)

For Ruth Alperson there was a double reflection. As she observed children's humor in a pre-school setting, that in turn led her to consider the role that humor was playing in the qualitative research course she was taking.

> Several weeks ago, in our qualitative research class, I turned to one of my neighbors and said, 'This is the funniest course I've ever

taken!' This is true. Our professor addresses us as 'folks' in a casual, personal way. She 'picks' on certain members of the class, lets us all in on the 'in' jokes right away. In regard to the topic at hand, the professor notes, 'I know that you have other aspects to your lives but they, of course, are not as important as this'. She makes a face, we laugh. 'If you don't like thematic analysis then we'll fail you, folks'. Are these attempts to keep us awake during three hours of learning about case study research? If so, then the strategy is working. I feel like we are fairly well integrated as a group. (In my five years' experience as a grad student, I would say that this is atypical.) Laughing together seems to have this effect. The professor blows a kiss to my neighbor, who says to me, chuckling, 'She's picking on me'. Meanwhile, we have learned more about how to do a thematic analysis.

What relationship this aspect of my qualitative research class has with my fieldwork is this: I chose to focus on children's humor. I realized, only recently, that the choice of humor as a topic had very much to do with my own enjoyable experience in class every week. Initially, I chose humor as a topic because in the pre-school class I was observing, I noticed many kinds of behavior that I would categorize as 'humorous'; as I watched more closely, I noticed further that there were several different kinds of humorous behavior, and that each child had his/her own particular brand of humor. This seemed, then, like a topic that had a great potential in extending beyond itself. At the same time, as I have mentioned, this topic functions thematically on a more personal level, as well; I am experiencing some uniquely humorous moments in my own class.

Ruth discussed her study in the pre-school setting in some detail and then concluded:

> This brings me full-circle back to the qualitative research class. I ask myself, what is so funny here, in what category does this type of humor belong, how does it function? (In short, I pose the very same questions here that I relate to the case study I have done.)

It is fortunate for us as qualitative researchers that often what we study shows itself in other slices of our lives, sometimes at the right time, as it did in Ruth's case, to help us deepen our insights in more than one area. As she reported to her support group, Ruth's reflections on humor also touched her own job as a teacher of eurythmics.

Dorothy Deegan's experience in the course on qualitative research became professional in-service to an extent that she had not anticipated because of the nature of her work. Here is her story in her own words:

> For the past three summers I have taught a course called *Writing Workshop* as part of an enrichment program at a suburban high

school.... The second unit requires the students to observe and record the people and events around them that may have been overlooked or taken for granted in the past. I encourage my students to leave their ideas and biases behind as they enter their field; I tell them that if they assume this objective posture they might very well find information that could not have been anticipated. Finally, I try to convince them that the data they are collecting will supply the raw material that can be transformed into a rich piece of writing. That's what I do. Notice what I don't do. I don't select a topic, enter a field, or observe. I don't write.

So this spring semester when an ebullient woman stood in the front of a class in which I was now a student and described an exercise she called 'shadowing', I experienced a *déjà vu* immediately followed by an overwhelming wash of fear. I was being told to do what I teach, or, in aphoristic terms, practice what I preach.

I do not mean to imply that I am a complete pharisee. I do write and am now writing in a variety of professional ways.... I always intended to write along with my students. I don't know how many lists of 'I'll never forget the time when....' that I've brainstormed right along with my group. I even have first drafts of stories they wanted to hear more about: the time my pocketbook got stuck inside a subway door with me outside, my first day teaching, my experiences in the 1965 New York City blackout. However, that's where my writing usually ends and where I reassume the role of teacher as the students demand more of my time to conference about topics, revisions, editings. So, positioned on the other side of the classroom, faced with this assignment reminiscent of my days in *Writing Workshop*, and having recovered from the initial shock, I thought about what I might choose to explore.

... Last summer one girl, a rather shy but persistent and bright Korean student, observed at the local police station. She was really shaken by the fact that, in her opinion, the policemen she saw were rude, racist, stupid. The myth she had bought into had been shattered. We talked about it and I tried to point out to her that she could not fairly generalize her experience; she saw three men who were part of one police force in one town in one county in one state and so on. She said she felt better and went on to produce a wonderful piece of writing.

As I sat pondering possible topics for my shadowing project I thought of this incident. I had personally felt bad about my student's experience because I have a brother who is a sergeant in the New York City Police Department. I mentally accessed what I thought would be interesting areas, but I found myself returning to the police.

I didn't think much of the danger even as I signed the forms which I did not read concerning, I suppose, the city's absolvement from liability. Gaining entrée was relatively easy. The system is well-instituted for civilians to observe their civil servants (are they still called that?) in action. I didn't really feel frightened until, standing behind one of the officers to whom I was assigned while his partner ascended the stairs where a suspected thief might be hiding, I realized the potential hazards attached to each radio call. This was real: this was life or death. That night, during the three hours I observed, followed, frantically scribbled down notes, or lazily documented moments filled with the sound of country-western music and male gossip, I learned what one aspect of ethnographic research was all about.

My experience was very different from that of my student. Or was it? I thought about that, then I thought about the fact that I had seen two men who were part of one precinct of one police force in one city and so on. Thank goodness I'm teachable.

As exciting as my field experience was, still a further lesson was to be learned in converting my notes into the form of a log. As I sat at my word processor with my notebook of scratchings in front of me, I wrote. And, as I wrote my words reconstructed the tension, the calm, the pathetic, the mundane of the night before. I felt as if I were writing a novel; my characters came to life as I quoted them; settings were recreated as I rebuilt city walls and colored them with the blackness of the night. It's difficult to explain but I have never felt such power over my words. The difference, I believe, between this and other writing experiences I've had is that this piece was not based on such flimsy material as is often found in memory but rather on hard data collected not twenty-four hours before. The tone of the piece was encapsulated in the nature of the subject. Riding in the back seat of a New York City police car officially on prostitute patrol but responsive to any calls is, in and of itself, exciting: therefore, an astute observer and careful recorder cannot miss capturing that excitement.

This summer I will be returning to the same suburban high school to again teach my two sections of writing. I am returning not only as a writing teacher but also as an ethnographer. I have newly acquired tools to share with my students and, more important, a new perspective on the process. I do what I teach.

The beginning researchers who were nurses, psychologists, therapists, often found themselves becoming uniquely aware of the therapeutic transaction from the patient's perspective — sometimes for the first time in their professional careers.

As a staff member of the psychiatric unit, I had to use the official labels for patients, knowing full well that each diagnostic label carried with it an explicit formula for interpreting patients' behaviors. If dianostic labels and the informed labels staff use distort and limit our perceptions and understanding of others, is there another way to approach human beings with the goal of trying to understand them? My research project helped me to become more aware of the kinds of labels I apply to patients, the criteria upon which I base my labels, and how those labels affect my perception of patients. (Gail Levine)

I was surprised to find out that the occupational therapists I interviewed prefer to deal with head trauma patients rather than CVA's (cerebrovascular accidents, commonly called strokes). I guess my surprise was due to my bias, not their perception. I prefer to work with patients who have a CVA diagnosis because they need me the most. The therapists I interviewed preferred the head trauma cases because they were younger, recover faster, and were less prototypic. I was surprised by my findings as well as my needs in a therapeutic relationship. My need to be needed superseded diagnosis, age, variety, or anything else.... (Beatriz Abreu)

In her next paragraph, Beatriz touches upon what we perceive to be universal professional issues of power and control and the fine line between them:

The therapist control issue was a surprise to me.... The therapist did 'for' the patient, not 'with' the patient.... How can therapists work with brain-injured patients in a less controlling manner?

A nursing educator and administrator, Joanna Landau, found that her field of study gave her a unique opportunity to see their work through the eyes of her staff members:

Most of my time in the field was spent sitting in the nurses' station, a very familiar and comfortable place, and yet I found that I was learning that I really knew very little about what the staff truly believed.

Kate Good's contribution to this theme has such integrity that I have found it impossible to pull apart more than I did in the segments from her field log that follow. Kate's piece is particularly useful as an example of how professional development and the qualitative research process intertwine, sometimes meld together, but consistently accrue to the benefit of both. What is more, the professional development described by Kate is very far-reaching. It is her own, that of the nurse she was observing, that of the patients she came in contact with, and that of the larger hospital administration, nursing, and other support staffs.

Kate, as a member of the 1990 qualitative research class, is working through her first experiences with the methodology as I am writing this chapter. Her field notes have the fascination of a novel in serial form, and I eagerly wait for each week's installment. Notice the way Kate relates to her staff, her sensitivity to body movement, her use of dialogue in the following account:

Today I met with staff members on the search committee to find a head nurse for one of our medical-surgical units, P. At the close of the meeting the three staff nurses were asking me to explain what I was doing the weekend before when I followed the transportation aide around. I explained that I was taking a course in case study or qualitative research.... I shared that the shadowing experience is designed to increase the researcher's understanding and grasp of a situation, to walk in another's shoes, so to speak, and try to see things from the other person's point of view. The nurses seemed fascinated, expressing their interest by turning their chairs and bodies to face me more directly, establishing and maintaining eye contact, and giving no observable recognition to the housekeeper who came in and began to clean the room. Of the three, A seemed most interested at first, saying 'Why didn't you follow me around?' then, 'I'd love to have you walk in MY shoes for a day'. A went on, 'You should see what we have to put up with every day'. 'I know that you're changing a lot of things around here and things are getting better, but you really have to see what really goes on to know what kind of things need to be changed....'

At this point, Kate noted in the margin of her journal, 'Might be worthwhile to follow up on what A meant by "things"'. This information could serve her in two ways, both as a researcher and as an administrator. The entry continues:

... At this point, C, the registered nurse who works nights on the same unit, actively joined the conversation. C invited me to follow her around, suggesting that a view of nursing on the day shift would not 'tell the whole story'. C seems less intense, even in this situation, than A, but I sense a feeling of serenity and calmness in C that draws me to her. Jody, the third nurse, participates by nodding her head in agreement and supporting the others to continue by phrases such as, 'You're right', and 'That's for sure'. I assured the nurses that the process of observation and interviews with staff were now being incorporated into my administrative activities and that I would be honored to share their experience and thanked them for their offer.

Three days later, Kate began participant observation for her pilot study on one of the medical-surgical units of the hospital. She scheduled her observations for Saturdays when she is off duty.

As I open the door to the nursing office, my nostrils are hit by a heavy odor of cigarette smoke. Jackie must be the weekend supervisor — J smokes 'like a chimney', as they say. Sure enough, Jackie is in the staffing office talking with Susan — the night supervisor. I think to myself, 'Why is S still here — she should have been off duty over an hour ago'. I would love to get into impressions of S and J, but that is really not my purpose today. S and J greet me and ask me what I'm doing here. I explain my purpose as previously described.... S and J cautioned me that the P staff were 'up in arms as usual', that one particular nurse, Doris, was rude and out of line with S earlier because S did not have any additional staff to send them. It seems that the P staff have, as a unit, acquired the reputation for being uncooperative, for overreacting, for demanding resources without justification with S and J.

In this segment, note that Kate as a supervisor is aware that S is in the office, although not scheduled to be on duty, but she files this fact away to look into it another time. In Chapters 2 and 4, we have discussed at some length the difficulties and ambiguities, as well as the intellectual rigor needed, to deal with doing research in a familiar site. Kate has thought this through well and is quite clear in her own mind, and in her explanations to her staff, of her dual roles:

S and J told me not to dare to go up there in a lab coat because they (the nurses) would put me to work. I seriously thought of changing back into my suit jacket — a little built-in protection — who could expect me to care for patients in a wool suit? I decided to wear the lab coat anyway because my original reason for the lab coat was still valid. To my mind, the lab coat would ease my presence for patients by identifying me as a health care or hospital-approved person. I had also ordered and obtained a different name tag — a generic one which simply said: 'KATE GOOD RN'. My permanent name tag identifies me as DIRECTOR OF NURSING. My thought was that the generic tag would reduce some of the role ambiguity for staff who traditionally or usually see me with the titled one. Anyway, my other reason for staying with the lab coat was this — if indeed there was a real shortage of staff, I would certainly assist with patient care and reschedule my observation for later — I still had Sunday and Monday. As an aside, while talking with S and J, I began to feel a buildup of anger and tension. Indeed, there were extra staff on other units that morning but S was 'teaching them (P staff) a lesson'. I must explore management approaches to conflict with the managers and supervisors at some point soon — maybe next Wednesday.

Kate's plans for her participant-observer role have extended to her uniform and name tag. As a professional with responsibilities in this setting, her first concern is for the welfare of the patients. By wearing an alternative name tag that omits the phrase, 'Director of Nursing', she signals to her staff that she is not present as a supervisor today. Notice also Kate's self-awareness that she would 'certainly assist with patient care' if it were necessary and reschedule her observations. Kate's final comments in that segment regarding the night supervisor and the weekend supervisor show her firmly in her supervisory mode within her own mind, and she has here as elsewhere included these observations in her journal while they are still fresh. They are valuable as data; they also demand her further professional attention. Notice, however, Kate's reasoned approach to the problem she observes — 'I must explore management approaches to conflict with the managers and supervisors at some point soon' — and this in spite of her 'buildup of anger and tension'.

> By the time I reached P, it was about 8:30 a.m. I approached the nursing station and greeted the unit secretary, Carol, the charge nurse, Daphne, and the nursing staff passing in the hall. I explained to Daphne why I was here and apologized that I hadn't given the staff advance notice. I told her that I had tried to reach her at home the day before (Friday) to clear it with her but that there was no answer. I assured Daphne that I would, at least for today, limit my observations to the activities around the nursing station but that I would also reschedule that observation if, in her opinion, it was 'not a good day'. I felt that it was important to give the charge nurse and staff some control over the decision since they had not been approached before this morning. Daphne seemed comfortable, saying, 'Great, this is the best day, we're really busy'. Daphne looked down at my feet then and said, 'You've got your running shoes on so why don't you just follow me. I'm in charge of the M side and have six patients of my own'. So much for observing at the nurses' station. P, a 40-bed medical-surgical unit, is known as 'hell'. I frequently (once a week) hear one of the nursing leadership staff say, 'I'm on my way to hell', or 'I'm going up to hell unit to....' Come to think of it, when quality assurance or quality of care reports are presented at various interdepartmental committees or meetings, there is often a chuckle among the members as the P data is displayed. The results on P are usually dismal compared to the other medical-surgical units. However, as I think about it, the chuckle often starts even before the data are displayed — many members anticipate poor outcomes, excessive variance, and unmet thresholds for P and start chuckling based on history. What a feat it would be to turn that unit and staff around — if we could only find a strong candidate for that head nurse position.

Again, Kate has woven through her notes background data on P — 'hell unit' — that will probably be of value in her study but that also lead to further professional musings — 'What a feat it would be to turn that unit and staff around'. She reins in, however, and continues her observational notes:

> ... On with today's observation. Daphne led me down to the middle of N hall and pointed out her assignment.... D administered a total of 25 pills between 9:00 a.m. and 9:39 to six patients (average = 4.01 pills/patient) and did not communicate with the

patients about what it was she was giving them or what it was supposed to do for them. In addition, none of the six patients asked any questions about their medications. In retrospect, perhaps the patients all knew what they were taking and D knew that, so there was no need for any further dialogue — but I doubt it. Next time I will follow up with select patients. At this point — about 10:15 a.m. — Dr W came on the unit to visit and see Ms T. Ms T was a 78-year-old woman (to be described more fully later) who had complained of nausea and abdominal pain the night before and had, in fact, vomited. The physician was notified by phone and prescribed an abdominal X-ray (which was done) and a naso-gastric tube (which was inserted). Her abdomen was very distended. I asked D about bowel sounds and she said, 'Oh, they're OK', but had not assessed them since I arrived at least. I was tempted to take her stethoscope and check myself but refrained. D did seem unsure of what she felt when she palpated Ms T's abdomen and I offered 'Would you like me to check?' D seemed relieved and I palpated Ms T's abdomen only to find her bladder distended clear to her umbilicus. I asked D when Ms T had voided last and D replied, 'Oh, she had hardly any urine all night'. I suggested that the patient was producing urine but was retaining it. I guided D through an abdominal palpation and she remarked, 'God, I've never felt a bladder that big before'. At that point it seemed necessary to reassure the patient that she had been getting medication for pain and that sometimes caused difficulty in passing urine. I assured her that we could relieve her discomfort if we put a small tube in her bladder and emptied the urine. After that, we have ways to keep it from happening again and would work with her. We catheterized Ms T of 1200 ml — 1.2 litres — of urine and she felt better. Ms T was disheveled with many layers of crumpled sheets under her, her teeth were caked with decaying food from meals consumed hours (and hours) before. I had already had three and one-half hours of observation and gave in to my own need to provide care for Ms T. I thanked D and told her that the three and one-half hours were enough for today. I arranged to meet with D on Wednesday ... to follow up on the observation. It will be good to share with D, to validate some impressions and to hear her perceptions of the morning. I then offered to complete the bath and care for Ms T in the hour I had left (I had to meet with a nurse-midwife at 1:00 p.m.). D seemed very appreciative. I said it was the least I could do and was sure I would enjoy it — WHICH I DID.

In observing Daphne, Kate notes details on which she plans to check later along with professional routines that need her attention. She has schooled herself to pause before intervening (as a teacher I recognize this as 'wait time') and then asks Daphne, 'Would you like me to check?' Kate guides Daphne through this learning experience with a combination of modeling and an opportunity for 'learning by doing'.

It often happens that events in the wider world of ideas parallel the evolution of our thinking. That we draw from and contribute to the meaning-making processes in our culture is part of the ongoing transaction. Even so, it can come as a bit of a shock to happen upon the writings of others who explore concerns that currently engross us. I was sitting in a summer workshop in my school district when my eye fell on a copy of Donald Schön's *The Reflective Practitioner* (1983) propped up on the windowsill as part of a display of current professional publications. Because I felt I had to examine it then and there, I spread it open in my lap under the table and surreptitiously skimmed it as the workshop continued. I was completing my dissertation that summer by writing up a section about myself as teacher-researcher, and describing the recursive, reflective, analytic processes as 'working within a hall of mirrors'. Schön's books, as I was to discover, document similar processes as they are realized in a variety of professions.

Schön and his colleagues have devoted themselves to developing structures for the education of professionals — particularly ongoing in-service education — that will enable them to become aware of the tacit knowledge they draw upon in their practice. Among other techniques, Schön *et al.* incorporate strategies for helping professionals become aware of gaps that may exist between their stated beliefs and their actual practice. For example, during in-service programs using the 'hall of mirrors' strategy (a term they use in a more closely defined sense than I had), they help psychotherapists in support group settings draw analogies between the client's sticking points in therapy and the therapist's own sticking points in treatment.

Educating the Reflective Practitioner is interesting reading — replete with case studies and vignettes about the art of coaching for reflective practice — in fields as diverse as architecture, musical performance, and psychoanalysis. It has been doubly fascinating to Margot and me as we have talked through this theme and found in it further confluence for the individual strands of honoring tacit knowledge, learning by doing, reflecting in and after action, the role of mentors, the pains of growth. We have underlined his quotation from Carl Rogers because it so aptly discribes our position: 'I have come to feel that only learning which significantly influences behavior is self-discovered, self-appropriated learning' (p. 89). Doing qualitative research offers opportunities for such learning.

Theme IV: Qualitative Researchers Often Feel as Though They Are Shouting across a Paradigmatic Rift

With time and experience, we hoped this theme would go away. It has not, however, as is illustrated by this following incident typical of many others.

The 'we' who are writing this book were engaged in a panel presentation at a professional meeting in another city. We had started the analysis of the papers by beginning researchers and were sharing some of the emergent themes, together with our own experiences, as topics for our panel. The talk turned to the difficulties that our students and we sometimes experienced in communicating with people who worked in the positivist paradigm. When we opened up the meeting for discussion from the audience, the stories poured forth. You will notice that we do not attribute authorship to most vignettes in this section, and the details are disguised:

> I wanted to do qualitative work in a field heavily dominated by quantitative studies. My favorite professor, after learning of the change in my research paradigm, called me 'defector' both privately and in public. This wouldn't have been so bad if he hadn't been my favorite and most respected teacher in the department. His kidding lost its jocular tone after the second time he said it. He considered me one of his brightest students, and he was both annoyed and disappointed that I chose to follow a research path of which he disapproved. Initially my confidence in what I wished to do was shaken, but I couldn't answer the questions that fascinated me in any way other than ethnographically. As I continued to work, my confidence returned, but a nagging sense of regret still lingers. (Anon.)

> I was sitting in the dissertation proposal seminar and the professor was asking each student, in turn, to discuss how statistics might be employed in his or her experimental research design. When my turn came, I said that I was going to use another methodology. He glared at me for a moment, then snapped '*What* other methodology?' (Anon.)

> In our department, during dissertation proposal reviews, one of the professors always agrees to the use of qualitative methodologies, *if* the candidate will do a couple of things, like choose a stratified random sample of subjects and establish inter-rater reliability. (Anon.)

Talking with Those Outside Academia

We have all felt, on various occasions, that we were trying to bridge chasms of misunderstanding when we talk about our work. At the most trivial, perhaps cocktail-party occasions, it becomes 'You're doing ethnography? Oh, that's where you examine how people's ethnic heritage still plays a role in their lives'. Ann relates her conclusions about such conversations: 'Generally, the more sophisticated the conversational partner, the more that person believes my dissertation took place in Samoa or the aboriginal outback of

Australia'. Margot tells of her mother, Erna, surely her greatest fan, who in conversation with friends was overheard to say, 'My daughter is writing a book. Something about qualitative research. Don't ask. I can't understand — but it must be something good'.

In my own setting, a small public school in a suburban community, few people, except the students and a few mothers, recognized my taping and transcribing activities as research. I tried out different explanations on faculty members or friends in the community when they politely inquired how my dissertation was coming. If I used the terms 'qualitative' or 'ethnographic', I saw by their faces that I conveyed nothing to any of them. I found that if I said I was doing a descriptive study of children's responses to literature in discussion groups, this made sense and sufficed for casual conversation. But I knew in that place I was alone.

Kate Good was also touched, and at a deep emotional level, when she attempted to explain her pilot study to professional co-workers:

> I was talking about my research with a group of colleagues. 'Oh', one said, 'you're doing that soft, easy qualitative stuff'. Soft! Easy! My heavens! I've never worked so diligently, so deeply. This research is *HARD*! How do I get through the heads of the people who really should know?

There are levels at which people's ignorance and misunderstanding about qualitative research matter a great deal. In Theme V we will discuss at greater length the concerns researchers feel when they sense that their participants are revealing more than they realize the methodology can uncover. For example, Teri has written in Chapter 4 of her worry that the female police officers she interviewed gave her more information than they would have wished. I have quoted Wolcott in Theme V where he describes a superintendent of schools dismissing an ethnographic study of his school as 'just pure anthropology'. In addition, the 'little learning' of some — participants or colleagues — with whom we work can impede or frustrate our work. In Chapter 5 we describe Stephen Ball's efforts at member-checking for his analysis in 'Beachside Reconsidered' only to have the head of the science department in the school he studied argue at length about method with him before discussing his account as 'honestly, absolute drivel'.

Jo Anne Bauer, whose experiences as a doctoral student comprise a substantial portion of the next section, recounts the following incident in which a participant considered the research too subjective until she could make positivistic meaning of its method:

> An interesting experience which speaks to this point occurred when I asked the family I was studying to keep a log of their computer

interactions over a week's time. The mother, who is a high school science teacher and promoter of scientific method, responded, 'That's a good idea; it will make the study more objective'.

Of course, we have found that people outside academia often do understand our research. Many times this has come about as we have shared some of our findings in concrete form. There is a difference between 'talking method' and reading a vignette about a person in a nursing home. The 'shock of recognition' that we have written about in Chapter 3 is not only the sole province of the researcher.

Talking with Those Inside Academia

Whenever our integrity as scholars and researchers is questioned, we are touched at a deep emotional level. Misunderstandings matter deeply. When they occur within an academic setting, they are most serious for beginning researchers, however, who not only want to earn the esteem of fellow students and colleagues in general but who also absolutely must assure faculty acceptance of their dissertation proposals. Jo Anne Bauer describes her gradual awareness and 'emerging fear' of this dilemma for herself and fellow doctoral students as follows:

> It is not uncommon for the beginning student of case study research methods to encounter and be puzzled by the dichotomy described by Rist (1982) as 'methodological' provincialism reflected in the reification of the terms 'qualitative methodology' and 'quantitive methodology' (p. i). Before fully understanding the larger context of this dichotomy, I, a novice researcher, began to feel that by engaging in qualitative research, I am aligning myself with certain assumptions, perceptions and cognitions suspected by many to be biased, subjective or less rigorous than quantitative orientation.
>
> To the degree that a beginning student feels a natural affinity with the qualitative methods she is learning, she may simultaneously feel challenged by the mainstream of an academic community oriented toward experimental models. It is not unusual to hear fellow case-study students within my research class report the skepticism of their faculty advisors, their committees and even of the subjects from their studies. One researcher, after interviewing an informant and then offering an explanation of the merits of open-ended interviewing, was told she should 'harden it up' by objectifying and quantifying her data.
>
> An emerging fear, then, of graduate students is that we may get caught between the 'research orthodoxies' of various departments and programs. An experience which alerted me to this tendency

occurred in my content seminar. During a class discussion of anticipatory schema theory, my professor used a quote from the text under discussion and chose to apply it exclusively to qualitative research, thus implying that ethnographic study is prone to a researcher bias which experimenters adroitly elude.

Occasions such as these alert the doctoral student to the shoals ahead. We return to the literature on qualitative research; we search out those points that buttress our proposed methodologies and work them into our designs. We learn that some faculty members articulate very specific concerns about and objections to certain aspects of qualitative methodology. If we are to succeed, we will try to learn, as Jo Anne did, to 'hear' what our dissertation committee members are saying:

> In order for real communication to occur between researchers of polarized orientations, it is important for student ethnographers to take their developing skills seriously. The human relations skills which enable the good qualitative researcher to establish necessary channels of communication with subjects are the exact skills required in communicating with quantitative researchers. The ethnographer who hones her listening skills to be able to hear and elicit the perceptions of participants must similarly 'hear' the questions, the worldview, the paradigm out of which quantitative researchers operate.

> LeCompte (1985) echoes this point while describing the communication challenge of her field — anthropology:

>> We spend a great deal of time thinking about how to communicate through and across cultures with our research subjects. We can put that training to good use trying to develop ways to make our peers from other disciplines understand the terminology and methods we use and how they are appropriate to the topics we study.

> One fruitful strategy comes from the success story of a nursing student, Amy, which she called a 'Show and Tell' experience. After her preliminary field visits to family planning centers, Amy participated in a dissertation seminar in which she needed to detail the parameters of her proposed study for her advisor. After Amy submitted her first draft of a proposal, the initial response from her professor was a lukewarm 'So what?' This obviously called for a new tactic. During her next session with the professor, Amy played an audiotaped interview to 'show' her data. From the tape, she was able to 'pull out' several coding categories and to suggest emerging themes. She even talked about developing hypotheses. This exchange engaged the professor in animated discussion, eliciting her observations about women who choose not to have abortions. Through the 'live data' of the taped interview, Amy was able to engage her

advisor into the specifics of the research, and thereby make a case for the merits of her proposal and its methodology. Thus, the ethnographer's 'emphasis upon accurate, almost photographic portrayal ... of immediate reality and dynamic processes within a setting' (LeCompte, 1985) allowed a very important outsider to 'get close to the data'.

Another approach comes from my own experience of communicating with a professor who explicitly wanted more than 'show and tell'. He required grounding of the naturalistic data in a review of related theoretical literature. In such cases, the task may be to convince quantitative researchers that ethnography 'is not merely descriptive narrative'; but that 'it is informed by theory, integrated with a corpus of previous work, and capable of generating and testing hypotheses'. (LeCompte, 1985)

One student tells about being caught between qualitatively and quantitatively oriented faculty advisors over the drafting of her dissertation proposal:

Professor L had discussed the concept of emergent design with me at length, but Professor N liked the sound of the study only when the questions were much more set. Then she asked, 'What theories will you apply and test?' Writing the proposal was a misery because I kept trying to find some theoretical construct I could use as a 'test'. When I next saw her, proposal in hand, Professor L pointed out, of course, that such tight beginning plans were not consonant with qualitative theory.

In negotiations such as these, support groups are of immense help. Not only do they furnish a sounding board, but they usually share a wealth of accumulated experience — very practical, very strategic — on how and when to negotiate the theoretical differences along with the personality and political currents that are sometimes flowing just below the surface.

A dissertation chair who is strong in qualitative methodology and has a reputation for 'getting people through' is the greatest help of all. The members of this writing team all had this good fortune. We have also noticed throughout the student articles notes of appreciation for such mentoring. When it is absent, if a student is working outside a center of qualitative research, he or she may find it impossible, both emotionally and technically, to produce a qualitative study. John Van Maanen, in the opening pages of *Tales from the Field* (1988), wrote tellingly of his earliest experiences without mentor support:

My own training as an ethnographer of a sociological sort reflects, I think, the training of many ethnographers and would-be ethnographers whose professional teeth were cut outside the more prominent and justly famous centers of fieldwork practice. For better or for worse, we lack a formal apprenticeship in the trade.... Without mentors or cohorts, our appreciation and understanding of ethnography comes like a mist that creeps slowly over while in the library and lingers with us while in the field.

This lack of tutoring is perhaps most telling at that still point in our studies when we have returned from the field and sit before the blank page that must eventually carry the story of what we have presumably learned. Aid, comfort, and confidence may be difficult to come by at this lonely and sometimes terrible stage. For instance, when returning to the university after a stay in the field that was to serve as the basis for my dissertation, I was told by my worthy academic advisors, whose interests and skills lay well outside ethnographic traditions, to simply 'write up' what I had 'discovered' in the field as if what was then in my head (and field notes) could be uncorked like a bottle and a message poured out.

My thesis was eventually written over a two-year period around some survey work I had accomplished in the field. My fieldwork-based materials were used sparingly to embellish and provide local color for a thesis straight from the land of multiple regressions and chi-squares. (p. xii)

We have used the metaphor 'shouting across the rift' for this theme. Sometimes we feel we are shouting because the distance seems so vast. Sometimes we metaphorically 'shout' as we debate issues through our publications. On other occasions, actual shouts echo across seminar and conference tables and into the halls of academia. But what of trying to bridge the rift? As I have noted before, the published accounts of established researchers have woven themselves into this chapter. One that seems particularly apropos here is 'On Seeking One's Own Clinical Voice: A Personal Account' by J. Richard Hackman (1988). In this essay, Hackman documents his personal intellectual journey from his beginnings as an experimental researcher in the field of social psychology to his present involvement with clinical, or field, research methodologies. His original uneasiness with experimental design arose, as he tells it, because 'I kept trying to figure out how to apply the dissertation findings, to use them to make a constructive difference in something I cared about'. He details ways in which he finds field methodologies useful, but he also documents his difficulties in communicating with and being taken seriously by some of those using qualitative methodologies from whom he had hoped to learn. Among other factors, he comments, 'To this outsider, the clinical establishment seems to have the quality of a priesthood: You are either in or out, and if you are in, you have to accept the doctrine' (p. 210).

Hackman's voice is that of one trying to bridge the rift, to have conversation with colleagues in both camps:

In fact, I do want to reengage with mainline social psychology. These people are my friends, and in a real sense my professional family of origin. Moreover, I am encouraged by what seems to be a renewed interest in relationships and groups among members of the social psychology establishment. But the guy who is coming back is different from the guy who left — and he is returning with some new tools and with a belief that the old homestead might be more interesting and durable if a few structural modifications were made. I wonder if the welcome mat will be kept out once that is realized.

From her experience 'inside academia', Margot has found the following to be useful in bridging the gap. She writes:

- Be available when co-workers wish to discuss qualitative research.
- When asked, be a guest lecturer about qualitative research in colleagues' courses.
- Help students to build a strong conceptual grasp of the methods.
- Set up student support groups that report their progress to faculty sponsors.
- Attend dissertation proposal defenses as a silent or not-so-silent advocate for the proposal and student.
- Write and publish.
- Do research in the field.
- Work on funded projects that need a qualitative lens.
- Network with other faculty interested in qualitative research.
- Support school-wide qualitative research in-service activities.
- Work actively on school-wide and university committees about doctoral issues.
- Stay current with trends in quantitative research and don't get too rusty with that language.
- Plan and run sessions about qualitative work with students, graduates, and other faculty for national, state, and local conventions.
- Keep a sense of humor.

What I have found to be *not* useful is to develop a precious I-am-not-understood attitude that maintains a separation between faculty who, while they take opposing research stances, need to work together in the service of students. It is so easy to develop such an attitude. I have books in me about my maddening, frustrating, sad experiences around qualitative research with other faculty, although at the same time I must say that, over the years, things have gotten better. Is is no wonder that 'qualitative people' band together. But not too tight. Not too exclusionary. Otherwise, we create more of the very camps we disdain.

Of course, there are fundamental issues at stake. The basic one is whether there can be a 'marriage' between the two paradigms (Goetz and LeCompte, 1984; Guba and Lincoln, 1989; Lincoln and Guba, 1985; Sherman and Webb, 1988). We hold that in terms of philosophic bases and their implications, such a marriage is impossible. But we are not now discussing marriages. We are discussing conversations. We are discussing tolerance for our neighbor, and the benefits of occasionally exchanging a tool over the back fence.

Theme V: Qualitative Research Is Value-laden Work, and Ethical Concerns Are Woven through Every Aspect of It

'Qualitative research is an ethical endeavor'. Margot repeated these words again and again as we worked over the sections on trustworthiness and made decisions about what should go where:

> Striving to be faithful to another's viewpoint is striving to be ethical. Striving to maintain confidentiality is striving to be ethical. Striving to be trustworthy is striving to be ethical. It is impossible to confine ethical considerations to a chapter or a section. Actually, they are present from the beginning and are woven throughout every step of the methodology.

Questions concerning ethics appear again and again in the writings of our students and our colleagues. Before I turn to the specifics of these, however, I would like to present a broader view of this area.

A few years ago I received, among other holiday greetings, a letter from a counseling and retreat center. As part of his year-end musings, the director voiced his gratitude for a life of 'value-laden work'. This phrase has stayed with me. I, too, am grateful for value-laden work as a teacher and as a reseacher. My sentiments are echoed in the words Jonas Soltis uses to introduce an article on 'The Ethics of Qualitative Research' (1989):

> . . . I want to make clear an assumption that undergirds my thoughts about the ethics of qualitative research that all of you may not share, but I think you should. It is that education is, at base, a moral enterprise. Education is ultimately about the formation of persons. It is about developing and contributing to the good life of individuals and society. Even though we may disagree about the specifics of what constitutes the educated person and

the good life, it is toward these high moral ends that the human enterprise of education in a democratic society is negotiated and directed. (p. 124)

Those of us who are writing this book are variously in the fields of education, communications, and psychology. Our students come from a wide range of professions, including nursing, arts, counseling, social work, librarianship, and other human services. It seems almost axiomatic to us that each profession has an ethical base analogous to that attributed by Soltis to education, since professions exist by definition for the service of society. We have noted that the interest of many professionals in exploring ethical considerations has received striking triangulation from a number of episodes related in Schön's *Educating the Reflective Practitioner* (1987).

The moral bases from which professionals work as they reach stages in their careers where they choose — or are required — to do research are expanded further by the nature of qualitative research itself. By definition, it is research through which we seek to understand more fully our fellow human beings. This overarching theme can be found expressed in various ways throughout the literature:

> To the extent that ethnography can complicate the simplified and often incorrect notions that one group has of another, it can play an important role in present and future worlds. (Agar, 1980, p. 204)

> Perhaps the most important force behind the quiet ethnographic revolution is the widespread realization that cultural diversity is one of the great gifts bestowed on the human species. (Spradley, 1980, p. viii)

Like the writings of experienced researchers, our students' papers are woven through — in some cases I could say freighted down — with ethical concerns. I see these as having three foci: for the integrity of the research itself, for the participants with whom one works, and for some broader social implications of qualitative research. The first two areas of concern are richly documented in the students' papers as well as in the literature as a whole. The last concern — for social implications — is one with which beginners doing pilot studies have little experience ... yet. Margot takes on that issue in her 'Last Word' that follows this chapter.

Concerns for the Integrity of the Study

The students of qualitative research used a variety of words — unbiased, fair, objective, accurate, representative, trustworthy, 'seeing what's really there' — and they applied them to a myriad of specifics. But whatever and however discussed, concerns for the quality, for the value, for the honesty of their work were by far the most prominent theme in all of their writings. This theme can be traced throughout the previous chapters because in many cases we have used quotations to illustrate aspects of the methodology that have also been coded for themes in this chapter — most particularly the one at hand. Here are some additional examples:

> Obviously my biases did enter into this experience after all, for what I perceived to be real revolved around my interests. What was important to my outside research unconsciously influenced initial perceptions. (Patricia Fogelman)

> In order to see 'what is', it is important not to be clouded with 'what I guess it's going to be'. (Ann Vartanian)

> I have become more aware of my own biases by checking similarities and differences in interpretations and the appropriateness of my conclusions with my support group. (Suzy Hahn)

> The findings in my analytical memo revealed that the themes I thought were evident in the data were not, and were manifested because of my preconceived impressions of what the data would disclose. The realization that the same emphasis on validity and reliability of data collection and analysis is as crucial an issue in qualitative research as it is in quantitative research had now become apparent to me in not just an intellectual sense but also in a very pragmatic comprehension. (Patricia Cobb)

Most of us come to qualitative research with attitudes toward 'objectivity' and 'subjectivity' as part of our cultural baggage. We have addressed this issue already in Chapter 3. Here I would like to highlight the ongoing work we undertake as qualitative researchers to rethink, and rethink again, considerations revolving around the objective/subjective fulcrum. I don't think that one needs to follow Guba and Lincoln to the further reaches of the philosophic position that 'reality consists of a series of mental constructions' (1989, p. 87) to function as a qualitative researcher. But I do think that one must accept that multiple interpretations exist, however one chooses to define reality, and that to be completely unbiased or 'objective' is impossible. So we work through for ourselves and negotiate with our students the functional understanding that complete objectivity is unattainable, that we strive to become less blinded by our own subjectivities, more self-aware. We work toward interpretive communities in which many different points of view are accepted. And, as researchers, we work to present the points of view of our participants, to see life through their eyes as well as our own, to attain that transcendent perspective (Lofland and Lofland, 1984, p. 119) which encompasses multiple interpretations.

Alan Peshkin writes of 'Virtuous Subjectivity: In the Participant Obser-

ver's I's' (1988). In this essay, he discusses the many I's, or personal subjectivities, 'stemming from one's class, statuses, gender, and values'. He illustrates
his point by analyzing two of his studies, one of a school district in a small
mid-western town he calls Mansfield, another of a private fundamentalist
school he calls Bethany. He concludes by pondering:

> Of course, as a white researcher I still see Mansfield's racism, and as a
> Jewish researcher I still see Bethany's successful school and community.
> Seeing, however, is not enough; it leads me merely to point out, not focus
> on, Mansfield's racism and Bethany's community. I concede that subjectiv-
> ity need not blind me to perspectives other than those following naturally
> from my subjectivity. However, since these other perspectives are not
> reinforced by my personal dispositions, they fail to get the same attention as
> those that are. They fail, therefore, to be explicated and connected to other
> aspects of the phenomenon under study, and expanded so that the promise
> of the perspective is most fully exploited....
>   The failure to exploit fully other themes than the one I have chosen
> may be seen as a shortcoming, but I see it as the reality of social research
> conducted in complex settings. Such settings support many stories, so to
> speak, not all of which can be told — or told most effectively — by any one
> researcher. Thus, my subjectivity is simultaneously enabling and disabling,
> as it impels me to entertain and develop some research possibilities and
> restrains and delimits me from developing others.

The questions that Peshkin raises seem echoed in an entry in one of our
student's logs:

> 'Symphonies in subjectivity' is the phrase this week. We talked
> about 'being fair', and I worry I'm too stubborn to be really fair.
> And if I'm really fair, will I miss something that being a little unfair
> might allow me to see? (Rena Smith).

Peshkin answers these concerns that at one time or another bedevil us all
when he says:

> When I disclose what I have seen, my results invite other researchers to look
> where I did and see what I saw. My ideas are candidates for others to
> entertain, not necessarily as truth, let alone Truth, but as positions about the
> nature and meaning of a phenomenon that may fit their sensibility and shape
> their thinking about their own inquiries. (p. 280)

We reconcile ourselves to the inevitable. We cannot be 'really fair'. But we
can uncover and make public our biases to whatever extent we are able,
inviting colleagues and participants to join us in the task. Growth in self-
awareness is in itself an ethical undertaking:

> 'Being fair' is having the courage to reconstruct, by way of language,
> what you have come to know, think, and feel. It is allowing yourself
> to experience research as a process of becoming, to experience the
> daily changes which arise in your thinking and understanding.
> Changes, which in and of themselves, often move in circular ways.
> Changes which turn in upon themselves — changes which repeat.
> (Wendy Hesford)

Throughout our chapters we ring changes (the wordplay is inescapable) on the same notes — coming to know, the processes of becoming, growing self-awareness — the courage and ethical rigor this requires, and the fact that these efforts and achievements touch all aspects of our lives, not just our research projects.

> Using oneself as instrument makes self-awareness a very high
> priority.... I have also had to struggle with this as a therapist, in
> terms of accepting my limitations as well as my strengths (Nancy
> Biederman)

I would hasten to add here again, as we have occasionally elsewhere, that for us as researchers and professionals this self-awareness, significant though it may be for personal reasons, is of paramount importance for the quality of our work, the service we render in the larger society.

Concerns for Impacts on the Participants

Sharon Lefkofsky was a coordinator for graduate work-study programs in physical therapy. Her work took her to a number of hospital and health care sites, and when she entered the qualitative research class, she had already planned to use one of these sites for her pilot study. Against the advice of her group leader, Diane, and of Margot ('The settings are too familiar; your questions are too narrow'), she went ahead until she, herself, saw the basic flaw in her plans:

> One aspect of the visits I hadn't resolved was how to set the limits
> for the different roles I was to manage: occupational therapist and
> researcher/student. After two weeks of agonizing, I realized that I
> couldn't enter these fields because I couldn't manage the dual roles
> honestly. For me, at that point, honesty meant representing myself
> without cover because I had to have ongoing relationship with the
> health care professionals after the exercises for class were finished. I
> didn't feel that I could protect all parties in such a way that trust
> wouldn't be threatened. Later, I learned that this feeling of discom-
> fort was a good guide.

The point here is not that one cannot study one's own workplace. In Sharon's case, however, her original research questions, already too narrowly focused, were such that she did not feel she could honestly explain them and justify her research role without compromising other interests. It is to her credit that she was attentive to her own ambivalence and devised a new, ultimately sounder plan. Kate Good, on the other hand, whose story is told in some detail in Theme III, had carefully thought through her 'cover' explanations, had ranked her priorities as nurse, supervisor, and researcher, and found that her different roles contributed to, rather than conflicted with, one another. Both of these researchers were concerned about impact on others, although their contexts and research solutions differed.

The literature is replete with discussions of those ethical considerations in conducting qualitative research that have to do with one's relations in the research context. Lofland and Lofland (1984) describe them in some detail in their chapters on 'Getting In' and 'Getting Along'. They compare dilemmas in qualitative research to analogous ethical questions that anyone might meet in everyday life and conclude that:

> These daily ethical dilemmas are no more readily resolved than the similar dilemmas of field research. But then, why should there be a difference? Fieldwork is not detached from ongoing social life, and the continuing ethical dilemmas of social life seem an inexorable part of the human condition. (p. 44)

There are three points that we think deserve special mention here, however. They have to do with preserving anonymity, with being aware of the effects, however unintended, our presence may have in the research setting, and with involving the participants more fully in the research process.

The very naivety of many research participants makes it the more imperative that we are careful to protect them. I find that the elementary school students with whom I work prefer to have their names used if they are going to be written about. When I tell them that 'this is not the way it is done', they often turn to a game of making up new names for themselves and each other. I usually listen as they fantasize renaming themselves, but I don't use those names either in my reports. I take pains not to identify other markers, such as the school year, so that readers who are familiar with my settings will not guess correctly.

We have all had experiences in which we wondered whether the participants were at all aware of the extent to which they were revealing themselves. Ball writes of the participants in his research setting, 'The majority of the staff clearly had little idea of what sociological research was and the sort of outcomes it might produce' (1984, p. 87). Teri has written in Chapter 4 of her ambivalent reactions to some of the data she recorded in interviews with female police officers, and of her emotional desire to shield or excuse them when she 'didn't like her findings'. For whatever reasons, then, researchers are often in a position to be more aware than participants of the vulnerability of research participants and possible consequences of the findings.

Wolcott (1988) offers an observation based on long experience that in spite of his care as a researcher to be honest in his representation of his role, the personnel in the schools he studied did not realize the implications of his explanations:

> Let me illustrate how educators use the term [ethnography] without neces-sarily understanding it. One large-scale, federally funded educational project completed in the 1970s made it possible to employ a number of full-time 'on-site' researchers to live in rural communities in order to document change processes in the schools and to study school-community interaction....
> ... After living somewhat apprehensively under the gaze of his resident 24-hours-a-day, 365-days-a-year ethnographer, the superintendent of schools in one of these rural communities received a preliminary copy of a report that had been prepared by the researcher. The superintendent's subsequent reaction, I'm told, was to note with a sigh of relief, 'The stuff's okay. It's just pure anthropology'. (p. 187)

At the close of 'Beachside Reconsidered', Stephen Ball relates his encounters with the news media as eager reporters vied unsuccessfully to uncover the identity of the school. He sums up these events surrounding the publication of his work:

> My experiences with Beachside would certainly affect the way in which I presented any future ethnographic work for publication. Apart from careful use of pseudonyms I fully intend to ensure that I actively mislead any readers as to the location or identification of the school or schools con-cerned.

In Theme II, I discussed ways in which researchers became aware of the transactional, or interactive, nature of the research process. Ann also discussed this aspect of participant-observation in Chapter 3. I introduce it here only briefly to note that beginning researchers are often not aware that inevitably they will in some way affect the research setting. They are then both surprised and abashed when this takes place. Leslie Rice recounts this incident:

> A researcher in my support group had been interviewing a woman about her role as wife and mother. In the process of the interview, the woman had described some of her unhappiness with her husband. Shortly after the interview, she told the researcher that things

were more clear now about her situation. Next week she left home. The researcher felt terribly guilty, feeling that she had precipitated the woman's actions because the interview had raised her consciousness.

Whether we like it or not, consciousness raising — our own and our participants' — is an inevitable piece of the process. If we are afraid that such awareness could be dangerous, better not to undertake the research. There are times, however, when it may well be of value. This seems to have been the case with Mary Porter's graduate student participants, mentioned in Theme II, who were inspired by what they learned during the interview process to inquire into benefits that might be available to them.

Julia Wollman-Bonilla grappled with an ethical dilemma of a different sort as she felt herself drawn into the life of a classroom in which the pupils saw the teacher as 'unfair' and in which she came to share in this perception:

> Because I knew how some of the children felt about their classroom experience and my observations corroborated their perceptions, I felt a sense of responsibility for fixing things. If they were being treated unfairly and this treatment impacted upon their learning, then shouldn't I, being aware of this situation, do something? However, in asking myself this question, I realized that not only did the quality of my data depend upon my commitment to description, not change, but also I was judging the teacher's behavior by my own standards rather than trying to make sense of that behavior by imagining her perspective alongside that of the students. I needed to think deliberately about the stresses of her job, her goals in the classroom, and the school culture as a whole in order to begin to understand Mrs Green. Therefore, while I felt it was important to provide her with feedback as to how I saw the situation, which might cause her to reflect upon what she takes for granted, I realized I had no right or power to try to make Mrs Green change. That would have to be her decision made within the constraints of her reality as a teacher.

Julie worked past the impulse to 'fix things' to a position that is not only more ethical for the researcher but is also probably more psychologically sound. She will provide a mirror in which this teacher can reflect. In the larger sense, Julie's study of this classroom can also contribute to the burgeoning body of qualitative research on classroom life. That such research needs to be more effectively marshalled and made public is highlighted in the concluding section.

Once they recognize the interactive nature of the relationship between researcher and participants as one of the hallmarks of qualitative research, many researchers are concerned that participants be accorded a more truly collegial role in the research process. At the conclusion of her study of kindergarten classrooms, Emily Kennedy (1975) described her ethical concern that the teacher and children of her study were not colleagues in the research process. In this, she sounded a prophetic note about qualitative research that she neither named nor had available to her at that time:

> A difficulty with the present study, as well as with the future investigations suggested here, is that the subjects of investigation are treated as objects. In a very real sense, research of this kind involves dominative interaction, not integrative. It does not involve either the teachers or the children in a participatory way, nor does it contribute directly to the understanding or development of either. It is highly likely that the teachers who volunteered their classrooms for observation would feel diminished by the findings of the study, even though those findings might be useful to them in their professional development. The increasing insistence by school boards, parent groups, and teachers' unions that classroom research be conducted only with the informed consent of the subjects or their representatives may resolve the problem by forcing the development of new kinds of research designs that include greater participation by the subjects and more feedback in both directions.

In this section I have considered qualitative research as an inherently ethical enterprise. I have also looked at some of the ethical dilemmas we face as they arise from our concerns for the fairness of the study and for fairness to our participants. In her 'Last Word', Margot will address some implications of qualitative research for commitment to the broader social arena.

Epilogue: Margot's Last Word

Writing about social commitment makes me as jittery as writing about love. While treatises about each of these can be informative, uplifting, even revolutionary, they are so much better understood by the doing.

It seems logical to me that the subject of the social responsibility of qualitative research does not emerge as a theme in the students' essays. When writing these, each student is immersed in immediate concerns that may well fix attention on extricating meaning from huge piles of data and writing a narrative that does splendid justice to the findings. It is reasonable, then, that they grapple with other methodological concerns and insights in their final reflective articles. Perhaps on a more essential level, however, most students are deeply concerned about social issues from their first qualitative thoughts forward, although this concern may not be articulated clearly. When we return to the roots of our earliest studies, when we look at the topics our students choose, we know that many of these arise from personal convictions about socially important issues: What can we discern about 'caring' nurses? How do those who are economically disadvantaged but who 'make it' account for their success? What happens when imprisoned juvenile offenders re-enter the larger society? What is the classroom experience of a child treated as an 'outsider', of students who perceive their teacher as unfair? How do runaway teenagers cope on the streets?

Often in the recursive process of qualitative research itself in living the 'circles within circles', what may have started as a general, rather amorphous commitment, takes on clearer shape, more urgency. This is especially true as we go through the cycles of ongoing analysis. It is one thing to study the re-entry from prison to their communities of Latino, juvenile males, but quite another to learn from first analysis forward that these people received no professional help in their transition, no guidance counselors, no job training, no support groups, no follow-up — nothing. What is more, it is a bitter epitaph that of these eight teenagers, two are back in prison, one has reverted to selling drugs, one has attempted suicide and then rejoined his gang, one has been shot and killed, one is on the run from the law, and two are seeking job training with such poor results that they are about to give up. These may seem to be uniquely dramatic cases, but feeling the pain of a child who is treated like an outsider in a regular classroom can be just as devastating, and just as influential, in moving the researcher to take more concrete social action. For some this means becoming a volunteer visitor in an AIDS hospital ward, a fund raiser for dignified housing to serve people labeled homeless, a political activist for day care for all children as well as for older adults. For others it means taking different routes.

In many cases the completion of a study becomes an end in itself. Certainly for doctoral students the completion of a qualitative research dissertation is eventually personally felt in terms of one's own life and career needs. Most often it is also felt in an expanded personal and professional sensitivity toward others. But, we ask further, 'Is there life after dissertation?' And for those of us who continue as researchers and writers, what is the meaning of that life in its broader social implications?

Researchers are fond of saying that their contribution to society is to the knowledge base in their respective field. This appears a valid, but limited stance. In academic circles it is easy to become involved in continuing theoretical debate over knowledge as an end in itself. Indeed, this end can be important and socially helpful. At times, however, doctoral students believe, perhaps naively, that their dissertations alone will get the message across. In my experience this is rarely the case. To communicate important information to our professions and wider society, it is necessary to keep on working, keep on speaking, keep on writing, and, in the process, keep on refining and redefining the nature of the information that one is contributing.

Further, when the results of a person's research can be placed in juxtaposition with those of others, we can make a more complete statement, and possibly a more important one, about the phenomenon we are studying. While the nature of qualitative research brings up questions regarding the uniqueness of each interpretation in a way that suggests that synthesis and generalization are impossible (Noblit and Hare, 1988), as a professional I am convinced that certain clusters of studies do make important statements. For example, I know that the reports from the teacher-as-researcher movement say something about how teachers become more effective and about those conditions that support their learning. Such information contributes to our social betterment. Because of this, I believe that more attention needs to be paid to reviews of qualitative research, to critiquing, comparing, and synthesizing, and then to bringing the results to the attention of broader audiences.

Beyond contributing after the study by personal, social action and by providing information, however, are activities integral to the qualitative research process that are seen by a growing group of people as critical hallmarks of social responsibility. For these researchers, and I count myself in this group, it is no longer ethically acceptable to study people in such ways that they provide the data for our major stepping stones — to earn degrees, write books and articles, lecture, complete funded research projects, and generally make our place in the world — while we provide them with far fewer and certainly more distanced benefits. At best these benefits to participants may involve some interaction with us, some feedback, some sharing, even some co-research — and certainly an expanded awareness (Lester and Onore, 1990). Often, in these ways, a qualitative researcher contributes as a much needed and appreciated interested other, a person who can be trusted to do what was promised, a person who creates a cooperative safety zone that will not be breached. In Chapters 3 and 5 we suggested a variety of ways to involve participants in what we consider ethical ways. These include seeking to tell their stories rather than imposing our own, to report their meanings, to involve them powerfully in the research process, to describe their social context, not as separate but as it is lived and understood by them, and to report their understandings of common as well as uncommon sense (Mayher, 1990). On the whole, however, although we may congratulate ourselves for not biting the hand that feeds us, we often give it only the merest pat.

On p. 226 Emily Kennedy speaks of the need to redress the balance of power between the researcher and the researched. Emily's statement alludes to the danger that if our participants remain more done to than doers, one result of the research process itself is that they become less resourceful and less powerful than they have a right to be. Guba and Lincoln (1989) develop this stance in their fourth generation evaluation paradigm. Indeed, their measures for the goodness of such evaluations, their 'authenticity criteria', are shot through with the sense that participants must be empowered by the research process. This holds true not only for their own integral involvement in every step during and after the research, but also for their understanding of an outreach in action with others. In Freire's (1970) terms, the social responsibility of qualitative researchers is to avoid seeing and treating participants as passive objects and, instead, to work with them so that they become increasingly knowledgeable, active, responsible, and, therefore, increasingly liberated. Others, some of whom are critical ethnographers or emancipation researchers, are also bringing us an ongoing dialogue about the social responsibilities of qualitative researchers. This embraces such issues as the very act of selecting topics for study, involving participants, and reporting. These issues consider both the overt processes and the covert messages inherent in them, both what is learned and how it is learned, both who is involved and how they are involved, both the researcher's product and the impact on and empowerment of participants to better their lives and those of others. In light of these issues, Anderson (1989) finds:

> ... There is little as yet practical advice. Critical ethnographers [and I, Margot, dare say all qualitative researchers] need to begin sharing insights from their research on such concepts as how to write a reflexive journal, how to negotiate outcomes with informants, how to gain and maintain site access when doing controversial research, and how to systematize reflexivity. (p. 263)

The call to systematize reflexivity points to perhaps our most serious need as well as our stickiest problem. However, the much-accepted vision of collaboration also needs a good hard look. There is an almost endless variety of such researcher-participant collaboration, from working as equal colleagues to any shade of imbalance, and I do not know of one expert who talks against the aim of involving research participants in responsible, important ways. In my experience, often such arrangements work well; sometimes they do not. Sometimes a participant co-researcher wants to move the study to areas the researcher colleague deems inconsequential, or downright silly. Sometimes the participant cannot stand one more bit of feedback. Sometimes the participant who seemed eager to do a personal log and daily sharing does not, or cannot, give the time it takes. Sometimes the person who seemed so open and flexible becomes irate at the first sharing of observations. Sometimes the participant does not agree that what is on the interview transcript is what was said. Sometimes what is crystal clear to the researcher about the lives of the people who are studied is denied vehemently by those very people. Sometimes the participant agrees with the researcher just to be nice because that is what one does. That is what one has learned is her or his place in life. Sometimes! Sometimes! Write your own example! All of these 'sometimes' have happened to me, to the writing team, to doctoral students. I am not urging that we do away with collaborative research — quite the opposite. I am saying that there are possible prices to be paid, lessons to be learned, and surprises when one sets out to empower the people one wishes to study because of the very process one has set in motion. What happens then, as qualitative researchers move with the flow of events, bring to bear their deepest insights about themselves and about working with others, and their greatest patience-creativity in helping to shape what needs shaping, what works and what does not, is perhaps the most valuable 'product' of doing such research.

Soltis (1989, p. 128) describes in his article on 'The Ethics of Qualitative Research' that the group known as critical researchers emphasizes '... that researchers be ethical in *purpose* as well as the *processes* of doing research'. I could not agree more. Soltis then raises what he terms '. . . the most fundamental question of all. Should the . . . purpose of human inquiry be directed primarily at securing the good of human being?' For me, there is no choice about the answer. However, I would push that question a bit further, as is the qualitative way, to '*How* should human inquiry be directed at securing the good of human beings?' There's the topic for another book! For now, our answer to Soltis's question is echoed in the metaphors introduced by Schön and Guba and Lincoln. It is Schön's (1983) position that professional schools in contemporary research universities give privileged status to 'systematic, preferably scientific, knowledge'. Schön likens this to 'the high, hard ground overlooking a swamp', and, he continues:

> In the swampy lowland, messy, confusing problems defy technical solutions. The irony of the situation is that the problems on the high ground tend to be relatively unimportant to individuals or society at large, however great their technical interest may be, while in the swamp lie the problems of greatest human concern. (p. 3)

To add to the process of triangulation by metaphor that continues to amaze us as we work, we noted Guba and Lincoln's (1989) discussion of the 'muddy boots syndrome' which they see as a fallacious argument for how qualitative and quantitative research should work together. This syndrome pictures the qualitative researcher:

> . . . in high boots, jeans, checkered shirt . . . mucking around trying to find things of interest. He or she reaches down, selects this clod, that stone, this artifact, all the while looking for something worth pursuing further. At last he or she finds it! Hands dripping with the mud and slop of the field, the constructivist passes the 'find' to the conventionalist, who stands at the edge of the field, safely up on a platform, in white coat, polished shoes, and necktie, wearing long rubber gloves. He takes the object we so enthusiastically hold up, being careful not to let the mud drip on any part of him or her. 'Look what we've got', we constructivists chorus! 'Yes, well', says the conventionalists, 'We'll soon see if you've got it right!' (pp. 113–14)

It is in the swampy lowlands where profession and research and social commitment are often indistinguishable that qualitative researchers seek the roots that nourish our growth. We know from our own lives that the job is often truly 'down and dirty'; I think of Laura Lee struggling to enter the world of a woman labeled schizophrenic, of Gail doing her best to interview a person high on drugs one sweltering day, of Debbie scrunched into the corner of a classroom, of Teri on police patrol, Diane rolling around on the playground with her students, Kate catheterizing Ms T. We qualitative researchers claim the muddy fields precisely because they are where the greatest human concerns lie. We prize what we find there. We are happy to share our findings, but we see no need to hand them over. We attempt to use what we find to reflect forward so that the fields may become more habitable.

Reinvigorating the fields entails that we engage in what David Dillon (1990) describes as the hallmarks of creative, critical learning:

> This kind of learning ... is what frees or liberates us from seeing things as they are to seeing them as they might be. It's ... what our imaginations are for — to remake the world by renaming it with our language and thus living differently in the world, and doing this over and over again in an endless journey. (p. 334)

In our writing, and particularly because of it, we now see in our mind's eye that the endless journey of 'circles within circles' of qualitative research makes a three-dimensional whole — a world. But it is a world always reconstructing, always spiraling, and so, a particularly fitting vision. After all, this book is not about research as set apart. It is very much about a way of life. In 'doing' qualitative research we enact what we value. In reflecting upon that, we can better understand our commitments. With awareness, we can act again as we see the need. Our guiding instrument is what Jerome Bruner (1990) calls openmindedness:

> ... a willingness to construe knowledge and values from multiple perspectives without loss of commitment to one's own values. (p. 30)

Such a stance is, to us, the heartback that powers both qualitative research and this book.

References

AGAR, M.H. (1980) *The Professional Stranger: An Informal Introduction to Ethnography*. New York: Academic Press.

ANDERSON, G.L. (1989, Fall) 'Critical Ethnography in Education: Origins, Current Status, and New Directions', *Review of Educational Research*, 59, 3, pp. 249–70.

ANZUL, M. (1988) 'Exploring Literature with Children within a Transactional Framework'. *Dissertation Abstracts International*, No. 49/08, p. 2132-A.

ANZUL, M., and ELY, M. (1988, November) 'Halls of Mirrors: The Introduction of the Reflective Mode'. *Language Arts*, 65, 7, 675–87.

ATKINSON, P. (1984) 'Wards and Deeds: Taking Knowledge and Control Seriously'. In R. BURGESS (Ed.), *The Research Process in Educational Settings: Ten Case Studies*. London: Falmer Press.

BALL, S.J. (1984) 'Beachside Reconsidered: Reflections on a Methodological Apprenticeship'. In R. BURGESS (Ed.), *The Research Process in Educational Settings: Ten Case Studies* (pp. 69–96). London: Falmer Press.

BECKER, H.S. (1986) *Writing for Social Scientists*. Chicago, IL: University of Chicago Press.

BERG, D.N., and SMITH, K.K. (1988) *The Self in Social Inquiry: Researching Methods*. Newbury Park, CA: Sage.

BOGDAN, R.C., and BIKLEN, S.K. (1982) *Qualitative Research for Education: An Introduction to Theory and Methods*. Boston, MA: Allyn and Bacon.

BOGDAN, R.C., and TAYLOR, S.J. (1975) *Introduction to Qualitative Research*. New York: John Wiley.

BRUNER, J. (1983) *In Search of Mind: Essays in Autobiography*. New York: Harper and Row.

BRUNER, J. (1990) *Acts of Meaning*. Cambridge, MA: Howard University Press.

BURGESS, R. (Ed.) (1984) *The Research Process in Educational Settings: Ten Case Studies*. London: Falmer Press.

BUSSIS, A., CHITTENDEN, E., AMAREL, M., and CARINI, P. (1978) *Educational Testing Service Data Integration Project*. Princeton, NJ: Educational Testing Service.

COWLES, K.V. (1988) 'Issues in Qualitative Research on Sensitive Topics'. *Western Journal of Nursing Research*, 10, 2, 163–79.

DILLON, D. (1990, April) Editor's Introduction to Theme. *Language Arts*, 67, 4, pp. 333–5.

DOUGLAS, J.D. (1984) *Creative Interviewing*. Beverly Hills, CA: Sage.

ELY, M. (1984) 'Beating the Odds: An Ethnographic Interview Study of Young Adults from the Culture of Poverty'. Paper presented at the Seventh Annual Conference on English Education, New York University, NY.

ELY, M. (1989) 'Qualitative Descriptions'. In L. MILLER (Dir.), *Project Gain Evaluation*. New York: Metropolitan Center for Educational Research and Development, New York University.

ELY, M., *et al.* (1989) 'Transformation of the Self in the Role of Professional Stranger'. Philadelphia: University of Pennsylvania Ethnography in Education Research Forum.

FETTERMAN, D.M. (1989) *Ethnography Step by Step*. Newbury Park, CA: Sage.

FITZGERALD, J. (1987) 'Research on Revision in Writing'. *Review of Educational Research*, 57, 4, 481–506.

FREIRE, P. (1970) *Pedagogy of the Oppressed*. New York: Seabury.

FRIEDMAN, T. (1989) 'The Experience of Being a Female Police Officer'. *Dissertation Abstracts International*, No. 50/09, p. 2834-A.

GALLAGHER, J., and ASCHNER, M. (1974) 'A Preliminary Report on Analyses of Classroom Interacting'. In R. HYMAN (Ed.), *Teaching: Vantage Points for Study*. Philadelphia, PA: Lippincott.

GARNER, D. (1986) 'An Ethnographic Study of Four 5-Year-Old Children's Play Styles'. *Dissertation Abstracts International*, No. 47/08A, p. 2880.

GIORGI, A. (1985). *Phenomenology and Psychological Research*. Pittsburgh, PA: Duquesne University Press.

GIORGI, A. (1989) 'One Type of Analysis of Descriptive Data: Procedures Involved in Following a Scientific Phenomenological Method'. *Methods*, Spring, 39–61.

GLASER, B.D., and STRAUSS, A.K. (1967) *The Discovery of Grounded Theory*. Chicago, IL: Aldine.

GLAZER, M. (1980, October) *The Threat of the Stranger*. Briarcliff, NY: Hastings Center Report (pp. 25–31).

GOETZ, J., and LECOMPTE, M. (1984) *Ethnography and Qualitative Design in Educational Research*. Orlando, FL: Academic Press.

GOFFMAN, E. (1989, July) 'On Fieldwork'. *Journal of Contemporary Ethnography*, 18, 2, 123–32.

GORDON, R.L. (1980) *Interviewing: Strategy, Techniques, and Tactics.* Homewood, IL: Dorsey Press.

GUBA, E., and LINCOLN, Y. (1989) *Fourth Generation Evaluation.* Newbury Park, CA: Sage.

HACKMAN, R.J. (1988) 'On Seeking One's Own Clinical Voice: A Personal Account'. In D.N. BERG and K.K. SMITH (Eds), *The Self in Social Inquiry: Researching Methods* (pp. 267–81). Newbury Park, CA: Sage.

HAMMERSLEY, MARTYN and WOODS, PETER (Eds) (1984) *Life in School: The Sociology of Pupil Culture*, Milton Keynes: Open University Press.

HUGHES, E.C. (1960) 'Introduction: The Place of Fieldwork and Social Science'. In B. JUNKER, *Fieldwork: An Introduction to the Social Sciences*, (pp. iii–xiii). Chicago, IL: University of Chicago Press.

JANIS, I.L. (1973, January) 'Groupthink'. *Yale Alumni Magazine*, pp. 16–19.

JERSILD, A.T. (1955) *When Teachers Face Themselves.* New York: Teachers College Press, Teachers College, Columbia University.

KENNEDY, E. (1975) 'An Investigation of Selected Kindergarten Teachers' Individual Integrative and Dominative Contact Patterns with Children and Their Relation to Teacher Assessments of Children'. *Dissertation Abstracts International*, No. 36/04A, p. 2158.

KUHN, T.S. (1970) *The Structure of Scientific Revolutions.* 2nd ed., enlarged. Chicago, IL: University of Chicago Press.

LAZARSFELD, P.E. (1972) 'The Art of Asking Why'. In P. LAZARSFELD (Ed.), *Qualitative Analysis.* New York: Allyn and Bacon.

LeCOMPTE, M.D. (1985, April) 'Insight, Hindsight and Pragmation: A Reflective Look at Anthropological Research'. Paper presented at the annual meeting of the American Educational Research Association, Chicago, IL.

LESTER, N.B., and ONORE C.S. (1990) *Learning Change: One School District Meets Language across the Curriculum.* Portsmouth, NH: Boynton/Cook.

LIGHTFOOT, S.L. (1973) 'Through the Eyes of Teachers and Children'. *Harvard Educational Review*, 43, 2, 197–244.

LINCOLN, Y., and GUBA, E. (1985) *Naturalistic Inquiry.* Beverly Hills, CA: Sage.

LOFLAND, J. (1971) *Analyzing Social Settings.* Belmont, CA: Wadsworth.

LOFLAND, J., and LOFLAND, L.H. (1984) *Analyzing Social Settings: A Guide to Qualitative Observation and Analysis.* Belmont, CA: Wadsworth.

MATHISON, S. (1988, March) 'Why triangulate?' *Educational Researcher*, 17, 2, 13–17.

MAYHER, J.S. (1990) *Uncommon Sense: Theoretical Practice in Language Education*. Portsmouth, NH: Boynton/Cook.

MEADOR, B.D., and ROGERS, C.R. (1979) 'Person-centered Therapy'. In R. CORSINI (Ed.), *Current Psychotherapies* (pp. 131–84). Itasco, IL: F.E. Peacock.

MERTON, R.K., FISKE, M., and KENDALL, P.L. (1956) *The Focused Interview*. New York: The Free Press.

MILES, M.B., and HUBERMAN, A.M. (1984) *Qualitative Data Analysis: A Sourcebook of New Methods*. Beverly Hills, CA: Sage.

MILLS, C.W. (1959) *The Sociological Imagination*. New York: Oxford University Press.

MISHLER, E.G. (1986) *Research Interviewing: Context and Narrative*. Cambridge, MA: Harvard University Press.

MUNHALL, P.L. (1988) 'Ethical Considerations in Qualitative Research'. *Western Journal of Nursing Research*, 10, 2, 150–62.

NOBLIT, G.W., and HARE, R.D. (1988) *Meta-ethnography: Synthesizing Qualitative Studies*. Newbury Park, CA: Sage.

PALEY, V.G. (1986) 'On Listening to What the Children Say'. *Harvard Educational Review*, 56, 2, 122–31.

PATTON, M. (1980) *Qualitative Evaluation Methods*. Beverly Hills, CA: Sage.

PESHKIN, A. (1988) 'Virtuous Subjectivity: In the Participant Observer's I's'. In D.N. BERG and K.K. SMITH (Eds), *The Self in Social Inquiry: Researching Methods* (pp. 267–81). Newbury Park, CA: Sage.

PORTER, M.A. (1984) 'The Modification of Method in Researching Postgraduate Education'. In R.G. BURGESS (Ed.), *The Research Process in Educational Settings: Ten Case Studies*. London: Falmer Press.

RICOEUR, P. (1979) 'The Metaphorical Process as Cognition, Imagination, and Feeling'. In S. SACKS (Ed.), *On Metaphor* (pp. 141–57). Chicago, IL: University of Chicago Press.

RIST, R.C. (1980) 'Blitzkrieg Ethnography: On the Transformation of a Method into a Movement'. *Educational Researcher*, 9, 2, 8–10.

RIST, R.C. (1982) 'On Qualitative Research: Issues of Design, Implementation, Analysis, Ethics and Applicability'. A bibliography prepared by R.C. RIST. 4th ed. Cornell University, NY.

ROSENBLATT, L.M. (1978) *The Reader, the Text, the Poem: The Transactional Theory of the Literary Work*. Carbondale, IL: Southern Illinois University Press.

ROSS, D.D. (1988) 'An Introduction to Curriculum Criticism'. In R.R. SHERMAN and R.B. WEBB (Eds), *Qualitative Research in Education: Focus and Methods* (p. 166). London: Falmer Press.

SACKS, S. (Ed.) (1979) *On Metaphor*. Chicago, IL: University of Chicago Press.

SCHÖN, D. (1987) *Educating the Reflective Practitioner*. San Francisco, CA: Jossey-Bass Publishers.

SCHÖN, D.A. (1979) 'Generative Metaphor: A Perspective on Problem-setting in Social Policy'. In A. ORTONY (Ed.), *Metaphor and Thought* (pp. 254–83). Cambridge: Cambridge University Press.

SCHÖN, D.A. (1983) *The Reflective Practitioner: How Professionals Think in Action*. New York: Basic Books.

SHAFFIR, W.B., STEBBINS, R.A., and TUROWETZ, A. (1980) *Fieldwork Experience: Qualitative Approaches to Social Research*. New York: St Martin's Press.

SHERMAN, R., and WEBB, R. (1988) *Qualitative Research in Education: Focus and Methods*. London: Falmer Press.

SOLTIS, J. (1989) 'The Ethics of Qualitative Research'. *International Journal of Qualitative Studies in Education*, 2, 2, 123–30.

SPRADLEY, J. (1979) *The Ethnographic Interview*. New York: Holt, Rinehart and Winston.

SPRADLEY, J. (1980) *Participant Observation*. New York: Holt, Rinehart and Winston.

SPRADLEY, J.P., and McCURDY, D.W. (1972) *The Cultural Experience*. Chicago, IL: Science Research Associates.

STEINMETZ, A. (1988) 'The Role of the Microcomputer in the Social and Psychological World of an Adolescent Male. *Dissertation Abstracts International*, No. 50/01, p. 269-A.

STERNBERG, D. (1981) *How to Complete and Survive a Doctoral Dissertation*. New York: St Martin's Press.

STRAUSS, A.L. (1987) *Qualitative Analysis for Social Scientists*. Cambridge: Cambridge University Press.

SWANSON, D.R. (1978) 'Toward a Psychology of Metaphor'. In S. SACKS (Ed.), *On Metaphor*, pp. 161–4. Chicago, IL: University of Chicago Press.

TABA, H., LEVINE, S., and ELZEY, F. (1965) *Thinking in Elementary School Children* (Report No. 1574). San Francisco, CA: San Francisco State College.

TESCH, R. (1987, April) 'Comparing the Most Widely Used Methods of Qualitative Analysis: What Do They Have in Common?' Paper presented at the American Educational Research Association Annual Convention, San Francisco, CA.

TESCH, R. (1990) *Qualitative Research: Analysis Types and Software Tools*. London: Falmer Press.

US GENERAL ACCOUNTING OFFICE (1987) *Case Study Evaluation* (Transfer Paper 9). Washington, DC.

VAN MAANEN, J. (1988) *Tales of the Field: On Writing Ethnography*. Chicago, IL: University of Chicago Press.

WALSH, D., SMITH., M.R., and BATURKA, N. (1990, Winter) 'The Growth of Teacher Reflection'. *The Commonwealth Center Newsletter*. University of Virginia: Commonwealth Center for the Education of Teachers.

WERNER, O., and SCHOEPFLE, G. (1987) *Systematic Fieldwork*. Vol. 1: *Foundations of Ethnography and Interviewing*. Beverly Hills, CA: Sage.

WHYTE, W.F. (1955) *Street Corner Society*. 2nd ed. Chicago, IL: University of Chicago Press.

WHYTE, W.F. (1960) 'Interviewing in Field Research'. In R. ADAMS and J. PREISS (Eds), *Human Organization Research*. Homewood, IL: Dorsey Press.

WOLCOTT, H. (1988) 'Ethnographic Research in Education'. In R.M. JAEGER (Ed.), *Complementary Methods for Research in Education*. Washington, DC: American Educational Research Association.

YIN, R.K. (1984) *Case Study Research: Design and Methods*. Beverly Hills, CA: Sage.

ZIGARMI, D., and ZIGARMI, P. (1980) 'A Personal View of the Stresses of Being an Ethnographer'. *Journal of Classroom Interaction*, 16, 1, 19–24.

Colleague Contributors

Beatriz Abreu
Ioannis D. Afthinos
Molly Ahye
Ruth Alperson
Marlene Barron
Jo Anne Bauer
Laura L. Berns
Nancy Biederman
Mathew Cariello
Patricia A. Cobb
Laura Cohen
Gerrie Colombraro
Gail Cueto
Steve Cullinan
Francia DeBeer
Dorothy Deegan
A. Richard DeLuca
John Devine
Marsha Diamond
Marie Del Carmen Diaz
Maryann Downing
Donna Flynn
Patricia Fogelman
Matthew Foley
John Forconi
Barbara A. Gagliardi
Joan Giansante
Debrah Goldberg
Kate Good

Suzy Hahn
Phyllis R. Hamilton
Wendy S. Hesford
Jim Hinojosa
Dorothea Hoffner
Ewa Iracka
Iris Kaplan
Emily R. Kennedy
Flora Keshishian
Ellen Klohmann
Hilary Knatz
Rita Kopf
Marcia Brumit Kropf
Deborah Lamb
Joanna Landau
Annie Hauk Lawson
Sharon Lefkofsky
Gail R. Levine
Laura Lee Lustbader
Donald McGuire
Andrea Mandel
Belén Matías
Francia M. Mercado
Nancy K. Montgomery
Raimundo Mora
Akiko Okada
Harriet Parnes
Allie Parrish
Diane Person

Colleague Contributors

Bernice S. Reyes
Leslie E. Rice
Melissa Rose
Beverly Rosenthal
Steven M. Rosman
Dalia Sachs
Jo Ann Saggese
Joseph S.C. Simplicio
Rena Smith
Steven T. Spitz
Rhonda Sternberg

Jackie Storm
Richard L. Stoving
Nicholas Surdo
Patricia Thornton
Mayumi Tsutsui
Elizabeth Ann Tucker
Ann Vartanian
Thomas Veltre
Laura E. Wilson
Julie Wollman-Bonilla
Ronna Ziegel

Name Index

Subject Index

Access to data sources. *See* Entrée to field sites
Analysis. *See* Data analysis
Analytic memos, 80–2
Audiotaping in data collection, 61, 71, 82–3, 84–5; transcribing, 82–3
Authenticity criteria, 95

Bracketing, 50
Bridging the paradigm gap, 210–18. *See also* Paradigms, research

Categories, 86–90, 145–7, 150. *See also* Data analysis
Coding. *See* Categories in data analysis
Computers in data analysis, 90–1
Constructs in thematic analysis. *See* Vignettes/Constructs
Credibility. *See* Trustworthiness
Critical ethnography, 229–30

Data analysis, 18, 78–82, 83–91, 110–12, 140–56, 158–9; characteristics, 177–8; numbers in, 155–6; starting, 86–90. *See also* Categories in data analysis
Data collection, 18, 42–69, 156
Data recording. *See* Logs
Discrepant case selection, 161
Dissertation advisement, 30, 213–16

Emergent design, 24–5, 30–1, 140–1, 214–15
Entering the field, 15–29, 35–7, 46–7; affect, 16–18, 38–9, 109–10, 186–8
Entrée to field sites, 17–18, 18–25, 38–9. *See also* Gatekeeper

Ethical considerations, 22, 38–9, 93–4, 218–26, 227–32
ETHNO, 90
Ethnograph, 90

Familiarity/unfamiliarity (with field), 15–18, 26–9, 33–5, 61–3, 123–32
Field logs. *See* Logs
Field notes, 69, 72–3
Flexibility, 33, 183

Gatekeeper, 18–22, 36, 71, 109–10
'Going native,' 114
'Grand Tour,' 55, 168

Heisenberg's uncertainty principle, 47
HyperQual, 90

Interpretation of findings. *See* Data analysis
Inter-rater reliability, 163–4
Interviewing, 42–3, 57–69, 89, 110–1, 128–9; characteristics of, 57–9, 59, 60, 65–9; distance/closeness, 60–3; planning of, 59–60
Interviews, formal, 53–4; informal, 53–4

Journal. *See* Log

Logs, 15–16, 17–18, 26–9, 48–9, 69–82, 92–3, 203–4; analytic memo, 80–5; beginning, 71–3; characteristics of, 69–71; content, 73–5, 75–80; format, 26–9, 73–77; hunches, 78